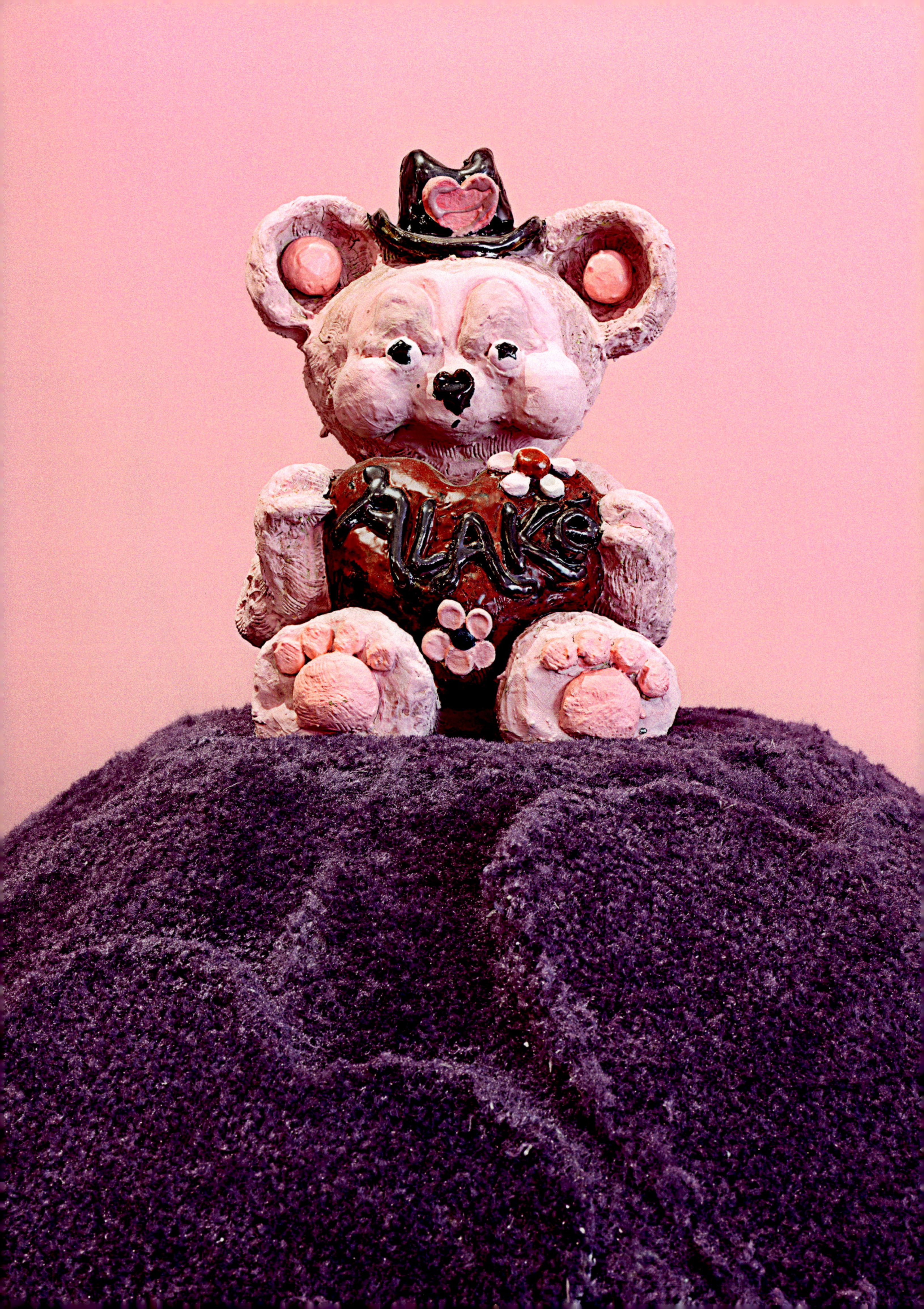
ALAKE

FUNK YOU TOO!

Humor and Irreverence in Ceramic Sculpture

MAD
museum of arts and design

HIRMER

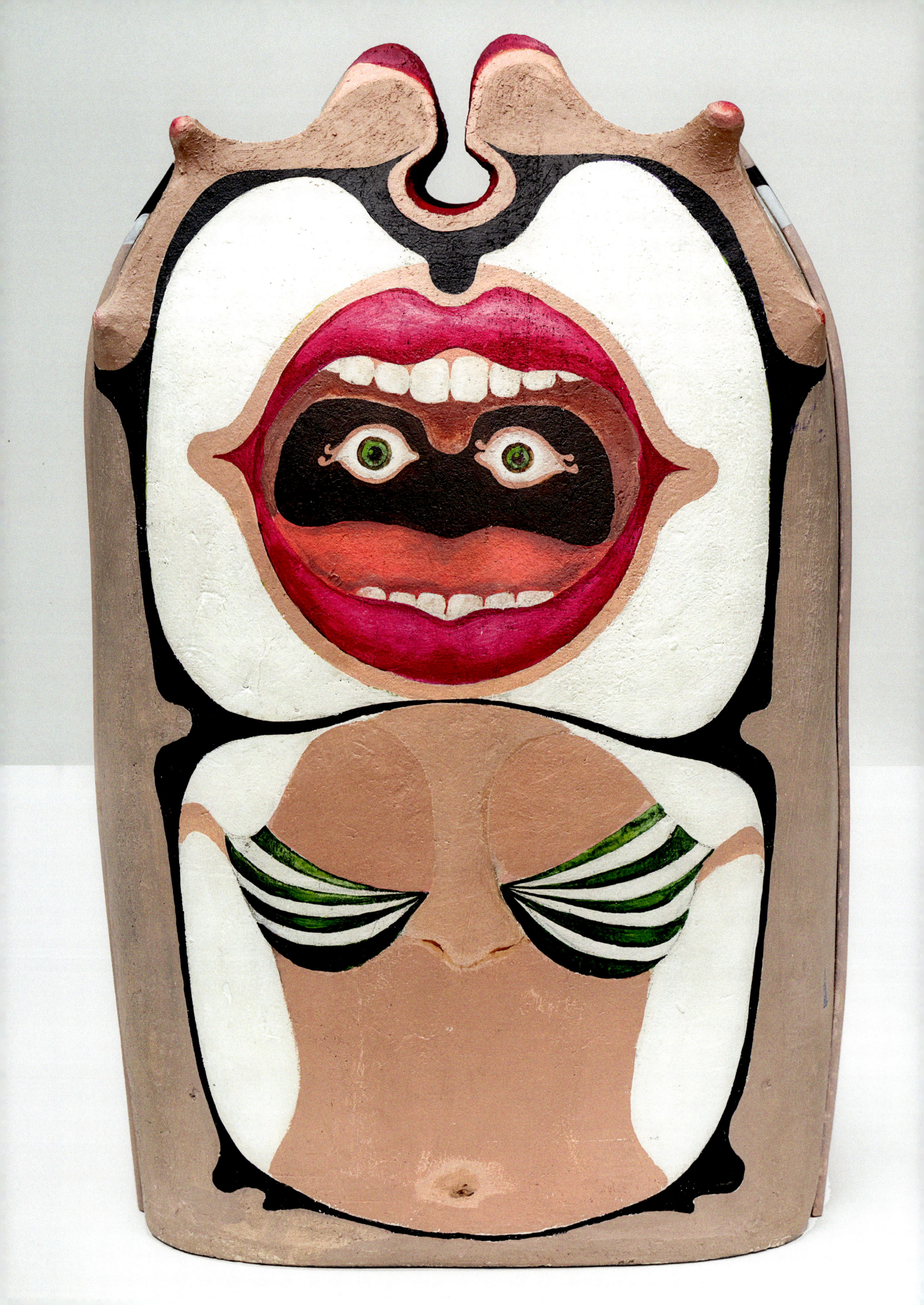

Contents

9
Angelik Vizcarrondo-Laboy
CURATOR'S ACKNOWLEDGEMENTS

17
Angelik Vizcarrondo-Laboy
FUNK YOU TOO!

77
Garth Johnson
FINDING FUNK

100
Biographies

106
Select Bibliography

109
Photo Credits

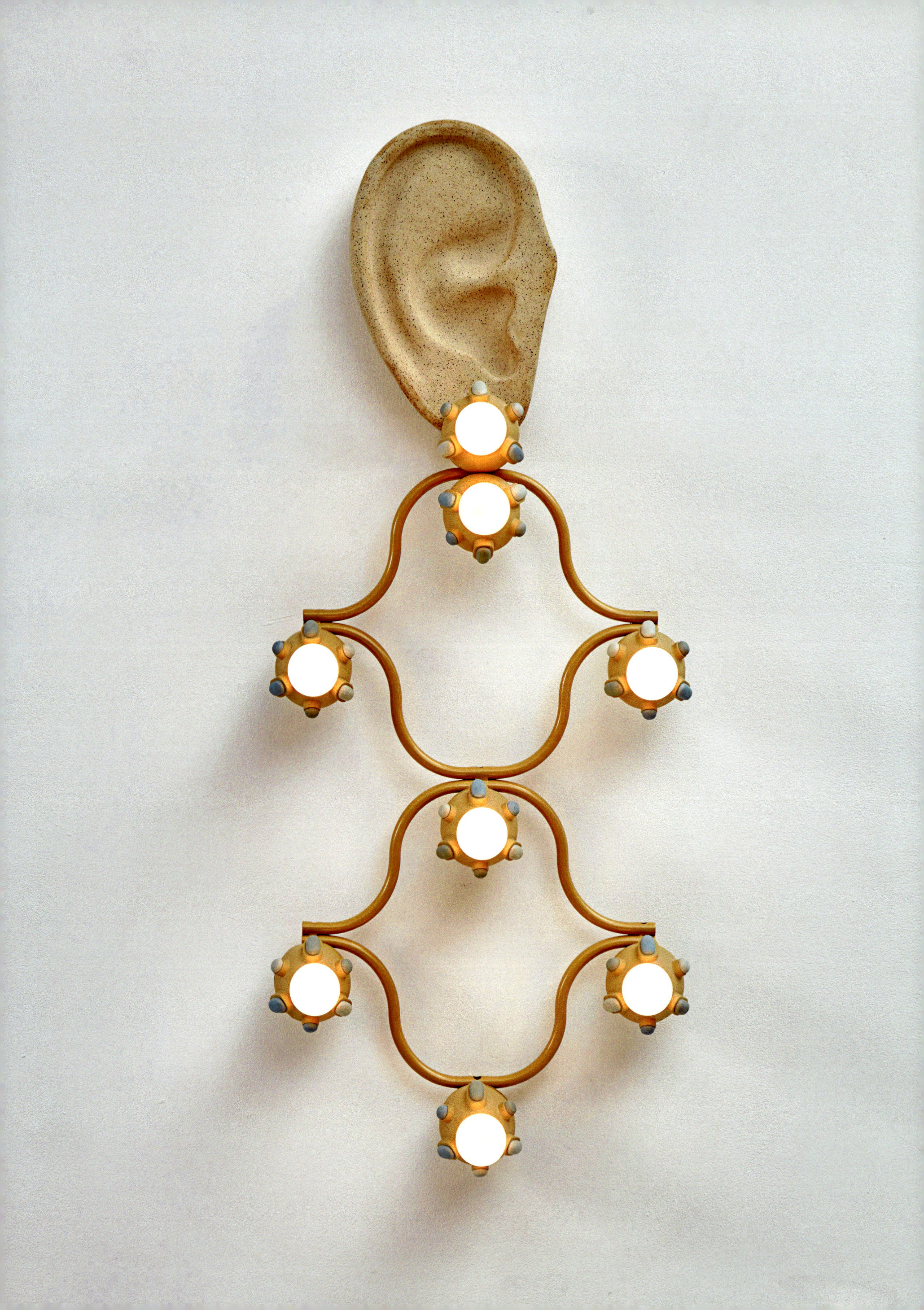

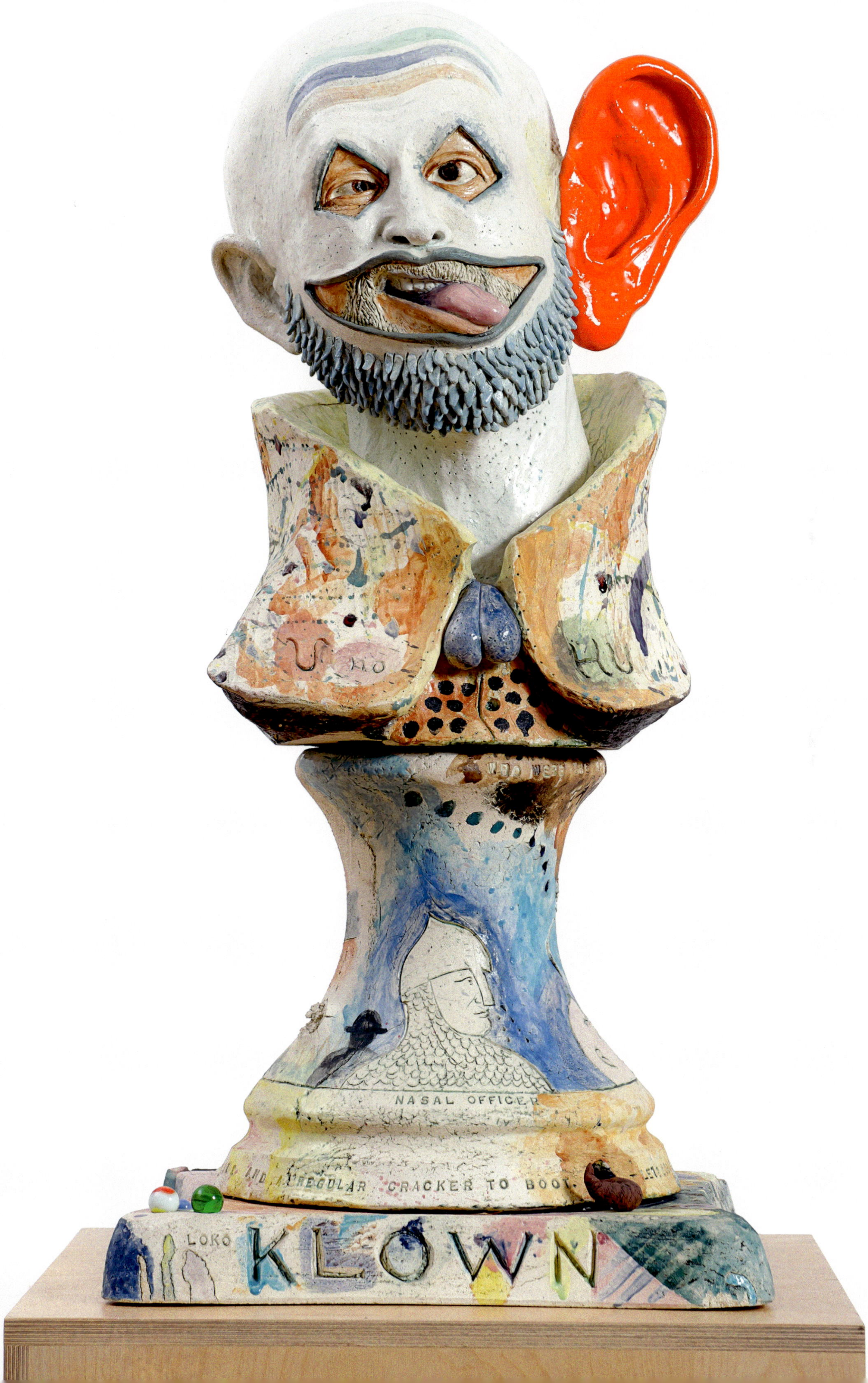
NASAL OFFICER
REGULAR CRACKER TO BOOT
LOKO
KLOWN

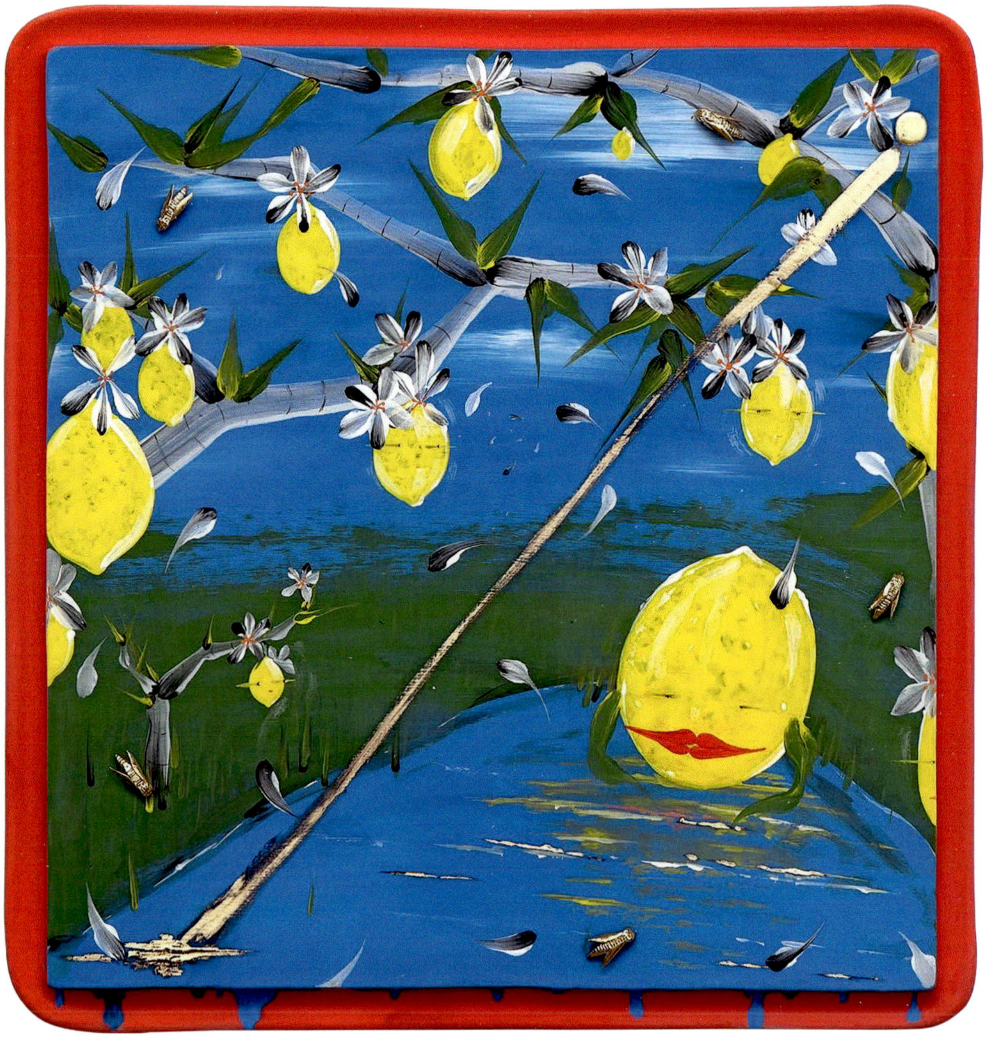

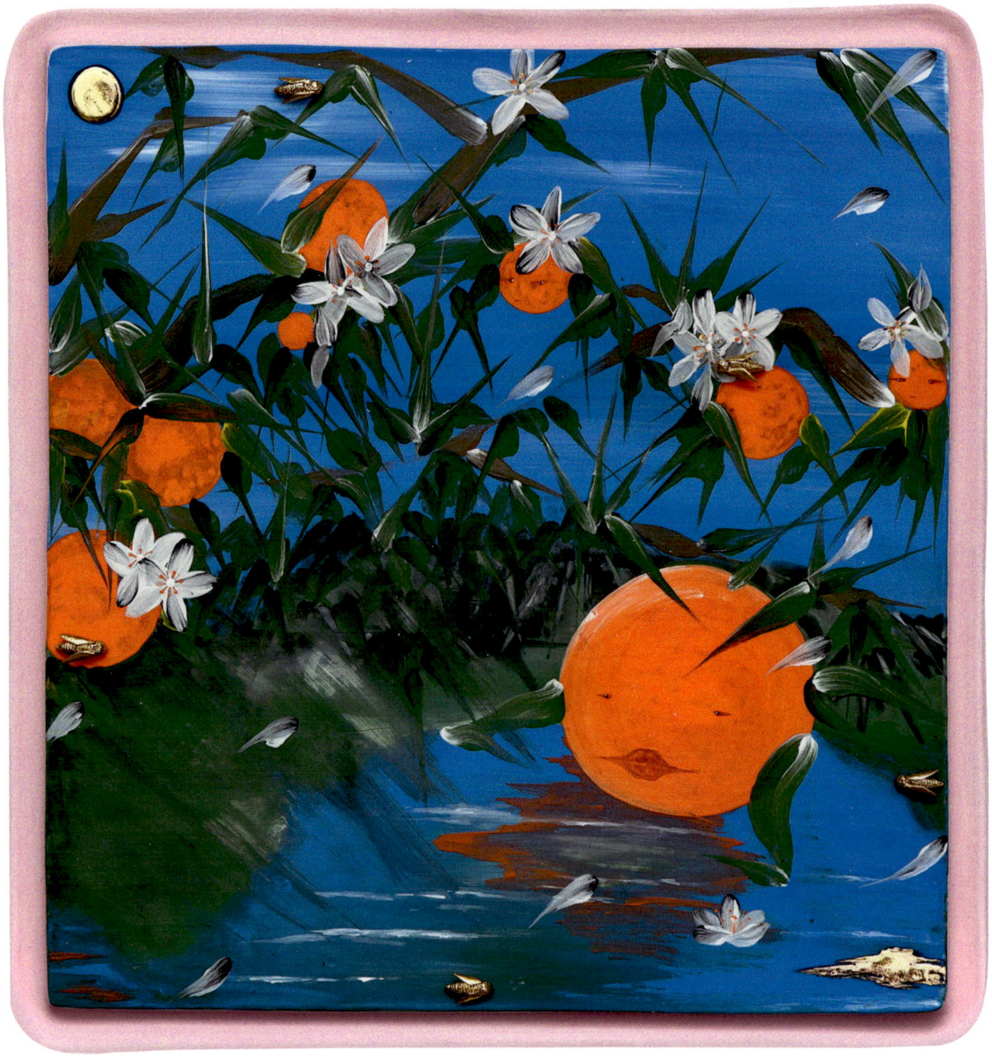

CURATOR'S ACKNOWLEDGEMENTS

Finally, funk! I have been working on this project in one way or another since 2017, and I am so thrilled to see it come to fruition where I began my curatorial career, the Museum of Arts and Design (MAD) in New York.

First, none of this would be possible without our dauntless artists. Thank you to all twenty-six of them for their vision and inspiring work, which so richly encapsulates life's joys and anxieties. I am immensely grateful to all the lenders who parted with their beloved artworks for a few months so that we could stage this exciting convergence. I also want to thank donors who contributed pieces or funds towards building MAD's permanent collection. Thank you to all who provided images and rights to illustrate this exhibition catalog. And a major thank you to the incredible team at Hirmer for putting together such a beautiful book!

My deepest gratitude to Elissa Auther, MAD's Deputy Director of Curatorial Affairs, and the William and Mildred Lasdon Chief Curator, for always supporting and encouraging my ideas and projects. I also want to thank the Center for Craft in Asheville, NC, for their generous support of this exhibition through a research grant and a curatorial fellowship in 2020, where I developed the exhibition *Sleight of Hand*, a glimpse into the concept for *Funk You Too!*. So many thank yous to fellow ceramics lover Garth Johnson for his contribution to this catalog and for always being a great sounding board for all things historical clay.

Thank you to the folks at the Robert Arneson Estate, lending galleries, and Perrotin, for helping me secure important loans. It was a joy to meet Kirk Arneson and Sandra Shannonhouse, who took me through Bob Arneson's archives and told me great stories about him. Thank you, Kirk, for your speedy responses to all my requests and questions. I also want to thank the Archives of American Art, Washington, D.C., and the Berkeley Art Museum and Pacific Film Archive, CA, for letting me riffle through their documents.

Nobody knows better than me how hard the team at MAD works. Thank you from the bottom of my heart for all that you do! Thank you to Tim Rodgers, Nanette L. Laitman Director, for supporting this project so quickly after taking the helm. I especially want to thank Willow Holdorf, Director of Exhibitions and Collections, who always goes above and beyond, Rachel Hansen, Registrar, and Sasha Nixon, Exhibition Design and Production Manager, the installation crew, and the mount-making team for coordinating the safe travels of all the artwork and ensuring a stellar presentation. I am grateful to Alida Jekabson and Lillian Stafford, Curatorial Assistants on the project, who helped manage the moving parts. And thank you to Elana Hart, Senior Grants Manager, and Ben Strauss, Director of Development, for their efforts to obtain funding.

To my friends Tyler Shine and Kat Kazlauskas, thank you for taking the time to read my essay and share helpful insights. I also want to thank Barbara Paris Gifford for being the best friend I could ever ask for. And finally, thank you to Frank Lopez, my California dreamer, who has supported me and my passions unconditionally.

Angelik Vizcarrondo-Laboy, Curator

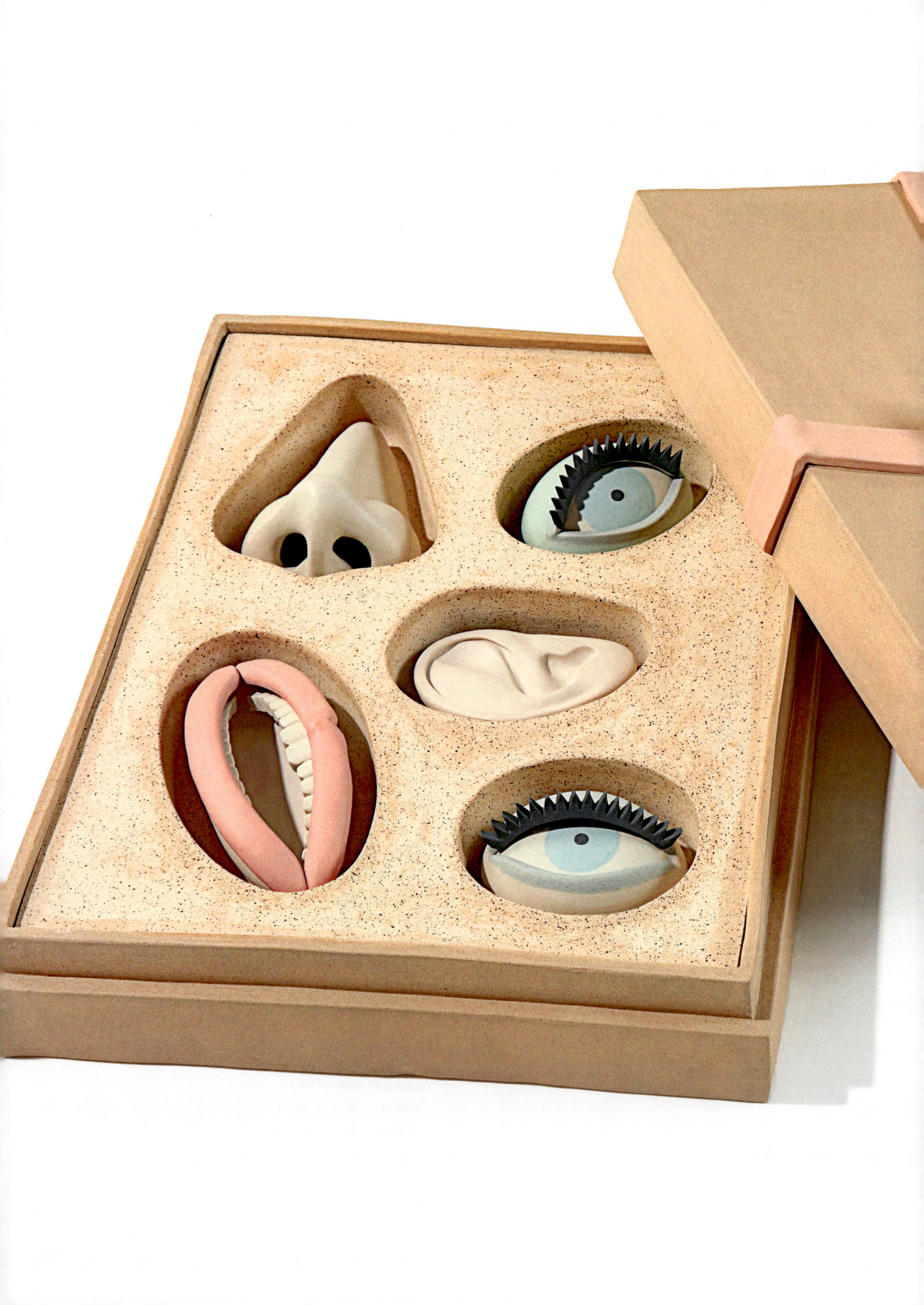

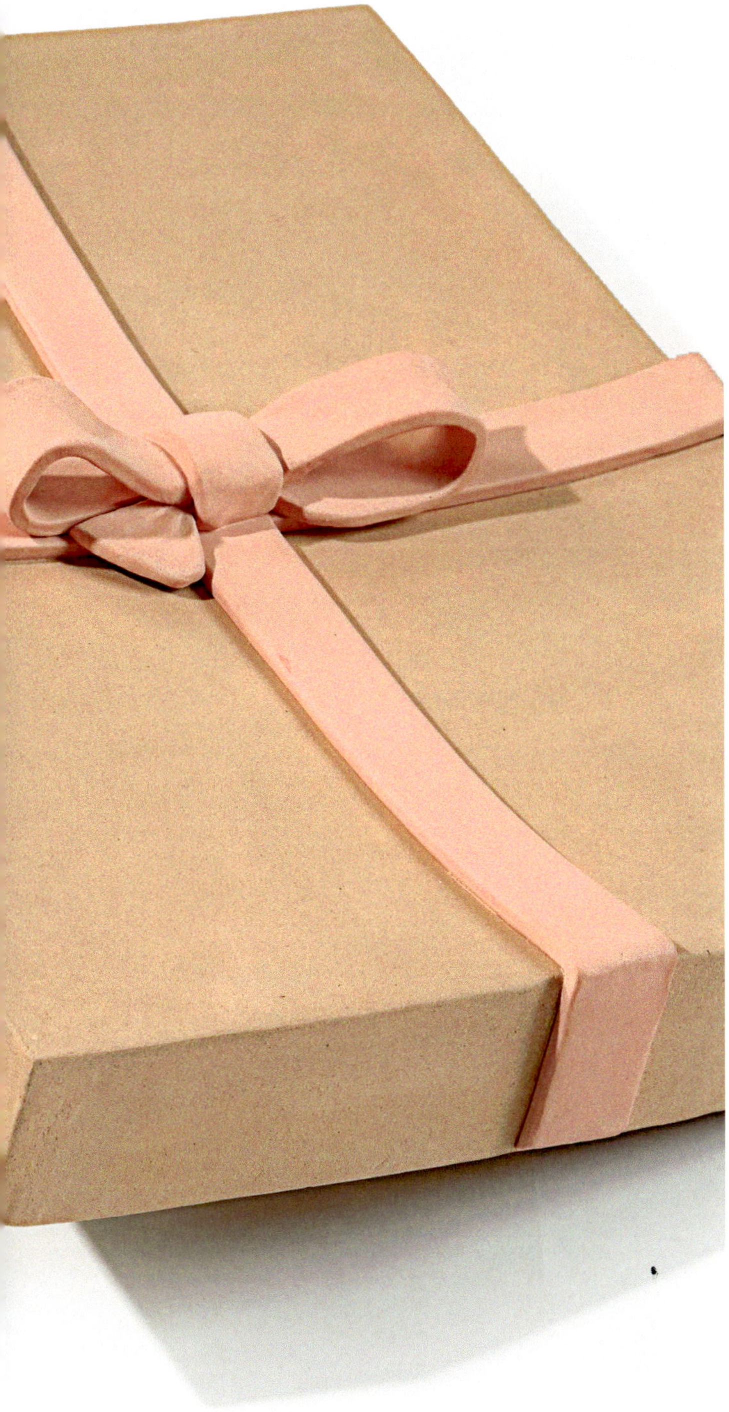

Lenders to the Exhibition:

Alake Shilling
Jeffrey Deitch, New York and Los Angeles
Alex Anderson
Collection of Ann and Argyris Vassiliou,
Stamford, CT
Collection of Emmanuel Perrotin
Collection of Howard and Judie Ganek
Collection of Jeff Rosa and Elizabeth Satterwhite
Collection of KAWS
Collection of Mr. Lorin Gu
Crocker Art Museum, Sacramento
Des Moines Art Center
Didi Rojas
Estate of Robert Arneson
Everson Museum of Art, Syracuse, NY
George Adams Gallery, New York
kaufmann repetto, Milan and New York
Kolodny Family Collection, New York
LGDR, New York
Magdalena Suarez Frimkess
Maryam Yousif
Melvino Garretti
Michael Rosenfeld Gallery, New York
Mindy Solomon Collection, Miami
Mindy Solomon Gallery, Miami
Museum of Arts and Design, New York
Natalia Arbelaez
Parker Gallery, Los Angeles
Private collection
Ruby Neri
Sally Saul
Salvador Jiménez-Flores
Sandra Shannonhouse
Sargent's Daughters, New York
The Museum of Fine Arts, Houston
The Pit, Los Angeles
Venus Over Manhattan, New York
Yvette Mayorga

Featured Artists:

ALAKE SHILLING

ALEX ANDERSON

CHRIS UNTERSEHER

CLAYTON BAILEY

DAVID GILHOOLY

DIDI ROJAS

DIANA YESENIA ALVARADO

GENESIS BELANGER

HOWARD KOTTLER

MAGDALENA SUAREZ FRIMKESS

MAIJA PEEPLES-BRIGHT

MARYAM YOUSIF

MELVINO GARRETTI

NATALIA ARBELAEZ

PATTI WARASHINA

PETER VANDENBERGE

RICHARD SHAW

ROBERT ARNESON

RUBY NERI

SALLY SAUL

SALVADOR JIMÉNEZ-FLORES

SANDRA SHANNONHOUSE

VIOLA FREY

SHARIF FARRAG

WOODY DE OTHELLO

YVETTE MAYORGA

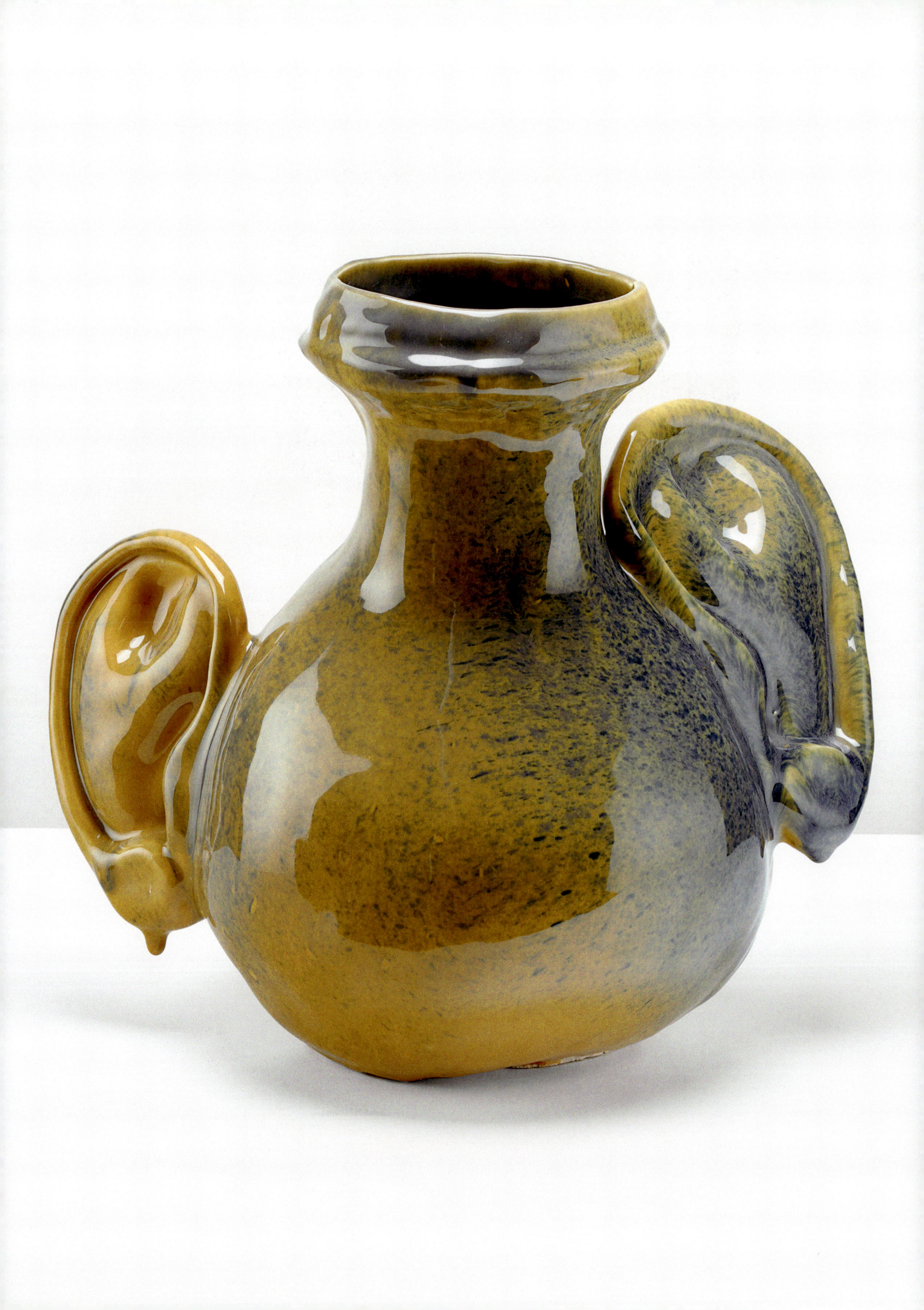

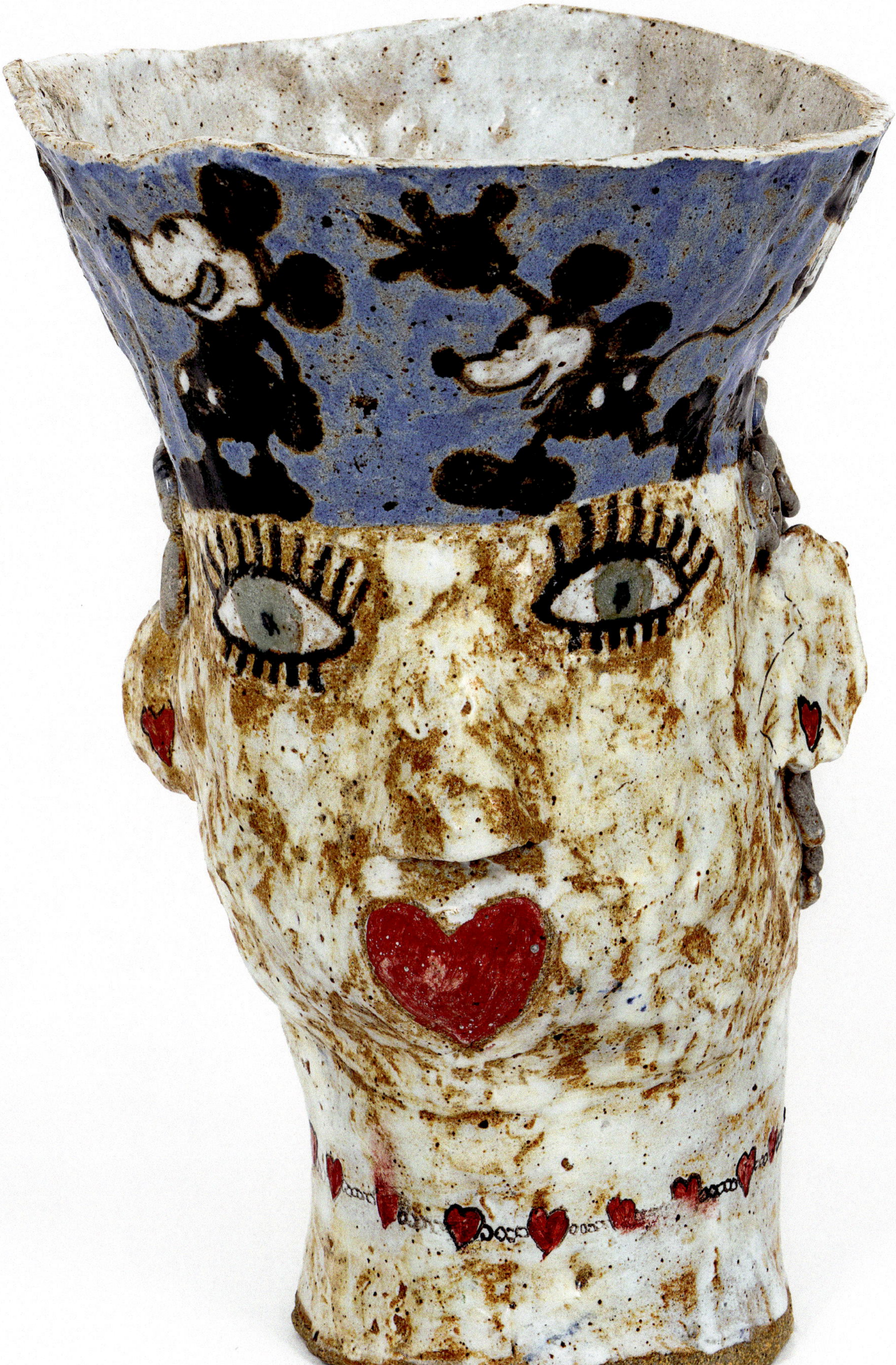

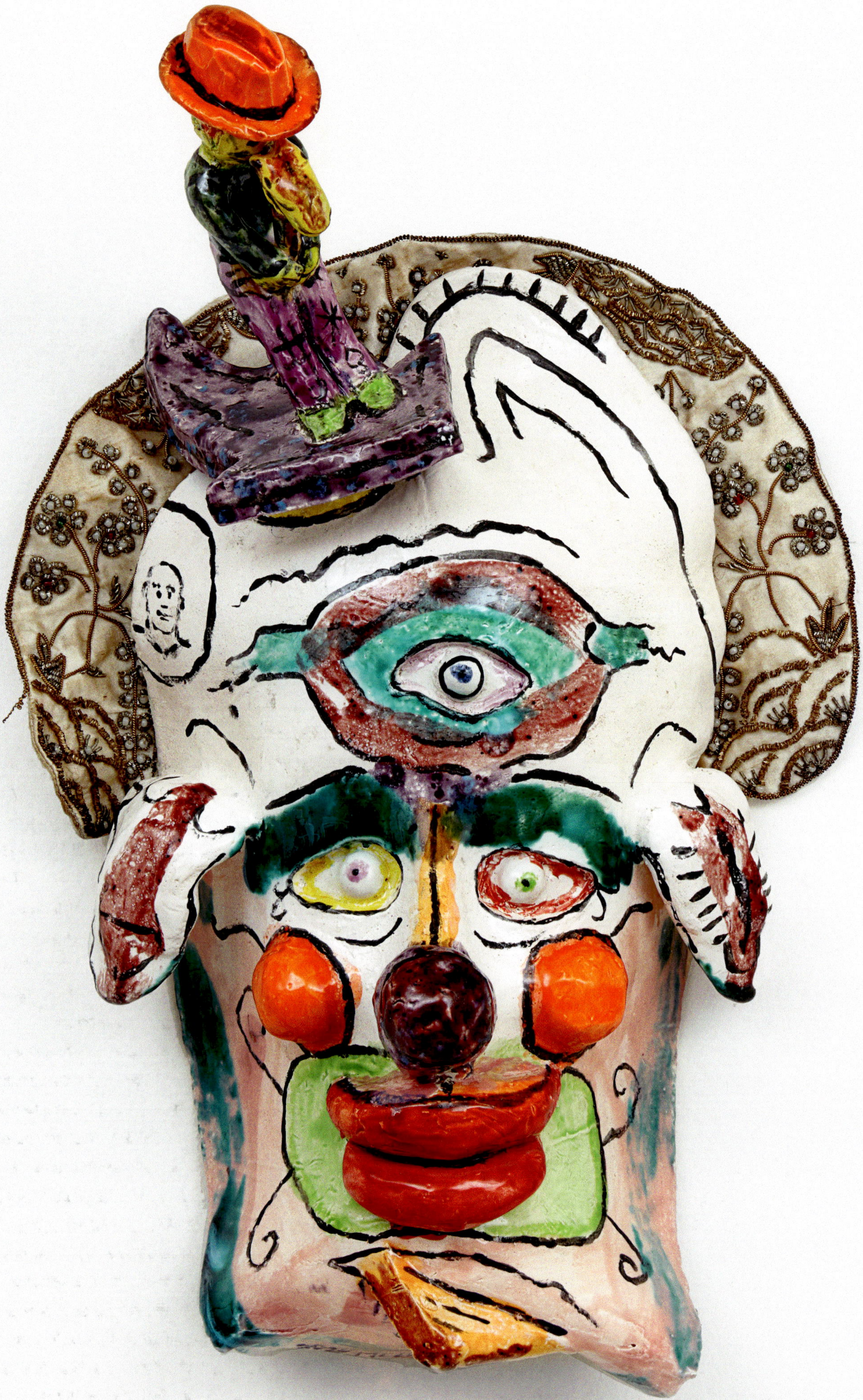

Funk You Too!

Humor & Irreverence in Ceramic Sculpture

The current contemporary art landscape evokes a trippy fever dream populated with vibrant ceramic sculptures of surreal everyday objects, anthropomorphic creatures, quirky animals, and cartoon-like figures. These objects appear to be letting you in on a joke, inviting laughter or at the very least a smile. This irreverent, animated scene is not without precedent and recalls the style and antics of West Coast "Funk ceramics" of the 1960s and 1970s and their makers. This sense of déjà vu is the impetus for the exhibition *Funk You Too! Humor and Irreverence in Ceramic Sculpture,* which brings together more than forty historic and contemporary works in clay that use humor as a tool of critique and personal expression to bridge the gap between ceramic practice of the 1960s and the present day.

This exhibition is not a comprehensive survey of all humorous ceramics in the United States, but rather an exploration of two critical contexts for this kind of work. Within these contexts, it highlights clay as a powerful tool for exploring personal and political narratives through strategies of humor, irony, irreverence, and cuteness. In doing so, it argues for the ongoing relevance of Funk ceramics to a new generation of artists working in the medium with figuration and subversive intentions. In the years since the formal recognition of Funk art in 1967, clay has emerged as a vehicle for storytelling, and a sensitive register for political, social, and aesthetic concerns, demonstrating that the radical shift the Funk generation created paved the way for a more diverse generation of artists working today.

Squishy and easy to transform, clay has an inherent comical quality and unavoidable scatological and infantile associations. Without proper contextualization, humorous art can be written off as superfluous or without depth. Artists who push against art world hierarchies risk dismissal through their use of humor, especially when using a material that has been marginalized throughout history, like clay. While satire and humor are effective subversive strategies in performative mediums such as film, theater, television, stand-up comedy, and animation, for addressing current events with a joke or irreverent suggestion, in sculpture it is a more complex endeavor. Without the format for the set-up and punch line, comedy is conveyed with subtlety through facial or bodily expressions, absurdity, amateur stylization, and fantasy imagery. *Funk You Too!* focuses on the rebels, troublemakers, and daredevils who have risen to the challenge of working in clay through the visual language of humor.

Constituting the earlier generation are Robert Arneson, Clayton Bailey, Viola Frey, David Gilhooly, Howard Kottler, Maija Peeples-Bright, Sandra Shannonhouse, Richard Shaw, Chris Unterseher, Peter VandenBerge, and Patti Warashina. Representing the current generation are Diana Yesenia Alvarado, Alex Anderson, Natalia Arbelaez, Genesis Belanger, Sharif Farrag, Salvador Jiménez-Flores, Yvette Mayorga, Ruby Neri, Woody De Othello, Didi Rojas, Alake Shilling, and Maryam Yousif. In an in-between category are Melvino Garretti, Sally Saul, and Magdalena Suarez Frimkess, who, age-wise, are peers of the first group, but their careers have taken off along with the second as part of a broader recovery of the work of underrecognized artists, especially women and artists of color.

Funk You Too! arrives at a moment when the medium of clay has unprecedented currency in the mainstream art world. Several contemporary artists in the exhibition have attracted widespread critical attention. Yet, their work has rarely been contextualized in relation to the history of ceramics, craft, and the broader history of Funk art. To connect the past and present, I discuss Funk art in the San Francisco Bay Area, associated issues of appropriation and race and the important venues for production and display. I will then address the prominence of humor in ceramics today as a vehicle for discussions of identity-based narratives that currently dominate the field. Finally, I will make connections between historical and contemporary work.

What the Funk? When You See It, You Know It

There is nothing neat about Funk art. It remains a controversial and contested subject matter with no consensus on when it was made, who made it, whether it constituted a movement, and even what it looked like. While so-called "funky" art had been around since the mid-1950s, it was not formally canonized until the 1967 exhibition *FUNK*,[1] curated by Peter Selz, founding Director of the Berkeley Art Museum and Pacific Film Archive at the University of California, Berkeley. At the time, Selz was a recent transplant from New York—where he worked as the Museum of Modern Art's curator of painting and sculpture for seven years—interested in showcasing art that was "very local."[2] *FUNK* ran from April 18 through May 29 (and traveled to the Institute of Contemporary Art, Boston, later the same year), showcasing fifty-eight sculptural works by twenty-six artists in various mediums, including clay.

Selz was not wrong in stating that "while it is much too early to make any claim for the historical or critical importance of this art, it seems appropriate to document its occurrence."[3] To the chagrin of many participating artists and critics, the exhibition became a defining moment for the establishment of Funk art. "Funk" was not a term that Selz coined but rather one he absorbed from the artistic community in the San Francisco Bay Area. In the exhibition catalog, Selz explained how participating artist "Bruce Conner and his friends in the Rat Bastard Protective Association (RBPA) put together ephemeral conglomerations of all kinds of uncombinable things, called them 'Funk,' and didn't care what happened to them."[4] Other artists used the term because of its connotation with body odor, such as Robert Arneson, who sculpted his first infamous toilet sculpture in 1963, retitling it *Funk John* in 1965. Selz provided yet another definition, "to be frighted and shrink back,"[5] an expected response to the funky art. According to RBPA artist Joan Brown, the point of Funk art was for artists to shock each other with the objects they made.[6]

The Director's emphasis on the word caused much dissent among artists, whose irreverent and sometimes downright angry answers to a pre-exhibition survey and remarks during a contentious symposium (April 28, 1967) made their grievances clear.[7] In James Monte's 1967 *Art Forum* review of the exhibition, Conner condemned Selz's curation by declaring that he was "trying to make Funk appear as a new thing happening now rather than a ten year old event. Selz's Funk is fake."[8] Harold Paris, Selz's "best artist friend" and exhibiting *FUNK* artist, wrote an article for *Art in America* titled "Sweet Land of Funk" to lay the critical foundation for *FUNK*. In it, he attempted to differentiate between Conner's and Selz's ideas of Funk by asserting that "Funk art [as presented in *FUNK*] has grown away from the funky art of the 1950s [referenced by Conner]."[9] Conner was vocal in stating that Paris was not "the spokesperson of Funk," and later

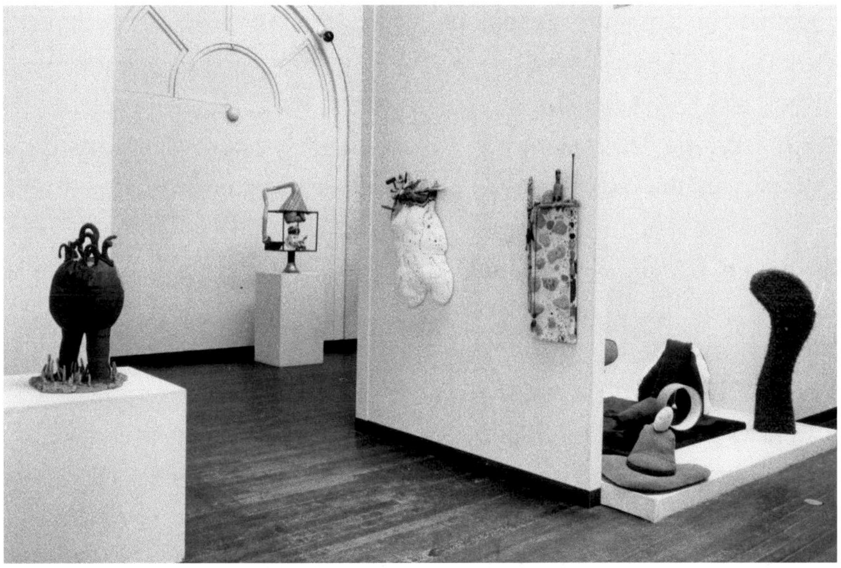

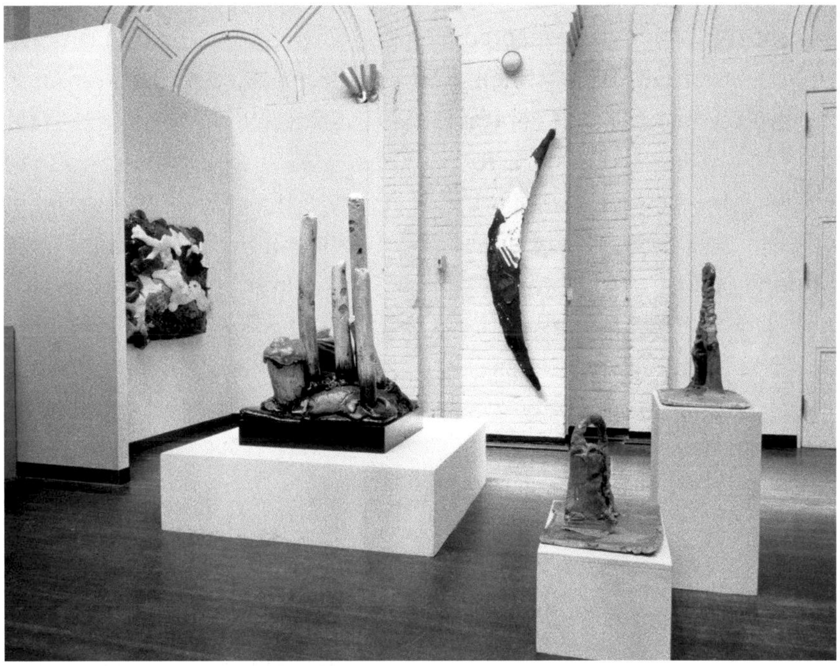

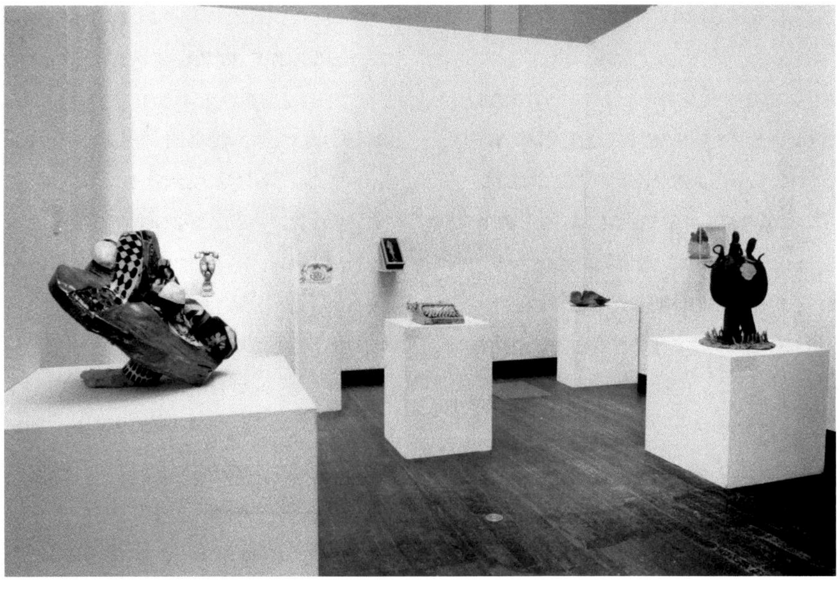

1–3 Installation views of *FUNK*, University Art Museum, University of California Berkeley, 1967. The University of California, Berkeley Art Museum and Pacific Film Archive

in life, Selz admitted that Paris was not "a Funk artist strictly speaking."[10] Paris was but a mere conduit for Selz's ideas.[11] Regardless of many artists' resistance to the label of Funk and public disagreement over the conceptual foundation of the exhibition, it was a commercial success with more than 18,000 visitors in the first few weeks of its run.[12] It crystalized the Funk label, which stuck.

The Funk ethos represented a shift in the art world. Many of the works displayed in *FUNK* would fit in a contemporary museum today, but in 1967 they were perceived as odd, unexpected, and at times off-putting [figs. 1–3]. The artwork was inherently political by defying modern art standards defined by the New York establishment, where Minimalism, Conceptual Art, and Pop Art ruled. Among the attempts by Selz to explain Funk art, this ambiguous and noncommittal description stands out: "Funk art is hot rather than cool; it is committed rather than disengaged; it is bizarre rather than formal; it is sensuous, and frequently, it is quite ugly and ungainly."[14] He added that the art "makes fun of itself," but is also "dead serious."[15] Although Funk had connections to Dada, Surrealism, California Assemblage, Bay Area Figuration, Abstract Expressionism, and even Pop Art, it was its own beast, difficult to categorize or define by any existing "fine art" standards of the time. Ultimately, some practitioners simply said that "when you see it, you know it."[16] Selz's *FUNK,* in particular, was an assortment of objects loosely connected by their eccentricity and an eclectic approach to materials and making. In his review, Monte described the exhibition as a "pastiche, incredible in its variety, of every painting and sculptural direction of the last twenty years."[17]

Although often called a movement, Funk had no definite group of artists, agreed-upon goals, materials, or aesthetics. In 2012 Selz agreed that he "would not use the term today."[18] Selz's common denominator among the artists was their relationship to the Bay Area, and while Selz recognized that similar artwork was being produced all over the country, he underscored that Funk "sprouted and grew" in the Bay Area.[19] It is not surprising that the Bay Area was a fertile epicenter for avant-garde art such as Funk, given the area's openness toward alternative culture, including the Beat movement and the 1960s counterculture. Important social and political movements of the period such as the Vietnam war protests, the Free Speech Movement, and the founding of the Black Panther Party, among other examples, demonstrate the Bay Area's progressiveness.

For Selz, funky ceramics were "useless pots."[20] By this criteria, a large number of 1960s studio ceramics qualified as Funk. Selz included ceramics by Arneson, Peter Voulkos, Ken Price, James Melchert, Manuel Neri, and Arneson's former student and studio assistant, David Gilhooly. Although most of the work contained some humor, Arneson's and Gilhooly's work stood out at a time when abstraction reigned supreme. While the artists were distinct, they shared an anti-establishment attitude about violating the expectations of "good pottery." If there is one thing scholars and artists, then and now, agree on is that Funk art was "largely a matter of attitude."[21]

A look back at *FUNK* is essential as a contextual foundation for *Funk You Too!* which focuses on the former's eduring legacy: the explosion of humorous and irreverent narrative content in ceramic sculpture. While this kind of work had already been in production by the early 1960s, the landmark *FUNK* propelled its recognition and catalyzed new work. Selz's wish to not "freeze or inhibit ... further development of Funk,"[22] was best realized in ceramics. As Brown explained, "the best funky things were those containing humorous elements that poked fun at sex, religion, pets, patriotism, art, and politics,"[23] which is an excellent description of Arneson's work and that of his friends and students, I will discuss later in this essay.

Arneson's figurative, kitschy, and rude sculptures became the epitome of Funk ceramics. As the leading exponent, many consider him the father of Funk. He was one of the few artists who embraced Funk as a label, writing in his 1970 artist "non-statement" that he was not afraid of "movements, attitudes, and labels," including Funk.[24] In the *FUNK* survey, Arneson takes great care to answer each question using different

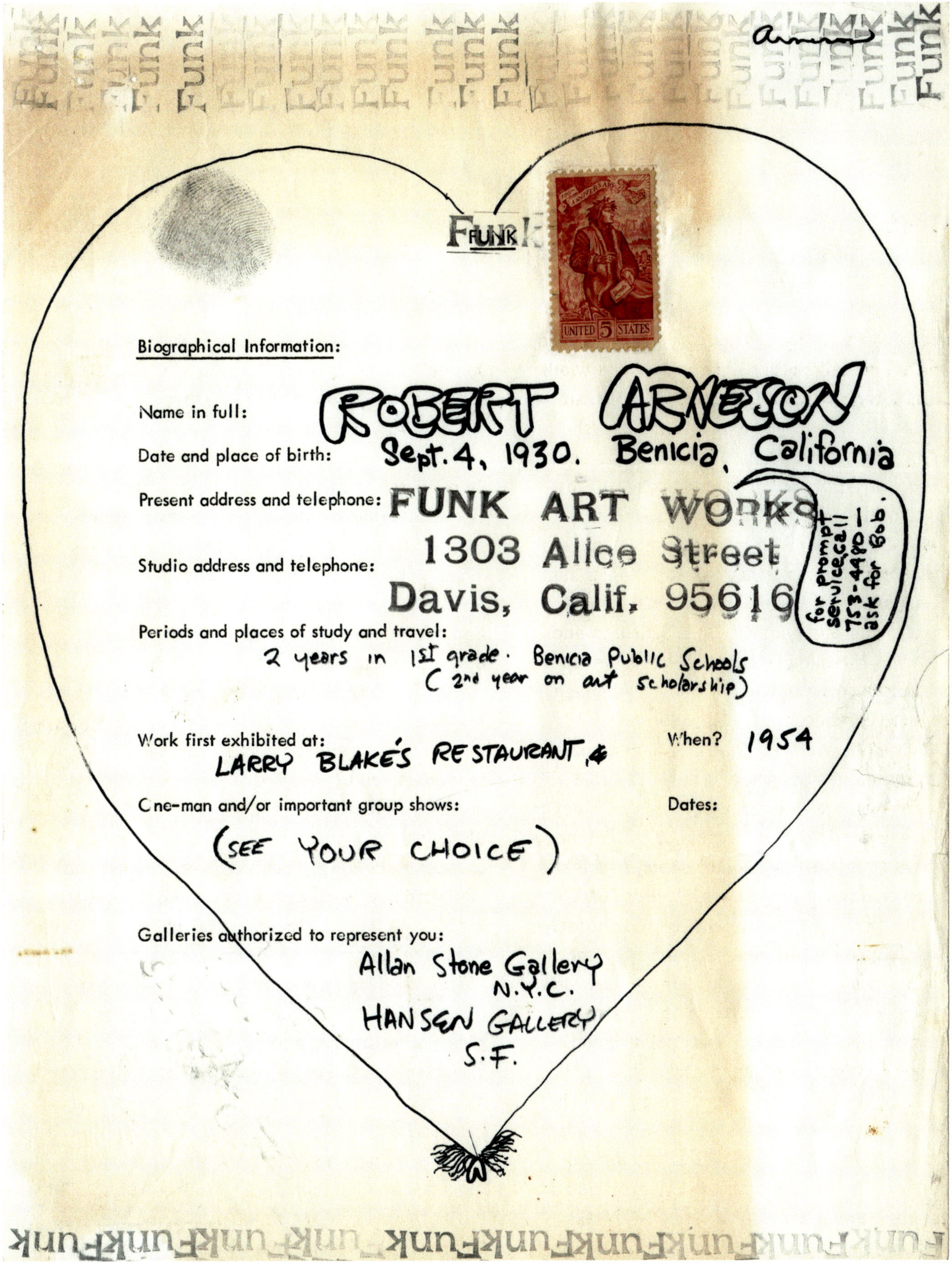

FUNK

Biographical Information:

Name in full: ROBERT ARNESON

Date and place of birth: Sept. 4, 1930. Benicia, California

Present address and telephone: FUNK ART WORKS

Studio address and telephone: 1303 Alice Street Davis, Calif. 95616

for prompt service, call 753-4480 — ask for Bob.

Periods and places of study and travel:
2 years in 1st grade. Benicia Public Schools (2nd year on art scholarship)

Work first exhibited at: LARRY BLAKE'S RESTAURANT, When? 1954

One-man and/or important group shows: Dates:
(SEE YOUR CHOICE)

Galleries authorized to represent you:
Allan Stone Gallery N.Y.C.
HANSEN GALLERY S.F.

4a–c Robert Arneson *FUNK* survey, 1967. The University of California, Berkeley Art Museum and Pacific Film Archive

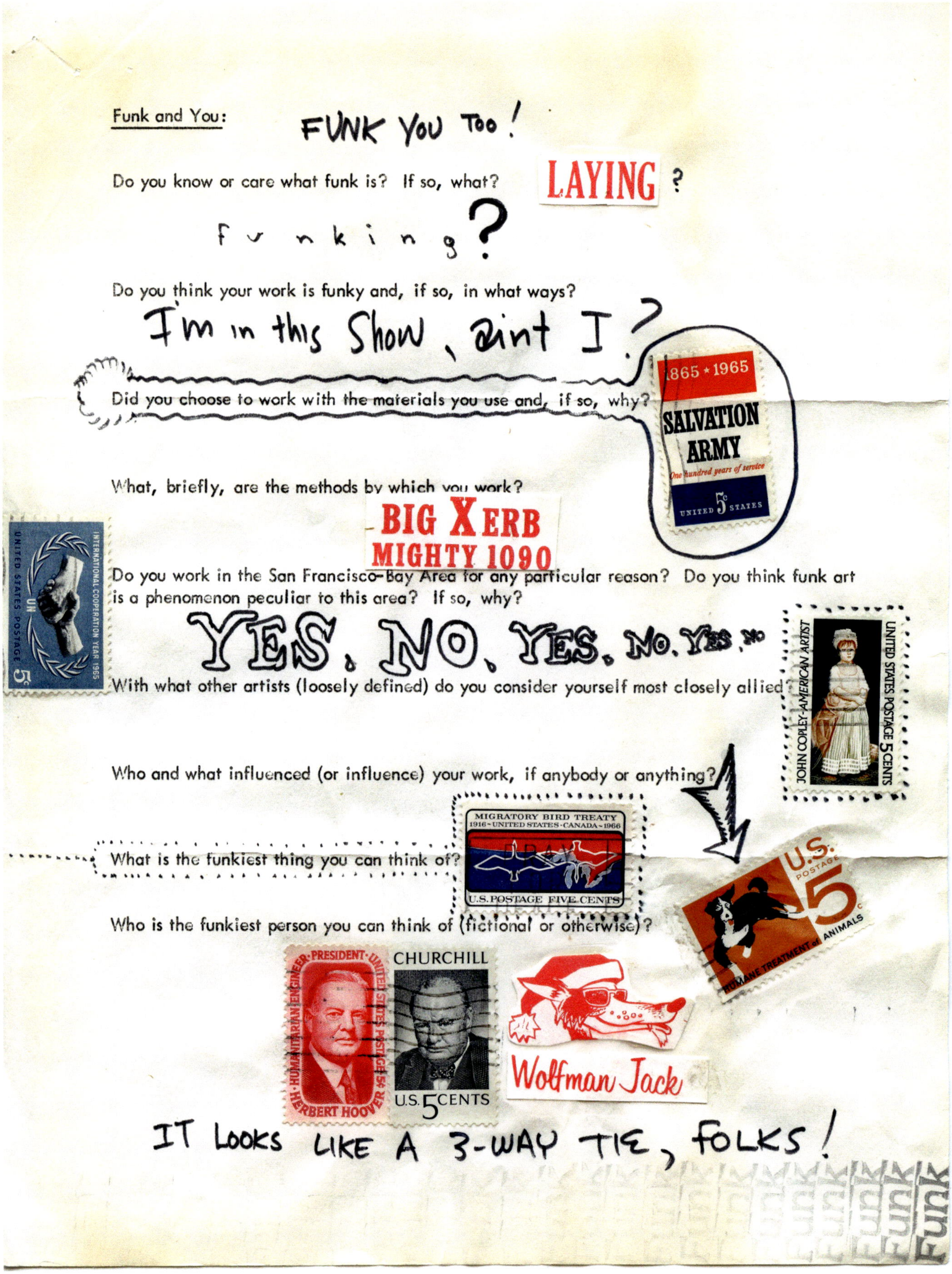

Funk and You: FUNK YOU TOO!

Do you know or care what funk is? If so, what? LAYING ?

Funking?

Do you think your work is funky and, if so, in what ways?

I'm in this Show, aint I?

Did you choose to work with the materials you use and, if so, why?

What, briefly, are the methods by which you work?

BIG XERB
MIGHTY 1090

Do you work in the San Francisco-Bay Area for any particular reason? Do you think funk art is a phenomenon peculiar to this area? If so, why?

YES, NO, YES, NO, YES, NO

With what other artists (loosely defined) do you consider yourself most closely allied?

Who and what influenced (or influence) your work, if anybody or anything?

What is the funkiest thing you can think of?

Who is the funkiest person you can think of (fictional or otherwise)?

Wolfman Jack

IT LOOKS LIKE A 3-WAY TIE, FOLKS!

How do you think funk art, and your funk art in particular, relates to other art -- past, present, and/or future? Or doesn't it?

SEE STAMP #1

It's Funkier
It's Funkier
It's Funkier

Do you think funk art is (circle your preferences):

fun	articulate	irrelevant
dirty	dumb	beautiful
clean	tasteless	ugly
sexy	anti-mechanical	paradoxical
colorful	low-brow	introverted
traditional	anti-intellectual	primitive
intellectual	political	masculine
moral	anti-political	unsophisticated
amoral	fuzzy	organic
immoral	sweaty	feminine
Renaissance	three-dimensional	messy
defiant	irreverent	raw
anti-	sensual	ill-made

VOID VOID VOID VOID VOID VOID VOID VOID VOID VOID VOID

Other: friendly

If you like, we would appreciate having a short statement about yourself and/or your work, which might be suitable for mass consumption through publication in our Funk catalogue.

Well,..yes. I think Ceramics *is* the World's most fascinating hobby!

fonts, postage, magazine cutouts, and stamping the word "funk" more than sixty times over the pages. *Funk You Too!* is titled after one of Arneson's tongue-in-cheek comments on the survey. The questionnaire portion was titled "Funk and You," and in response, Arneson wrote "Funk You Too!," a pun on the similar sounding four-letter expletive which encapsulates the humor, irreverence, and the contextual foundation for this exhibition in three simple words [figs. 4a–c].

A Funky Note: Issues of Appropriation and Race

In revisiting the history of Funk art through a contemporary lens, it is important to address the overlooked issues of appropriation and race in the 1967 exhibition. While Selz's curation of *FUNK* was subject to hostile critique, the title's appropriative nature and lack of diversity among the exhibiting artists were never questioned.

Selz notes that he borrowed the word "Funk" from the jazz scene, where it represented "the unsophisticated deep-down New Orleans blues ... which give you that happy/sad feeling,"[25] despite Harold Paris's claims that he picked the word out of the dictionary for his pre-exhibition article.[26] Yet another story goes that sometime in the 1950s, RBPA artist Manuel Neri heard trumpeter Miles Davis say, "Man, that's a funky note," while playing in a San Francisco jazz club, and he began applying it to artwork along with his peers.[27] While Funk music, as we recognize it today, was nascent in the mid-1960s through the work of musicians like James Brown, it preceded Selz's *FUNK*. Descriptions of Funk music by historian Rickey Vincent are amusingly similar to those given by Selz about Funk art. "Funk is funkiness, a natural release of the essence within .... Funk is at the extremes of everything. Funk is hot, but can also be cool .... Funk is impossible to completely describe in words, yet we know the funk vibe when we see it."[28]

I contend that Selz appropriated the word from the African-American music vernacular, already used by Bay Area artists, to denominate a group of predominantly white artists.[29] This form of racial appropriation was typical of 1950s and early 1960s Beat culture, a scene many Funk artists participated in. Although there were Black Beats, the most prominent proponents were white poets and writers deeply influenced by their interactions with African-American culture, particularly its traditions of improvisation in language, poetry, and music.[30] The Beats often referenced jazz in their writing, and the word "funky" was part of their lexicon.[31]

While many of the Beats' writings reflected a superficial understanding of Black life, such as Allen Ginsberg's infamous poem "Howl," which describes the "negro streets" as a place to obtain drugs, they generally advocated for interracial culture in a time when segregation was pervasive. Although they could never fully understand the reality of being Black in America, the Beats embraced an associative marginalization tied to their appropriations of and interactions with African-American culture. As scholar Mona Lisa Saloy puts it, the "reversals, oppositions, aesthetics, and values that are different from the larger society" were viewed within Beat circles as tools of "liberation, resistance, and loyalty" that politicized abjection.[32] In this vein, Glenn Adamson has argued that Robert Arneson welcomed the association of marginality that came with the label of Funk.[33]

There is no known comprehensive list of artists Selz considered to be a part of *FUNK*. He shared that he and his team visited "a great many studios," but did not elaborate on how they decided on the twenty-six artists to showcase.[34] The inclusion of Los Angeles-based artist Ken Price, who had no connection to the Bay Area, complicates matters, as the funky work of African-American artists in Los Angeles such as Melvin Edwards, John Outterbridge, and Noah Purifoy would have fit well within Selz's exhibition. Although I could speculate many possible reasons for their exclusion, there is no record of anyone asking Selz why there were no Black artists in the exhibition.[35] Despite the exclusion of African-American artists from the 1967 exhibition, Black cultural contributions are essential to the foundation of Funk art, Selz's *FUNK*, and Funk ceramics. Black communities originated the language, the approach, and the attitude that shaped this moment in clay.

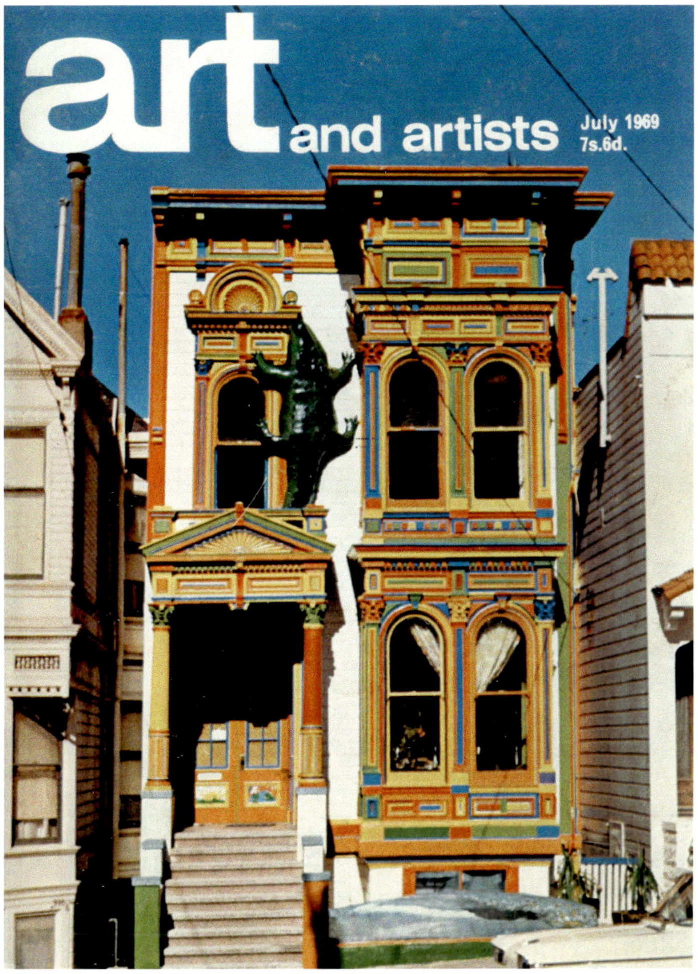

5 Rainbow House (908 Steiner Street), San Francisco, on the cover of *Arts and Artists*, July 1969

It's Nuts! From Funk to Nut

At least five years before Selz's *FUNK*, Arneson, along with friends and students, were actively building and sharing irreverent and humorous sculptures at three key venues: Temporary Building 9 or TB 9, the art department where Arneson taught at the University of California, Davis (UC Davis, 1962–91), the Candy Store Gallery, founded in 1962 in Folsom, CA, and Maija Peeples-Bright's Victorian Rainbow House in San Francisco [fig. 5]. Within these nuclei, they set the terms for the creative scene from which Funk ceramics as a genre emerged.

Arneson's work better aligned with his students' than with *FUNK* artists, except for Gilhooly, his student, teaching assistant, and friend. Consequently, many of his students became known as makers of Funk ceramics, including Peeples-Bright, Sandra Shannonhouse, Richard Shaw, Chris Unterseher, and Peter VandenBerge. As such, TB 9 became a breeding ground for Funk ceramicists. This cohort also included Clayton Bailey, who taught briefly at UC Davis when Arneson invited him to take over his classes while he was on a leave of absence.

Arneson and his comrades found a nurturing haven to develop their ceramics at the Candy Store Gallery (1962–92). Adeliza McHugh and her sister bought the house that became the gallery, intending to open a confectionery shop specializing in almond nougats.[36] After a failed state inspection, McHugh pivoted to selling the next best thing: the quirkiest art of the day. In 1962, she approached Arneson at UC Davis about providing her work for consignment. Although he was hesitant, he gave her some "raunchy funky" cups and small works to get her "off my back," which she quickly sold, returning for more two weeks later.[37] Impressed, he became a pivotal artist at the Candy Store,

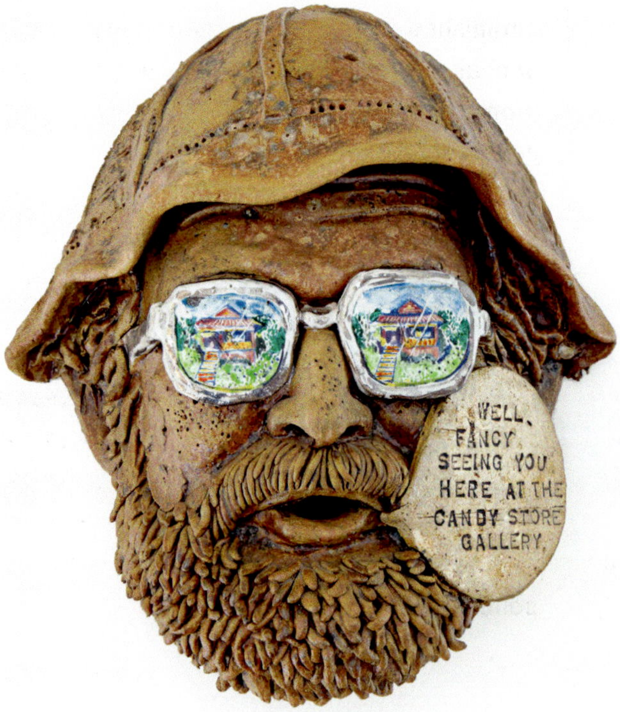

6 Robert Arneson, *Well, Fancy Seeing You Here at the Candy Store Gallery*, 1973. Stoneware, glaze, and luster, 13 × 12 × 6 in. (33 × 30.5 × 15.2 cm). Private collection

bringing other artists along and even making the gallery's sign in ceramic. Illuminating the significance of the gallery to his practice, in 1973, Arneson made a self-portrait with a speech bubble reading, "Well, fancy seeing you here at the Candy Store Gallery," with a double reflection of the colorful house on his sunglasses [fig. 6].

In her fifties, and without previous art world experience, McHugh cultivated a strong roster of multidisciplinary artists that included Jim Nutt and Gladys Nilsson of the Chicago Hairy Who!, who relocated to California in 1969; Chicago-based "outsider" artist Joseph Yoakum; Roy De Forest, and William T. Wiley, both part of *FUNK*; along with Arneson and his circle [fig. 7]. The thriving art dealer was described as the "first lady of Funk" in a 1981 local newspaper article and was beloved by the artists she championed.[38] Arneson's sculptural tribute to McHugh from 1976, *House Mother for Odd Birds*, captures the smiling gallerist with colorful birds flying around her head representing her quirky artists [fig. 8]. The gallery became well known in the Bay Area for its consistent presentation of avant-garde work that was laugh-out-loud funny and the subject of multiple exhibitions at the nearby Crocker Museum of Art in Sacramento.[39]

A few years after *FUNK*, many Candy Store artists, especially the ceramicists, began to refer to their work as Nut art. Art critic David Zack, Peeples-Bright's then husband, and painter De Forest coined the term at the Rainbow House, where the artists often gathered. Unlike "Funk," this label was self-appointed, accepted, and used by an organized group of artists who sought to create humorous work. "The Candy Store Bunch" was featured in the 1972 exhibition *Nut Art* at the California State University Hayward Art Gallery, whose accompanying catalog contained a collection of ramblings, musings, statements, artwork images, doodles, letters, and photographs which helped solidify the circle's intended aesthetic and ethos.[40] Together they formed a band of misfits on the outskirts of the mainstream art world, but nevertheless successful, with countless exhibitions, acquisitions, and publications. Fun and funny, Nut ceramics often conveyed information through tongue-in-cheek titles, revealing an inner dialogue between group members. Bright colors and absurdity ran rampant within the walls of the Candy Store Gallery. The artists used humor disarmingly to discuss the silliest and the most taboo topics alike.

Contemporaries making kindred work included Viola Frey in the Bay Area; Howard Kottler and Patti Warashina in Washington state; and Magdalena Suarez Frimkess and Melvino Garretti in Los Angeles, among others nationally, like Sally Saul in Texas and then New York, and internationally. Funk or Nut ceramics have remained present in the field since their inception, although with diminished presence as artists have passed away or changed styles. Funk has gained renewed momentum and visibility in recent years with a generation of young artists working in clay and established artists receiving greater recognition today.[41] While conscious of their predecessors, this new cohort has re-examined the potential for humor in clay through a rainbow of perspectives, forming the basis for an expanded exploration of narratives that goes beyond historical precedent. In this way, the new guard carries Funk into the future, reinvigorating the use of satire, irreverence, and subversion as a lens through which to address some of the most pressing social and political issues of our day.

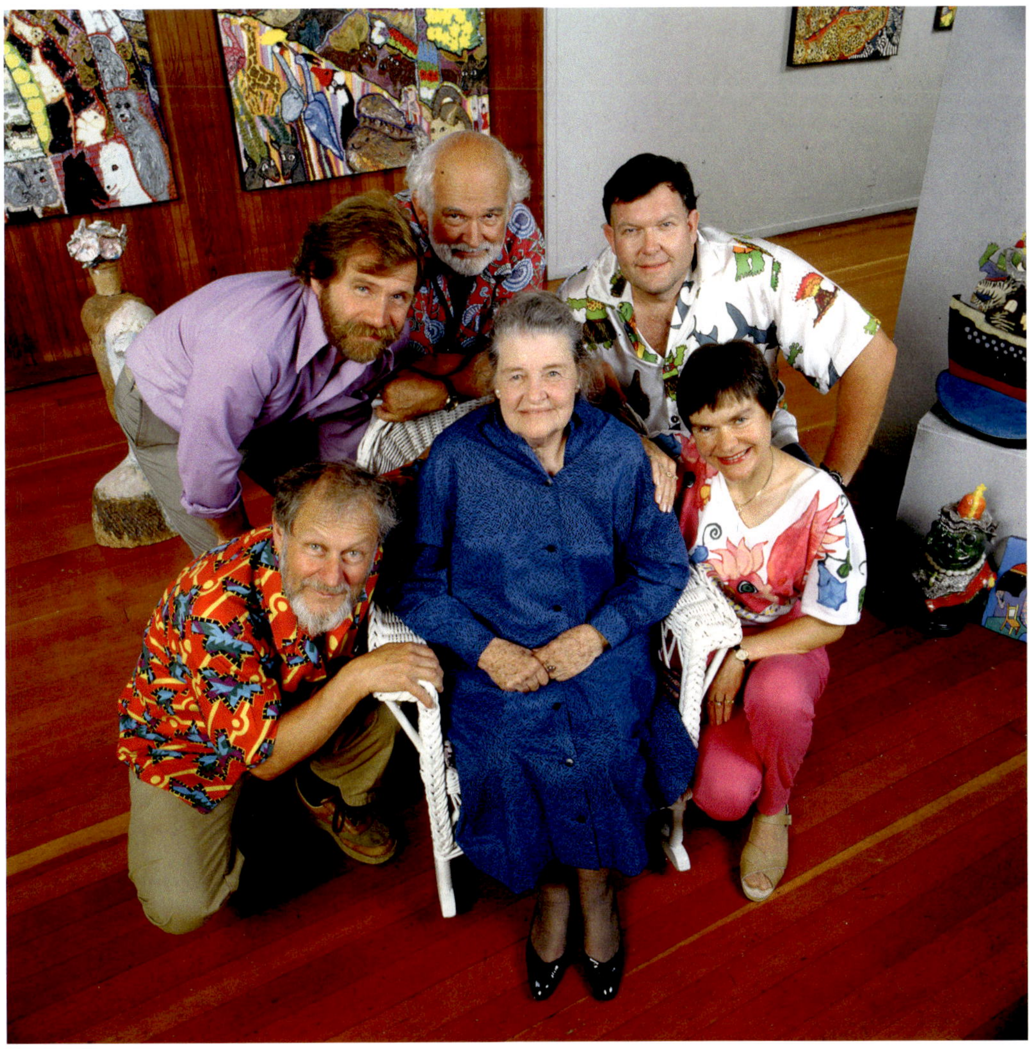

7 Group photo at the Candy Store Gallery (clockwise from bottom left: Roy De Forest, Peter VandenBerge, Robert Arneson, David Gilhooly, Maija Peeples-Bright, Adeliza McHugh), 1987

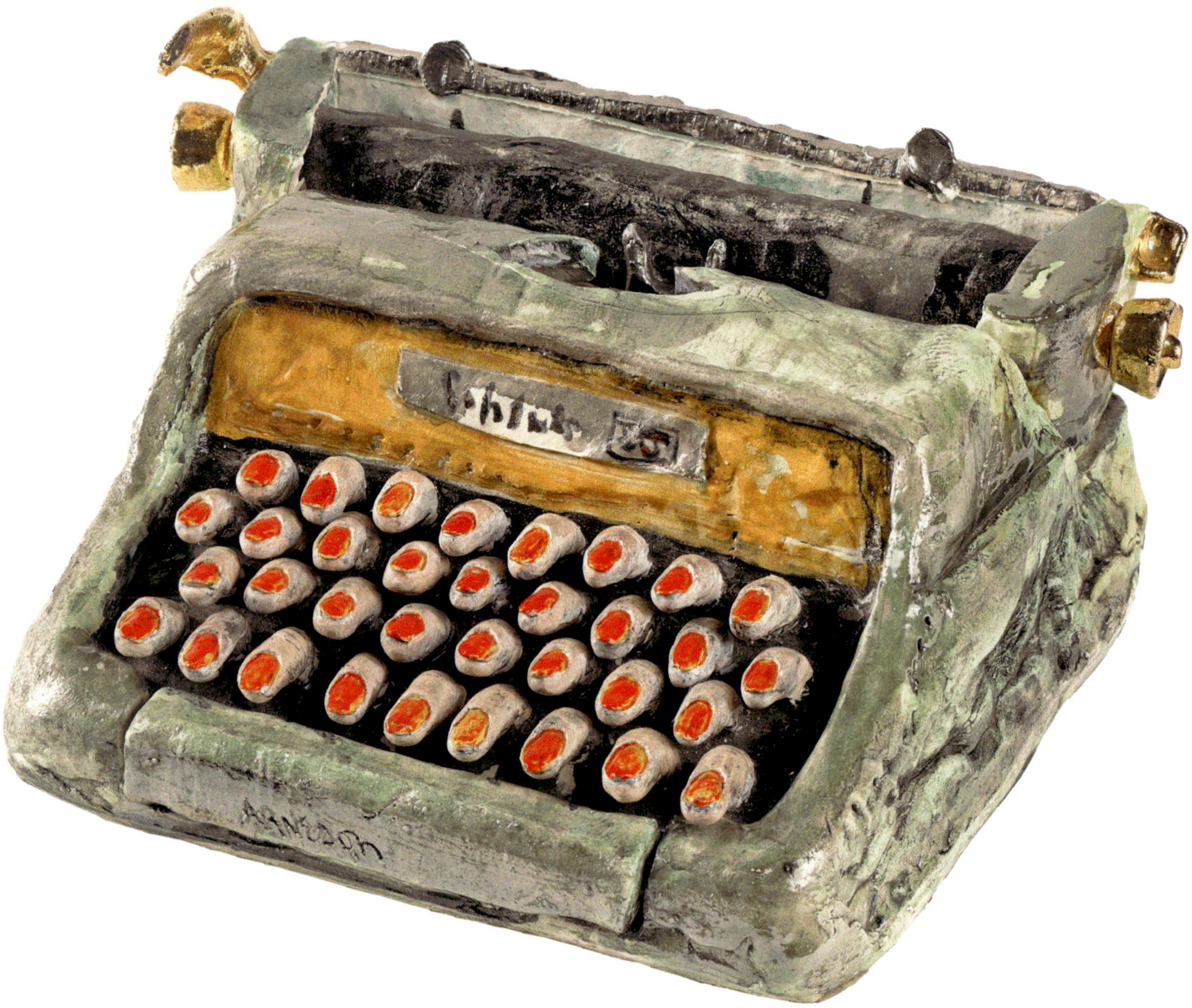

9 Robert Arneson, *Typewriter*, 1965. Earthenware, glaze, and nail polish, 6 ⅛ × 11 ⅜ × 12 ½ in. (15.6 × 28.9 × 31.8 cm). The University of California, Berkeley Art Museum and Pacific Film Archive; gift of the artist, 1967

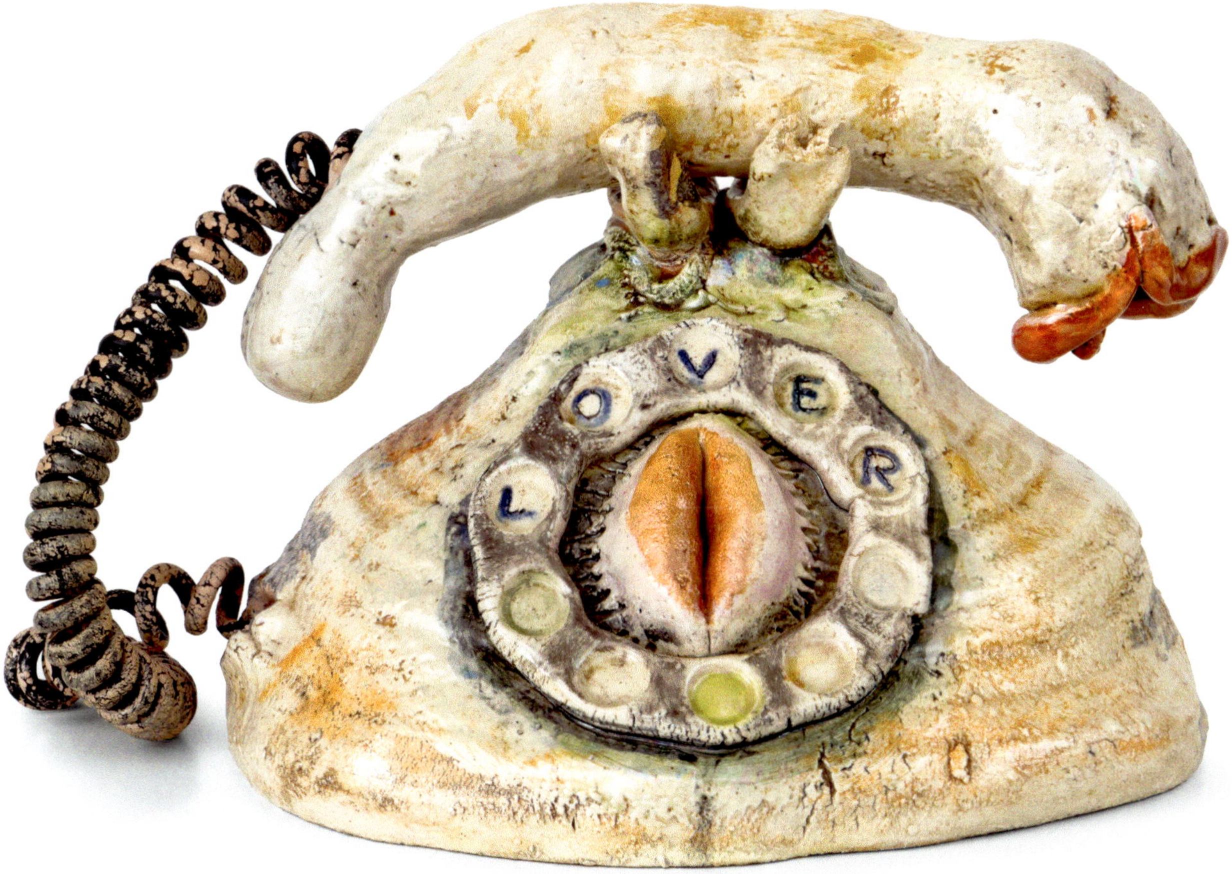

10 Robert Arneson, *Call Me Lover*, 1965. Ceramic and glaze, 8 × 11 × 9 in. (20.3 × 27.9 × 22.9 cm). Kolodny Family Collection, New York

landscape of grazing cows painted onto a miniature couch and chair. While the tiny furniture makes a silly canvas for the bucolic painting, it demonstrates Shaw's profound interest in establishing ordinary objects as "fine art." His pursuit echoes Arneson's self-consciousness about his status as an artist working in ceramics, or "the world's most fascinating hobby,"[45] as he self-deprecatingly put it. Arneson referred to his work as "white mud calling itself art," belying a very successful career.[46] His attitude was one way of deflating the power of the hierarchy of the arts.

The Funk bug also infected Seattle, where Patti Warashina and Howard Kottler used Surrealism to address identity politics in their art practices while running the ceramics program at the University of Washington. Kottler visited *FUNK* which gave him the "freedom to let my craziness run amok," and expand his already subversive vessels positing the pottery form as homoerotic.[47] An exploration of his sexuality, he focused on the mouth of the vessel as a proxy for bodily orifices.[48] The sexy pots became more suggestive through the addition of fur. The dainty *Hole Grabber* (1967) consists of a circular base decorated with decal flowers from which a furry stem protrudes, crowned by a golden disk with a hole at its center [fig. 12]. Cast Barbie arms surround the hole, appearing to grab it as the title suggests.

For her part, Warashina began making feminist work in 1971 to critique the culture of ceramics programs at universities that cultivated boys' clubs. At the time, male students were encouraged to learn kiln-building while female students were expected to focus on decorative techniques. This gendered division of labor reflected the expectation that the former would become professional artists while the latter would abandon their careers to pursue marriage, childrearing, and the domestic arts. Warashina proved them wrong by demonstrating mastery of the kiln through a series of sculptures depicting the equipment, such as in *Metamorphosis of a Car Kiln* (1971) [fig. 13]. She combined the iconography of classic cars (also considered "macho") with bricks to create visual puns for kilns used in schools, known as "car kilns." This series is in sharp contrast to Arneson's *Kiln Man* (1971) [fig. 14], where the artist showed dominance over the kiln by transfiguring it into

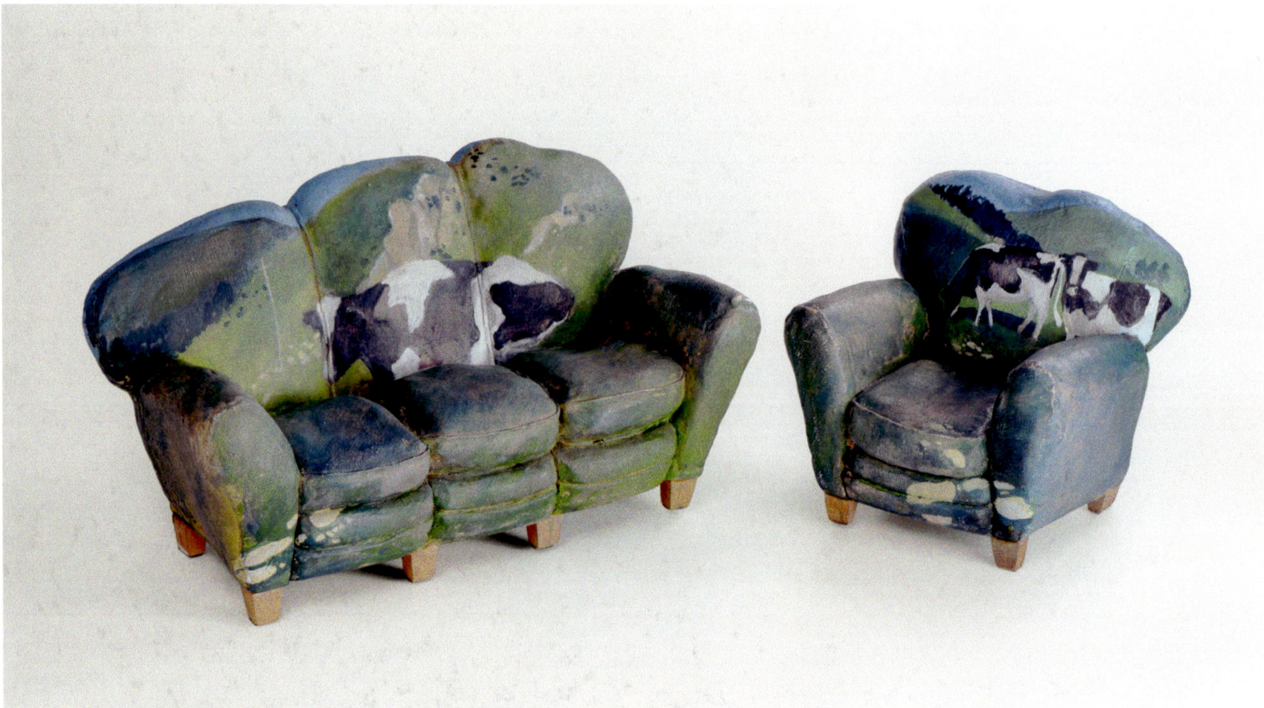

11 Richard Shaw, *Couch and Chair with Landscape and Cows*, 1966–67. Earthenware, acrylic paint, and wood, chair: 9 × 10 × 5 ¾ in. (22.9 × 25.4 × 14.6 cm); sofa: 9 ¾ × 18 ½ × 10 in. (24.8 × 47 × 25.4 cm). Museum of Arts and Design, New York; gift of the Johnson Wax Company, through the American Craft Council, 1977

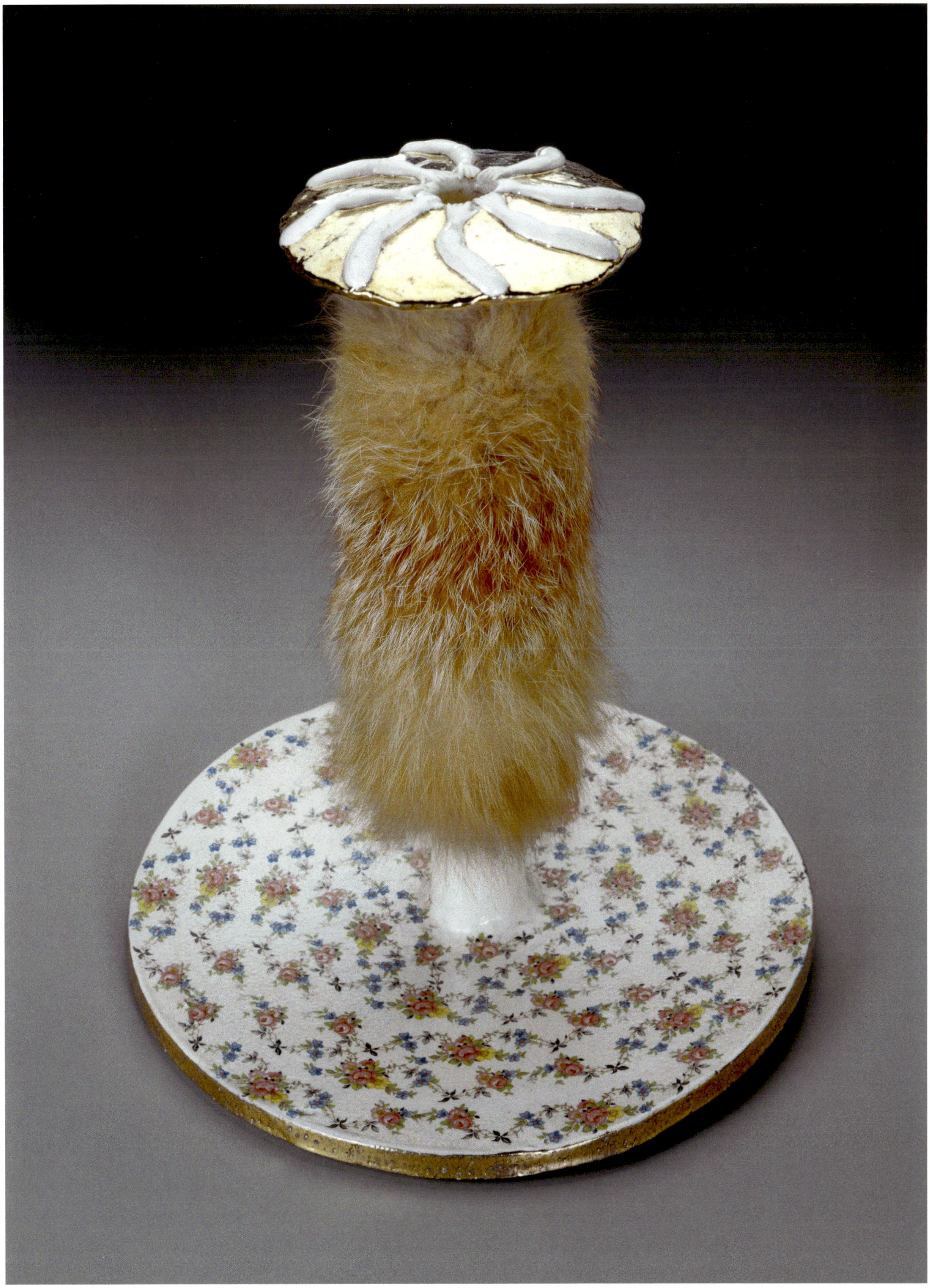

12 Howard Kottler, *Hole Grabber*, 1967. Earthenware, luster, decals, and fox fur, 15 × 13 × 13 in. (38.1 × 33 × 33 cm). Museum of Arts and Design, New York; gift of the artist and Manolides Gallery, through the American Craft Council, 1972

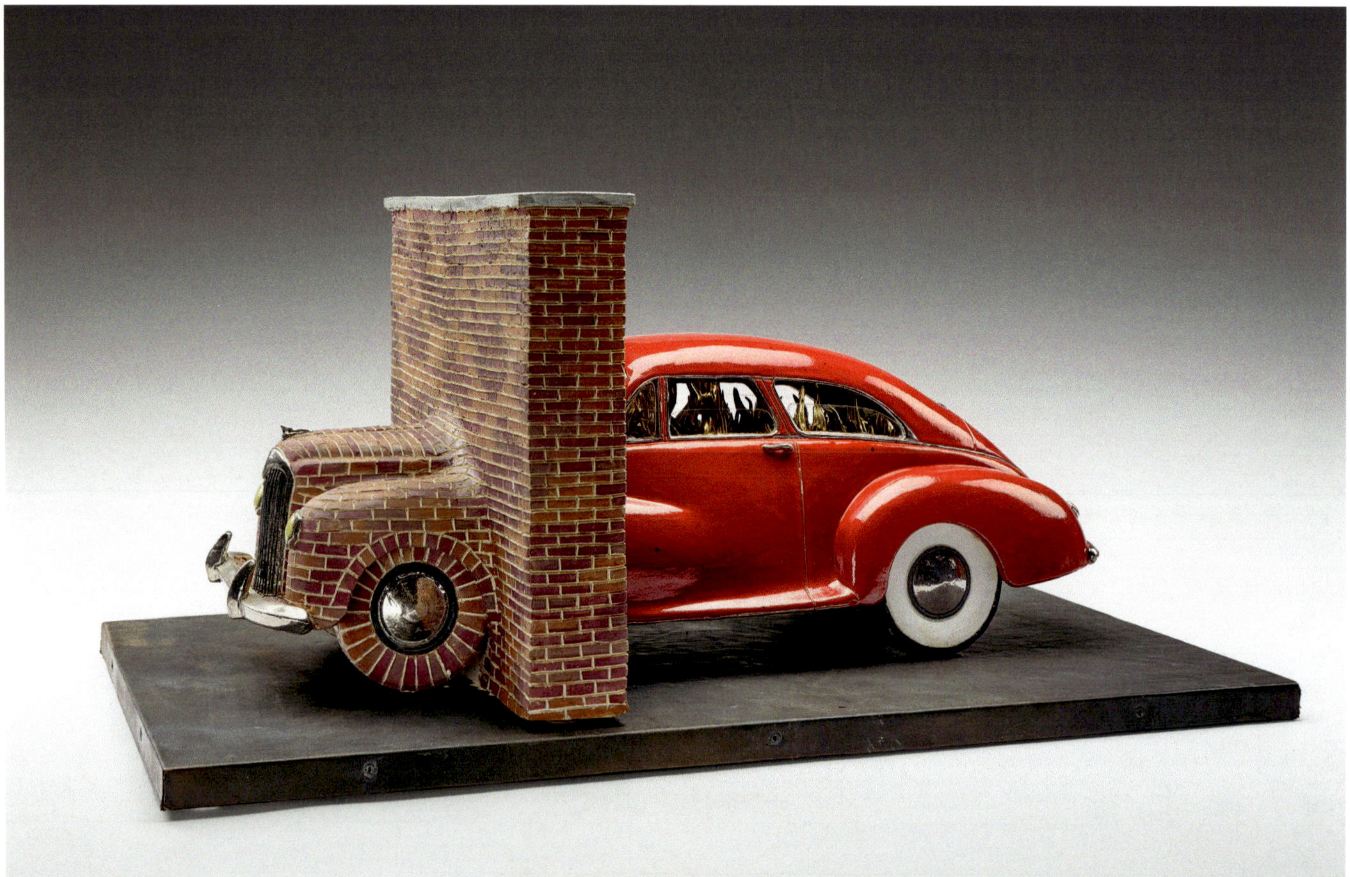

13 Patti Warashina, *Metamorphosis of a Car Kiln*, 1971. Earthenware, acrylic paint, and luster, 20 × 36 × 20 in. (50.8 × 91.4 × 50.8 cm). The Museum of Fine Arts, Houston; purchase funded by Sara and Bill Morgan in memory of Clint Willour and in honor of Cindi Strauss; the GRITS Foundation; Nina Zilkha; the Decorative Arts Endowment Fund; Cecily Horton; and Joan Morgenstern, 2021

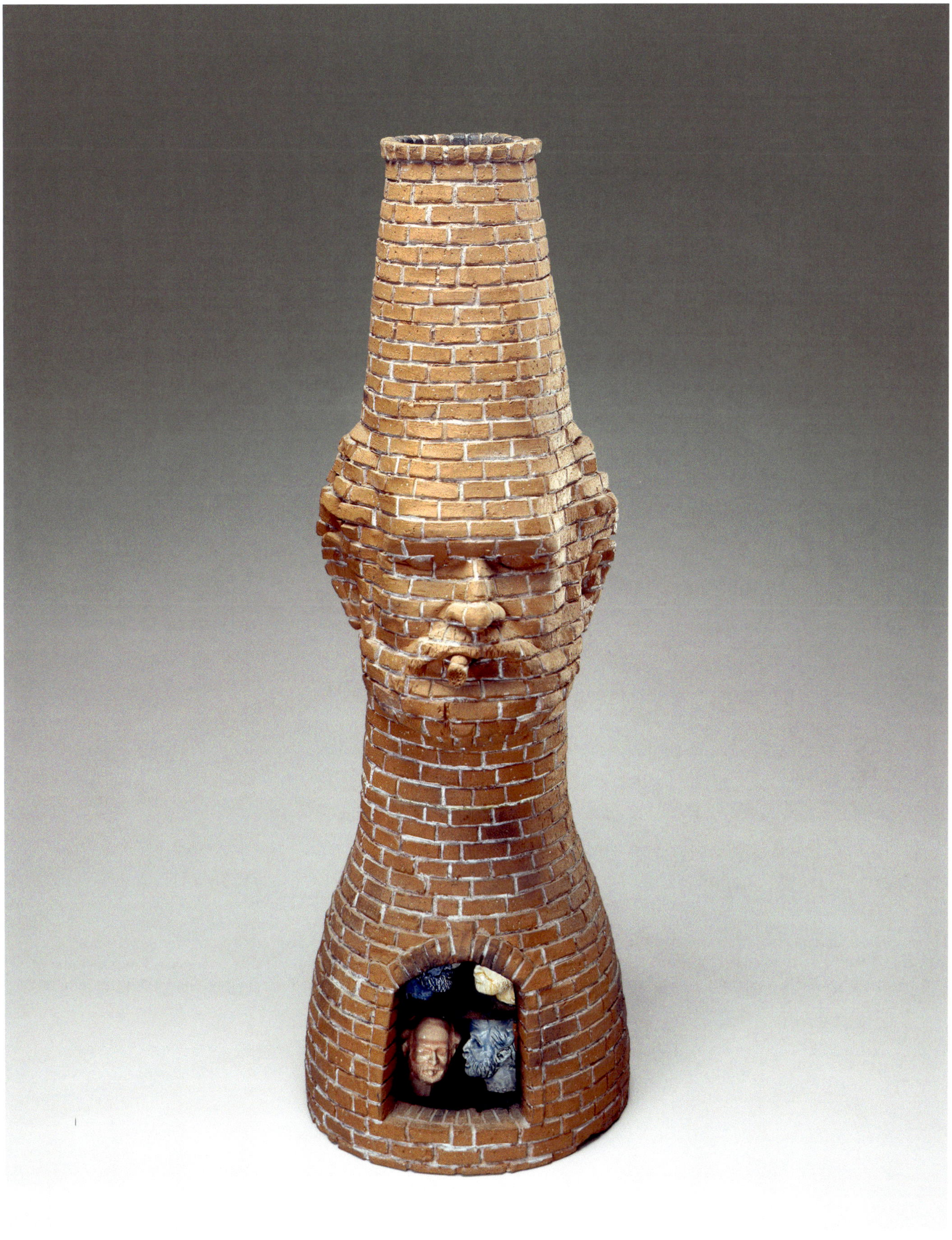

14 Robert Arneson, *Kiln Man*, 1971. Earthenware, glaze, and paint, 36 × 12 × 12 in. (91.4 × 30.5 × 30.5 cm). Hirshhorn Museum and Sculpture Garden, Smithsonian Institution, Washington, D.C.; Joseph H. Hirshhorn Bequest Fund, 1998

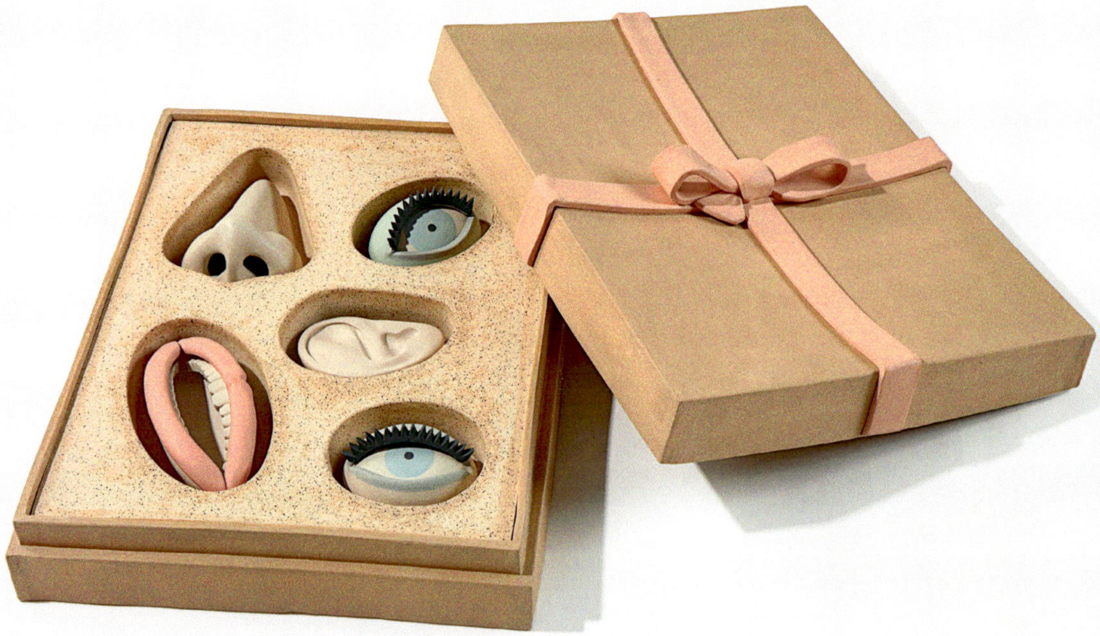

15 Genesis Belanger, *You Never Know What You're Gonna Get*, 2020. Stoneware and porcelain, 5 × 27 × 23 in. (12.7 × 68.6 × 58.4 cm). Collection of Emmanuel Perrotin

his likeness and filling its cavity with tiny self-portraits. Arneson's classroom has been described as a "clubby masculine garage workshop."[49]

The Surrealism of the everyday continues today in the work of New York-based contemporary artists Genesis Belanger and Didi Rojas, who comment on our society's social media-fueled obsession with luxury and consumerism. Belanger's sleek pastel sculptures of uncanny domestic objects are inspired by 1950s American advertisements, particularly their manipulative appeal to sentimentality gendered as feminine. Through this lens, Belanger explores the inadequate ways people support each other in moments of grief by relying on what she calls "tokens of condolence,"[50] such as buying flowers or candy, instead of expressing genuine empathy. In *You Never Know What You're Gonna Get* (2020) [fig. 15], a title borrowed from Forrest Gump's "Life is like a box of chocolates" speech, Belanger renders a neat box of ceramic sweets containing the deconstructed elements of a face. Like the puzzle pieces of a Cubist painting, the box holds two wide-open eyes, a smiling mouth, a nose, and an ear. The captured moment underscores the futility of consumerism in the face of grief, encouraging reflection on our coping mechanisms.

Rojas tackles the importance people place on objects through her renditions of footwear. Having grown up in an immigrant household, Rojas values resourcefulness and considers her practice a way to gain access to otherwise unattainable luxury items, through the transformation of humble clay.[51] Her shoes are proxies for the wearer. Typically displayed in groups, the sculptures appear to be social gatherings. With a playful scale, the shoes step or stack on each other, conveying human emotions such as tenderness and anger [fig. 16].

Oakland-based contemporary artist Woody De Othello makes the ordinary extraordinary through

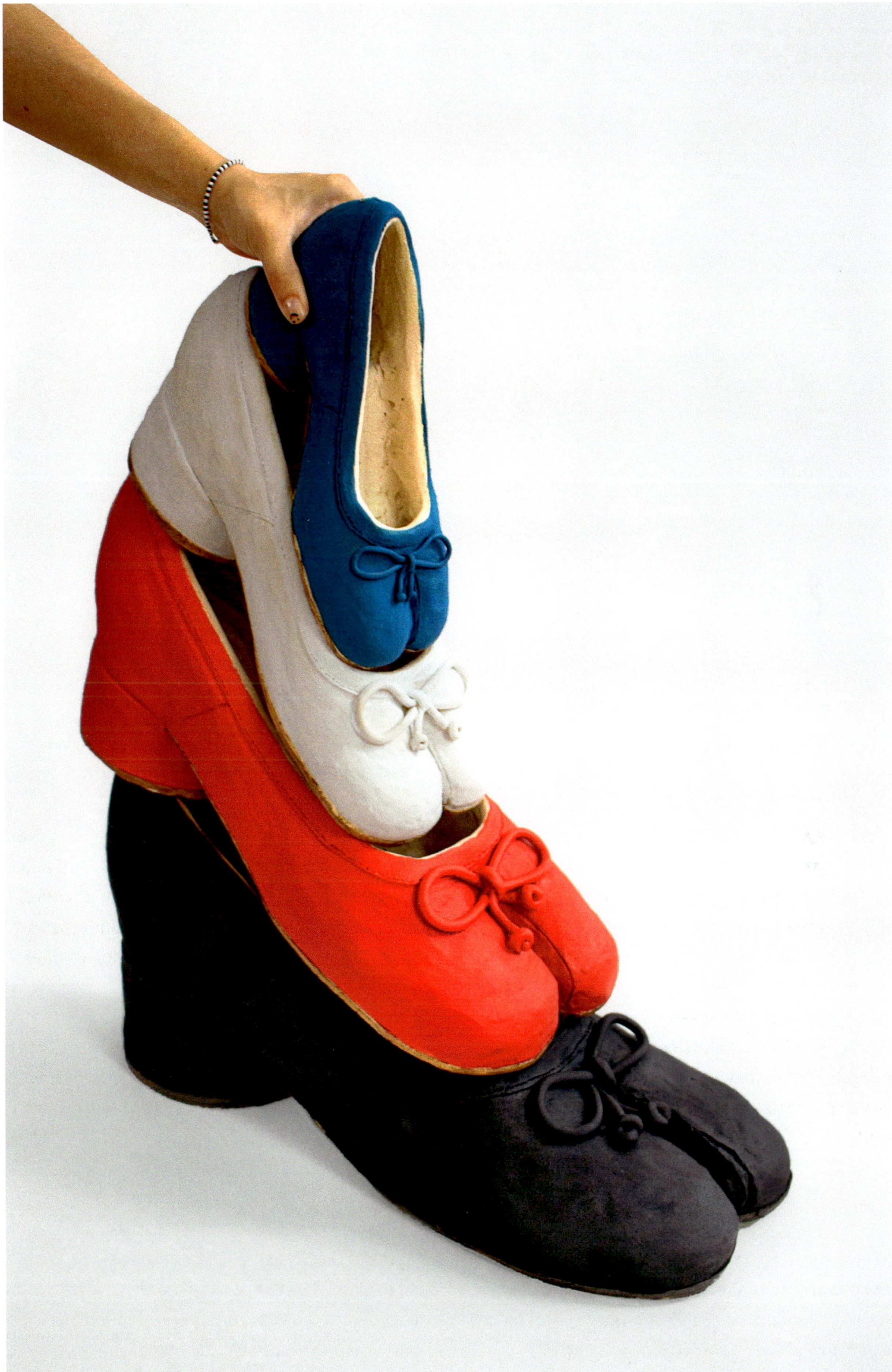

16 Didi Rojas, *I Pledge Allegiance to... I'm Baby*, 2022. Ceramic and underglaze, 22 × 9 × 23 in. (55.9 × 22.9 × 58.4 cm). Courtesy the artist

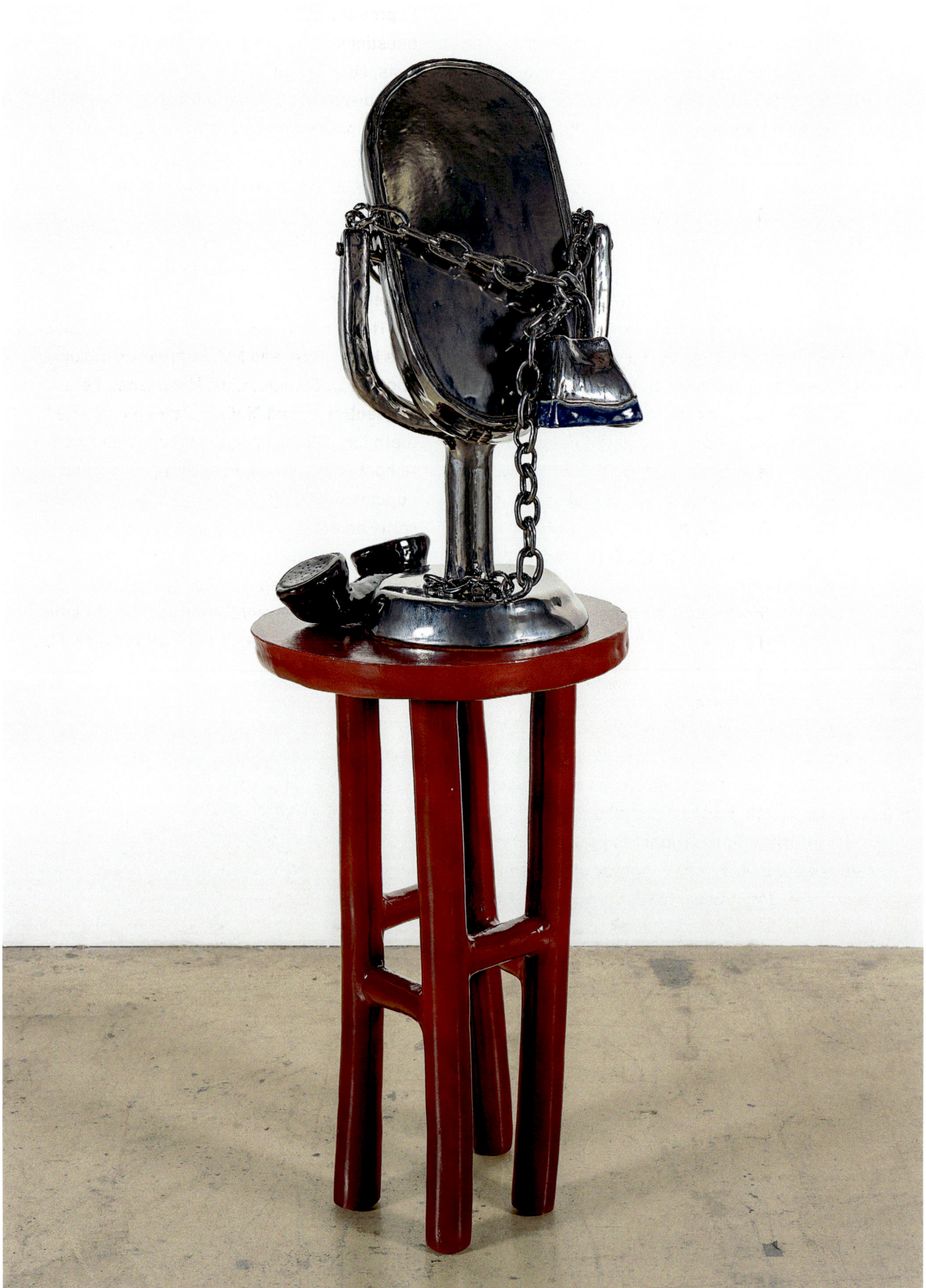

17 Woody De Othello, *Still on Hold*, 2021. Ceramic and glaze, 61 × 29 × 29 in. (154.9 × 73.7 × 73.7 cm). Crocker Art Museum, Sacramento; gift of Kevie Yang, 2021

sculptures of television remotes, clocks, and telephones, and anthropomorphic vessels in cartoonish proportions with droopy mannerisms. The humorous objects aim to ease the burden of processing trauma from daily indignities and the historical mistreatment of Black bodies in the Caribbean and United States.[52] *Still on Hold* (2021) [fig. 17] is a lustered ceramic mirror wrapped with a chain on top of a red stool. A telephone handset lies at its base, suggesting the irritation of being put on hold by customer service. Paired with the mirror, the handset conveys the frustration of being unable to attain self-actualization. However, for Othello, the stool "represents access to something you can't reach,"[53] and the open lock suggests hope. His sculptures serve as a form of *nkisi*, power figures from West Africa, and continue the Yoruba practice of making spontaneous sculptures out of found objects, both for the purpose of protection.[54]

Like Kottler, the eccentric Clayton Bailey, a self-described "artist serious about critiquing the conventions of serious art," found encouragement to develop his already jocular ceramics further in 1960s Funk ceramics, particularly Arneson's toilets.[55] Bailey's 1966 "Nite Pots," a series of periscope-shaped chamber pot sculptures with thick, shiny lips around the peepholes, were eroticized forms meant to prevent function through arousal, much in the way of Arneson's telephone. Both Bailey and Arneson pushed the boundaries of expression, often obliterating societal taboos. In 1968 Bailey and his family settled in Port Costa, CA, from Wisconsin, where he embraced the dogma of Nut art and, like De Forest, his neighbor and friend, adopted an alter ego named Dr. Gladstone—a performance that lasted throughout most of his career.[56]

Fascinated by sensationalized stories in tabloids, Bailey claimed to have made scientific discoveries in the persona of the doctor and anthropologist. Adding curator to his resume, he opened the Wonders of the World Museum to house his ceramic fossils, specimens, machines, robots, and creatures, such as *Monster "Burping Bowl"* (1977) [fig. 18], in which a dinosaur-like figure inside a bowl gurgles water to produce burping sounds. The irreverent ruse questioned the perceived authority of anthropologists, curators, and doctors and the power of their discoveries. Bailey's most extraordinary validation for his elaborate hoax came in the form of a nomination for the 1976 Nobel Prize in physics by Dr. Charles Schwartz of the University of California, Berkeley, who said, "Here is the amazing Dr. Gladstone, of whom I can say with confidence that his scientific genius will not be turned against mankind."[57]

The anthropomorphism of animals and food was key in Funk and Nut ceramicists' arsenal, and Bailey, Gilhooly, Chris Unterseher, Peter VandenBerge, and Maija Peeples-Bright used them for building compelling imaginary worlds. Gilhooly was devoted to crafting his own universe populated by frogs. Before he accidentally became an artist, having signed up for art classes in 1962 as a ploy to court a beautiful art student, he pursued degrees in biology and anthropology.[58] *Cynthia Camel Trophy* (1966), a camel head sticking its tongue out, part of Selz's *FUNK*,

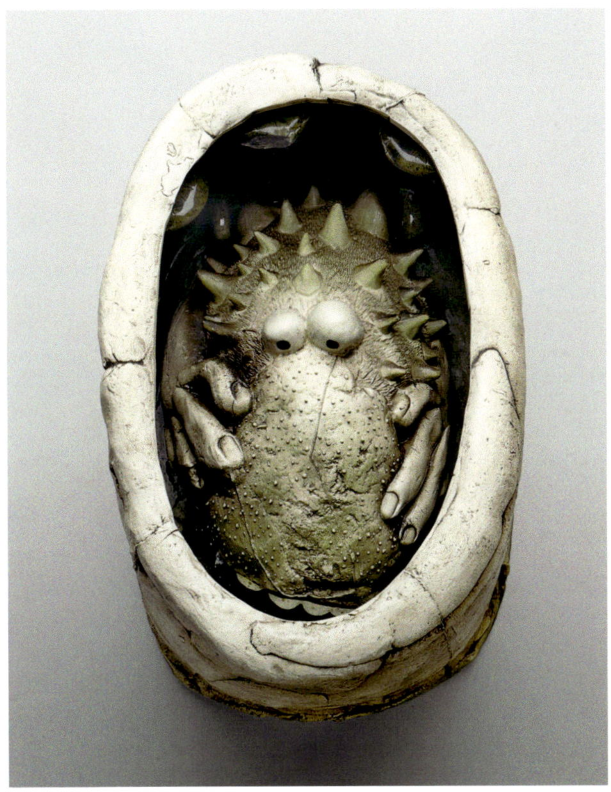

18 Clayton Bailey, *Monster ("Burping Bowl")*, 1977. Ceramic, 9 ½ × 13 × 19 in. (24.1 × 33 × 48.3 cm). The Museum of Fine Arts, Houston; The Leatrice S. and Melvin B. Eagle Collection; purchase funded by the Caroline Wiess Law Accessions Endowment Fund, 2010

precedes the thousands of quirky amphibian sculptures in Gilhooly's Frog World. His artistic practice combined his passions to reimagine human history. The innocuous green actors provided infinite flexibility to address philosophical and social issues.

In the 1970s, Gilhooly's amphibians began frolicking among food, swimming leisurely in chocolate, and sleeping between burger buns to channel the artist's fixation with food.[59] He prolifically made ceramic food sculptures to sell at "bake sales" at the Candy Store and other galleries. Later on, Gilhooly's frogs suffered an identity crisis, transfiguring into versatile bread. In *Bread Frog as a Coffee Break* (1981–82) [fig. 19], the doughy frog freckled with authentic poppy seeds balances donuts and coffee atop its head. Pulling the curtain back on the artistic dialogue between the Nut artists, Unterseher, another of Arneson's students, made sculptural dioramas of everyday and nature scenes, especially of surfers, such as *Champion Surfer Mike Doyle Teaches Dave's Frogs a Few Tricks* (1967) [fig. 20], in which a small figurine of a man is surfing with Gilhooly's iconic frogs.

Although now better known for making stylized heads inspired by puppets, earlier in his career, VandenBerge took on food as a subject. Together with Gilhooly, he frequented the San Francisco farmers market, where VandenBerge found inspiration in the produce.[60] He embraced humor as an essential component of his art and began to anthropomorphize the vegetables, particularly carrots.[61] He infused human emotion into them to convey scenes such as a mother caring for her child, a couple entwined watching a movie, and a woman lounging in *Carrot on Divan* (c. 1971) [fig. 21]. While VandenBerge sculpted veggies, Peeples-Bright had a penchant for animals, or "beasties," as she calls them. A true maximalist, she has had a bountiful practice making paintings and ceramic sculptures with fun alliterative titles, layers upon layers of happy animals, bold colors, and full of childlike exuberance, which continues to this day. A recurrent character in her practice is her beloved late dog Woof W. Woof, portrayed in *Woof with Whale Vessel* (c. 1978) [fig. 22].[62] Born in Latvia during World War II, she was forced to live with her family in a refugee camp in Germany until 1950, when they relocated to California. A reflection on her childhood, *Beast Map* (1965–66) [fig. 23], a colorful impasto painting, personifies the continents as creatures baring their teeth at each other to underscore fraught global relationships. Given her background, it is not surprising that Peeples-Bright has spent her career focused on joy and abundance through "meticulous worldbuilding," as Catherine Wagley puts it.[63] She was a vital member and one of the few women of the Candy Store Gallery, opening her Rainbow House (replete with wall-to-ceiling beastie paintings) to her peers.

Often achieved through anthropomorphism and the infantilization of an image, cuteness has become a prominent aesthetic of contemporary art, social media content, and retail for the past few years in the United States.[64] Los Angeles-based contemporary artists Alake Shilling, Diana Yesenia Alvarado, and Alex Anderson use cuteness to explore power dynamics. Like Peeples-Bright, Shilling's preferred subject matter is animals, characterized by a style recalling Lisa Frank and Hello Kitty. Her cast of melancholic and mischievous characters is affective and emotive, from a suspicious ladybug to a sad bear wearing a flowered cowboy hat in *Baby Bear Loves Alake* (2021) [fig. 24]. Scholar Sianne Ngai describes cuteness as the eroticization of powerlessness, which triggers a desire to care intimately for and aggressively protect a non-threatening object.[65] Animals, real and stuffed, often provide comfort to people. Shilling is turning that relationship on its head by inviting viewers to comfort her characters instead.[66] Her mixed-media paintings, such as *Buggy Bear on a Star-Studded Beach Adventure* (2021) [fig. 25], expand her reocurring characters' narratives, in this case by adding a sense of wonder and trepidation as the bear hesitantly dips its toe in the water.

Cuteness incites a power struggle between the feeling of dominance over an unthreatening object and the influence that object can exert over us.[67] The big, watery "puppy eyes" of Alvarado's angels, demons, and clowns exemplify this manipulative phenomenon by conveying vulnerability and,

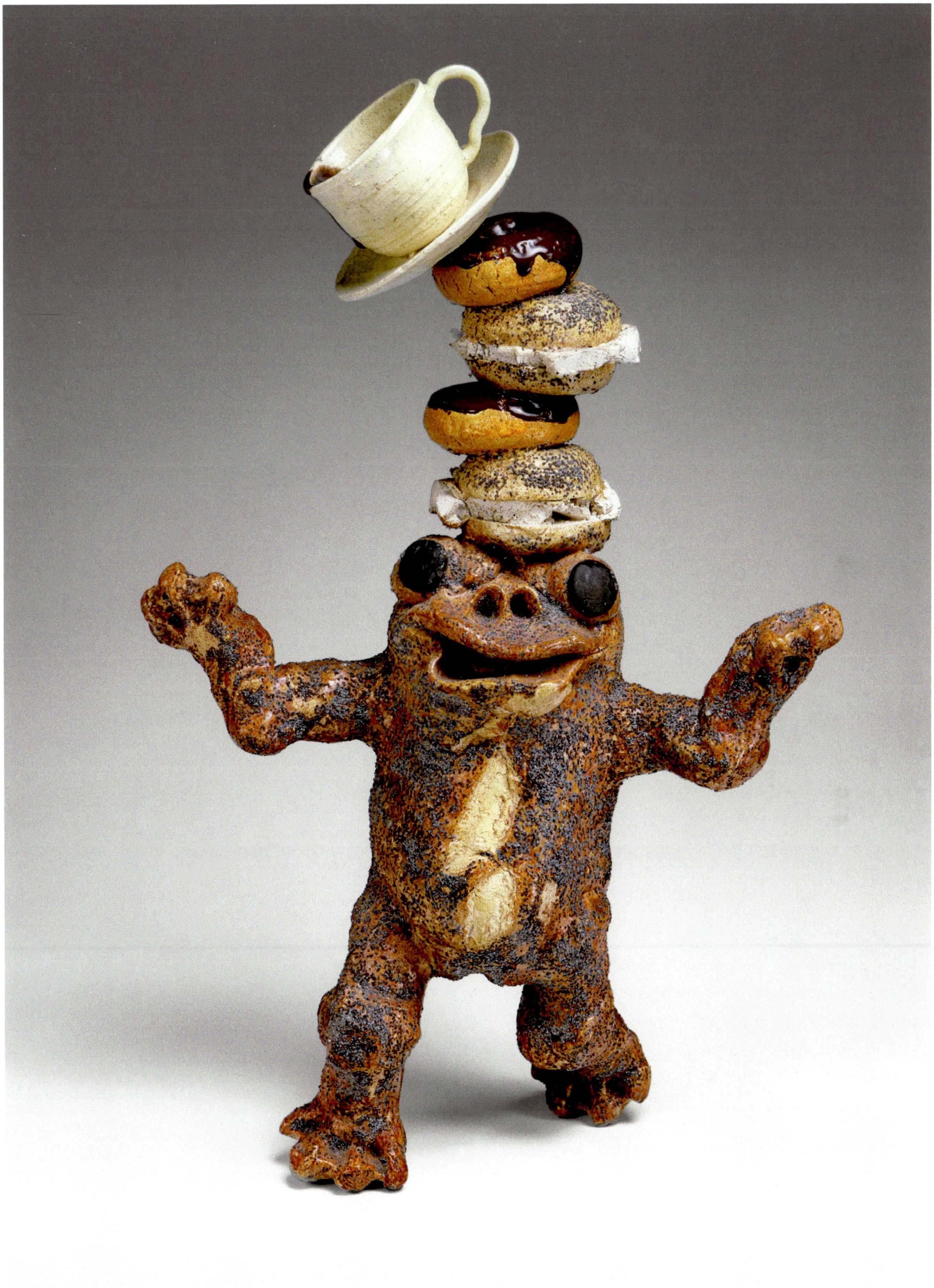

19 David Gilhooly, *Bread Frog as a Coffee Break*, 1981–82. Earthenware and glaze, 23.5 × 15.5 × 6.5 in. (59.7 × 39.4 × 16.5 cm). Museum of Arts and Design, New York; gift of Rebecca Cooper Waldman, through the American Craft Council, 1986

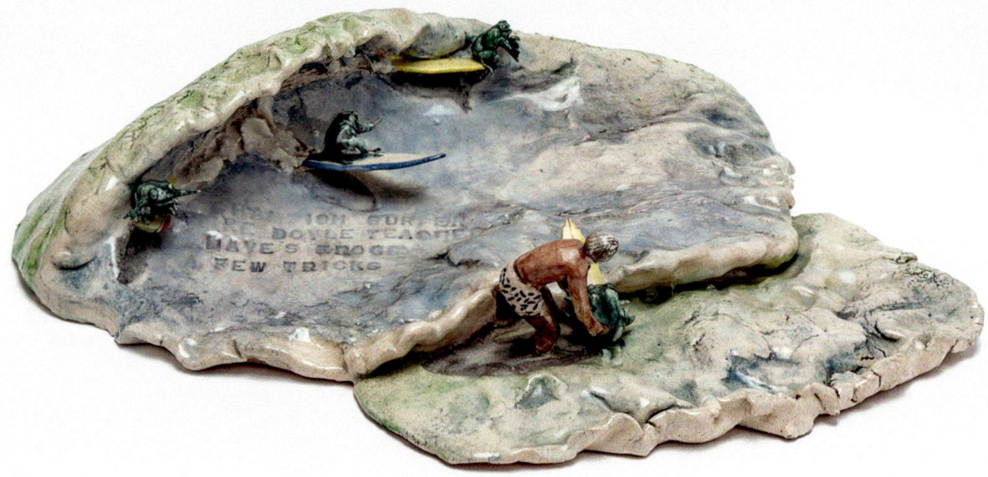

20 Chis Unterseher, *Champion Surfer Mike Doyle Teaches Dave's Frogs a Few Tricks*, 1969. Ceramic and glaze, 4 × 15 × 15 in. (10.2 × 38.1 × 38.1 cm). Everson Museum of Art, Syracause, NY; museum purchase with Deaccession Fund, 2021

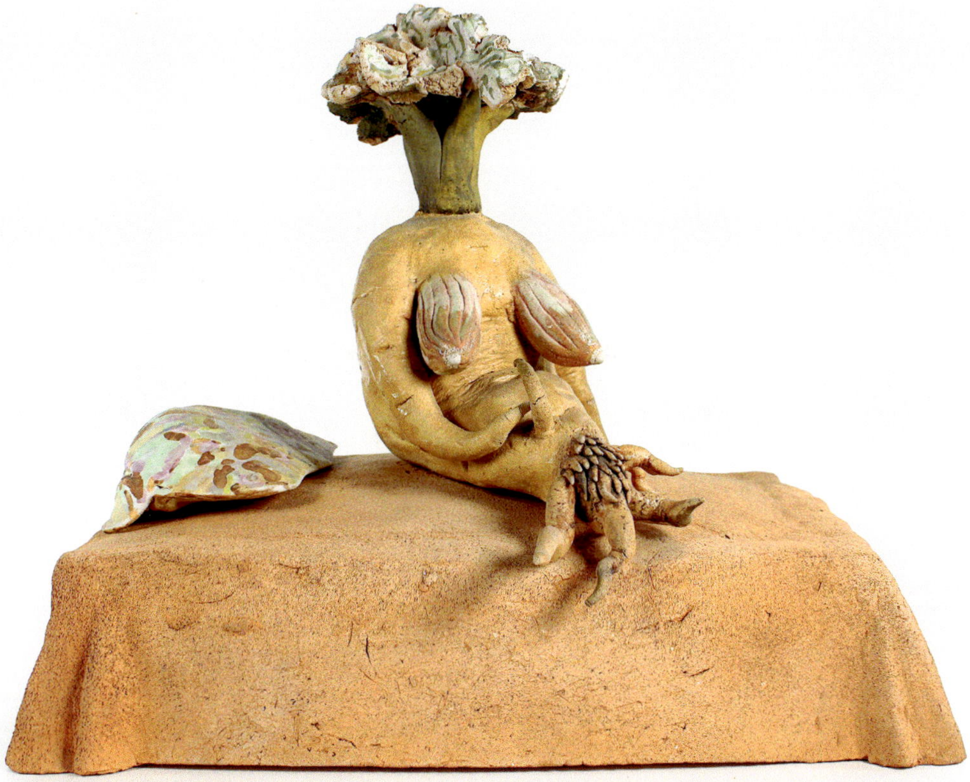

21 Peter VandenBerge, *Carrot on Divan*, c. 1971. Earthenware, 13 × 15 ¼ × 12 ¼ in. (33 × 38.7 × 31.1 cm). Everson Museum of Art, Syracuse, NY; gift of Les Levine, 1983

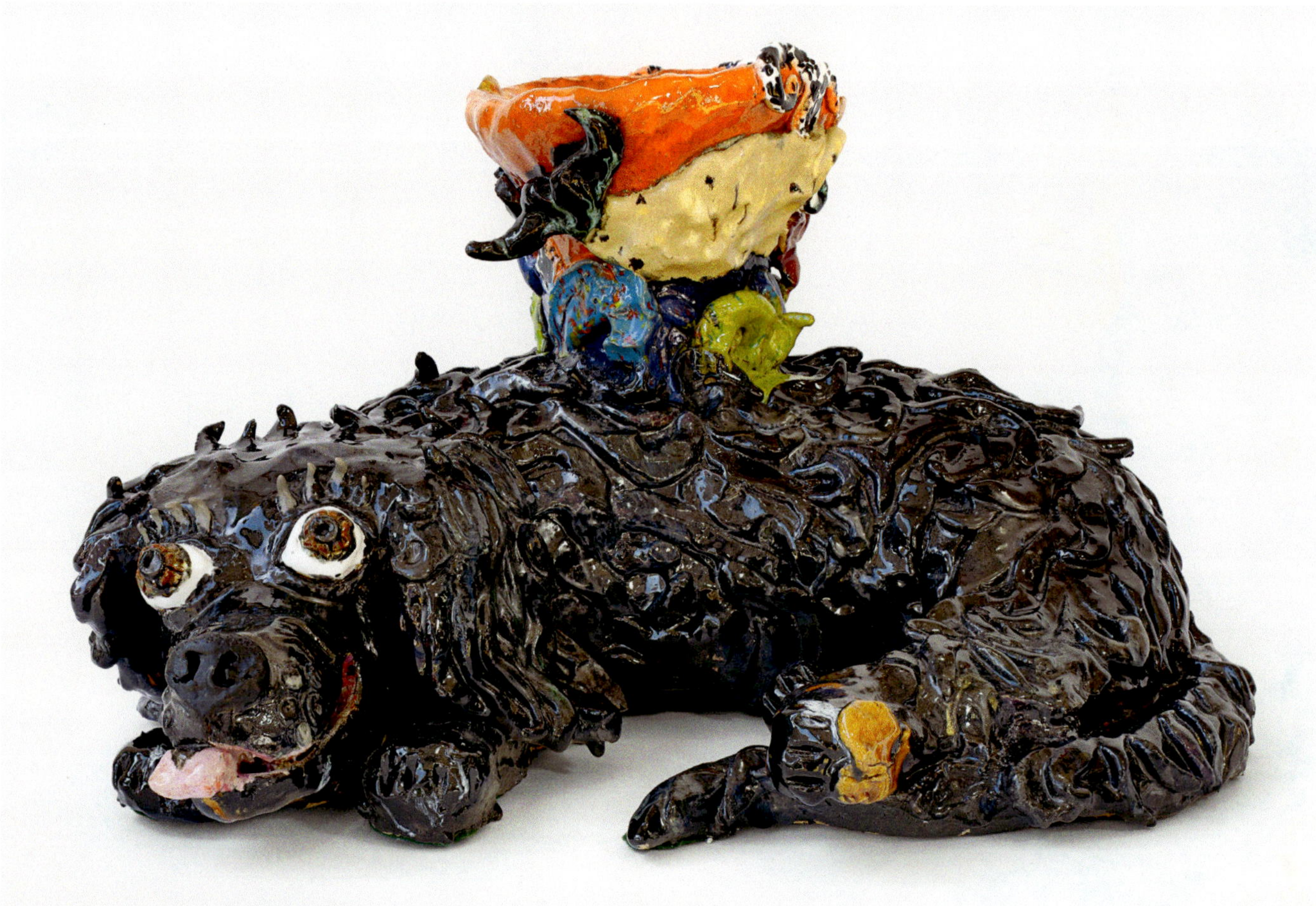

22 Maija Peeples-Bright, *Woof with Whale Vessel*, c. 1978. Stoneware and glaze, 18.5 × 14.5 × 11.5 in. (47 × 36.8 × 29.2 cm). Everson Museum of Art, Syracuse, NY; museum purchase with Deaccession Fund, 2021

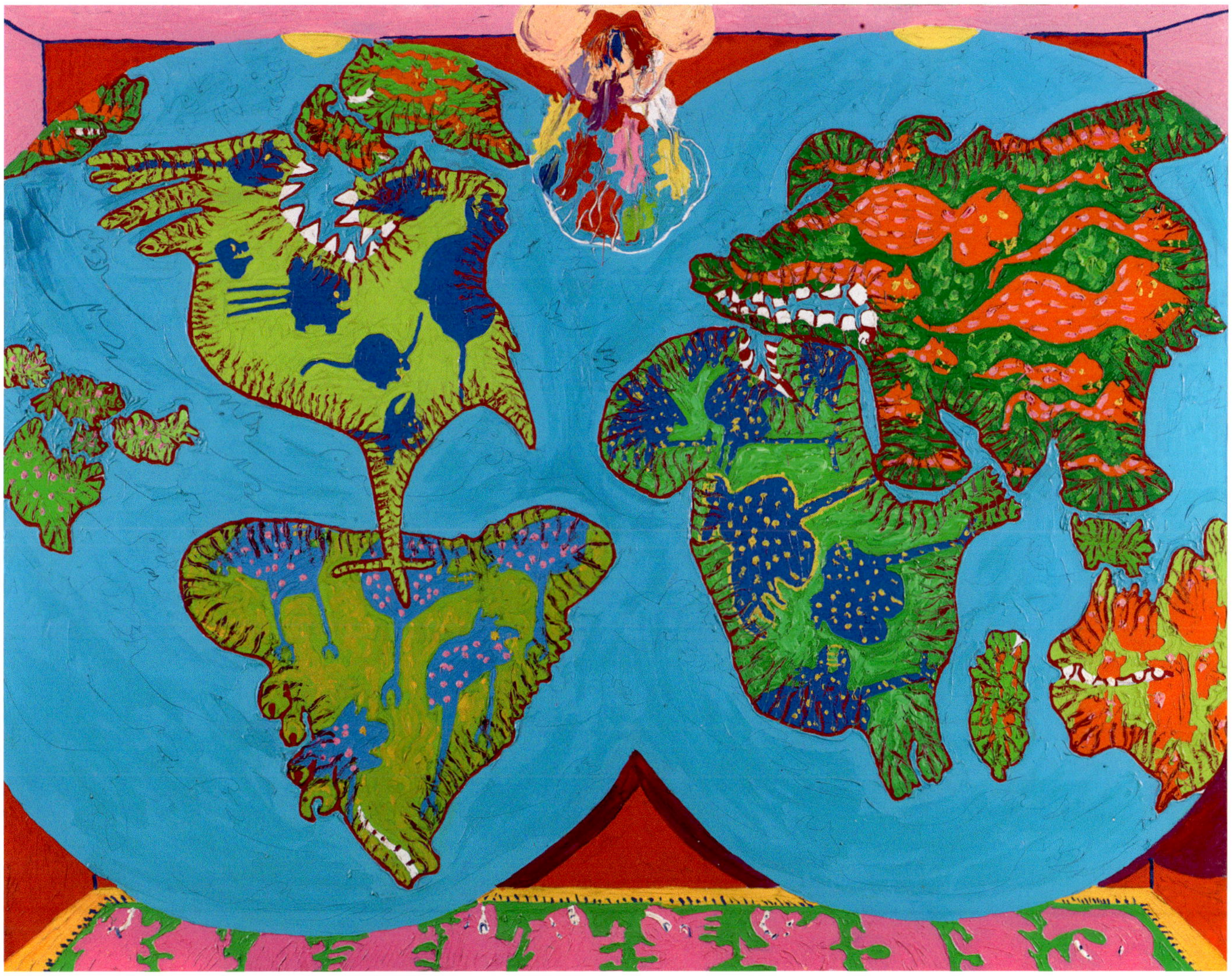

23 Maija Peeples-Bright, *Beast Map*, 1965–66. Oil on canvas, 55.5 × 72 in. (141 × 182.9 cm). Crocker Art Museum, Sacramento; gift of Mr. and Mrs. Norman Jones, 1981

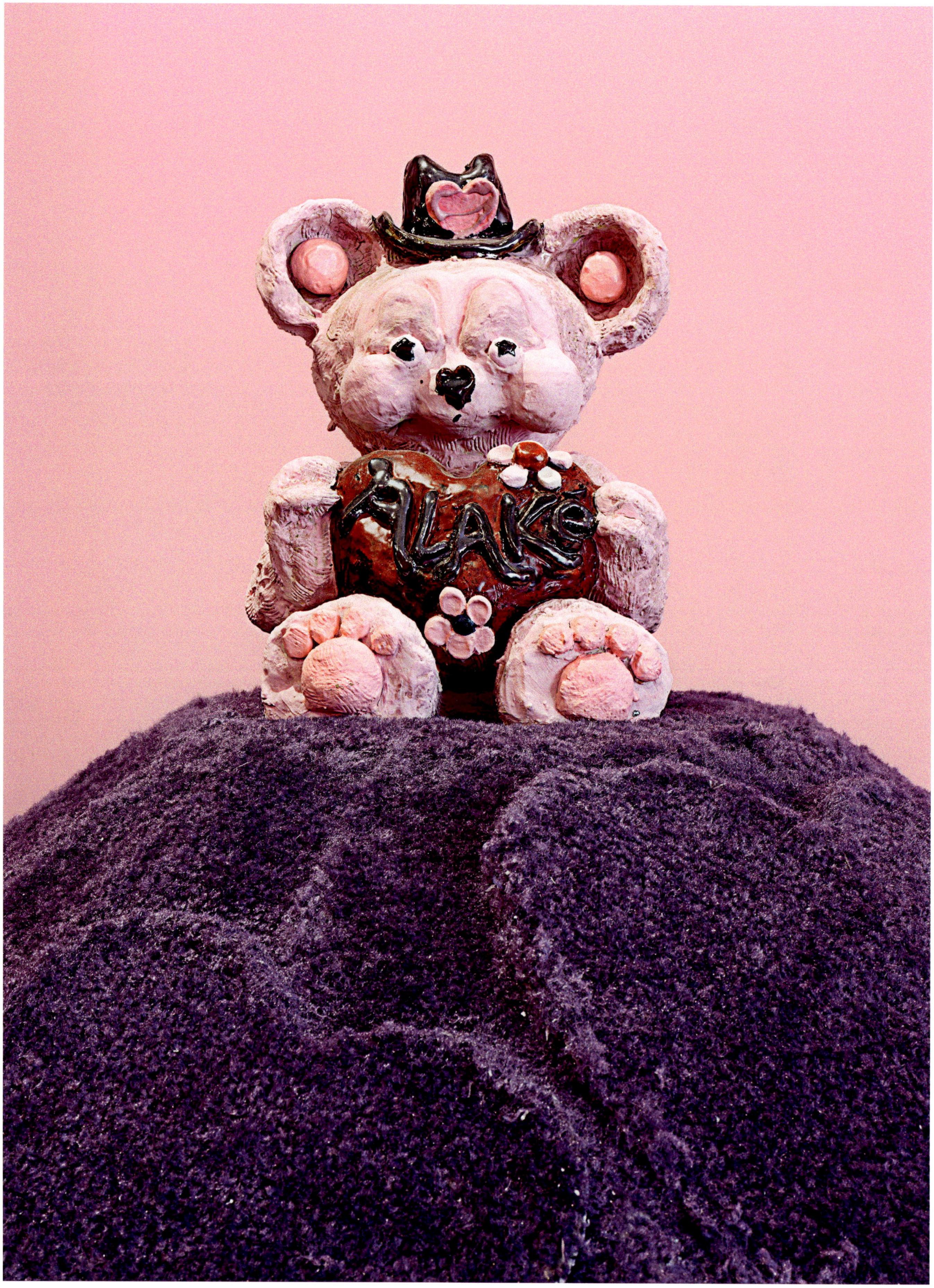

24 Alake Shilling, *Baby Bear Loves Alake*, 2021. Ceramic, glaze, and enamel paint, 11.5 × 8 × 9 in. (29.2 × 20.3 × 22.9 cm). Courtesy the artist

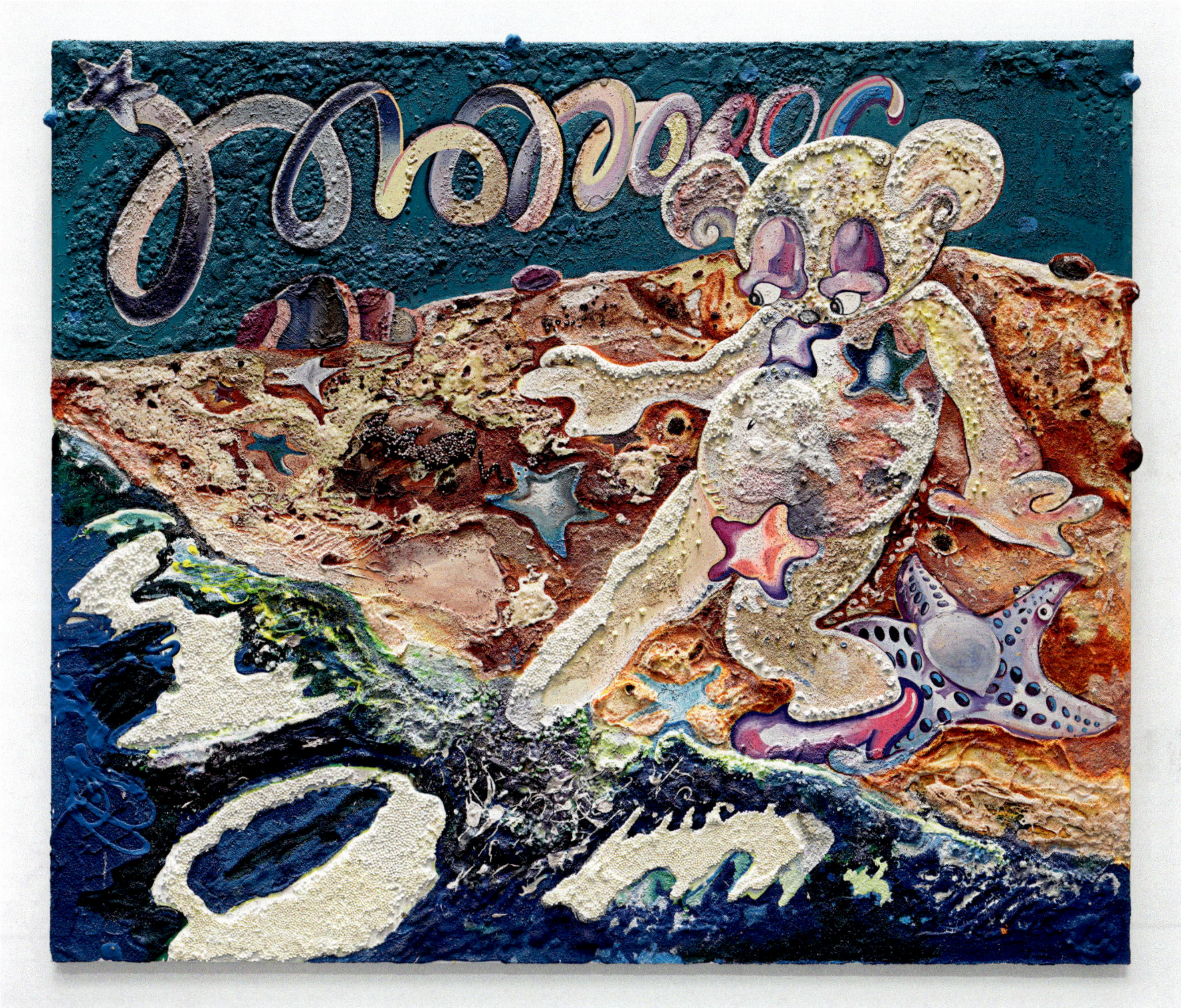

25 Alake Shilling, *Buggy Bear on a Star-Studded Beach Adventure*, 2021. Oil paint, glitter, sand, styrofoam balls, and salt on canvas, 60 × 72 × 2.5 in. (152.4 × 182.9 × 6.4 cm). Courtesy the artist and Jeffrey Deitch, New York and Los Angeles

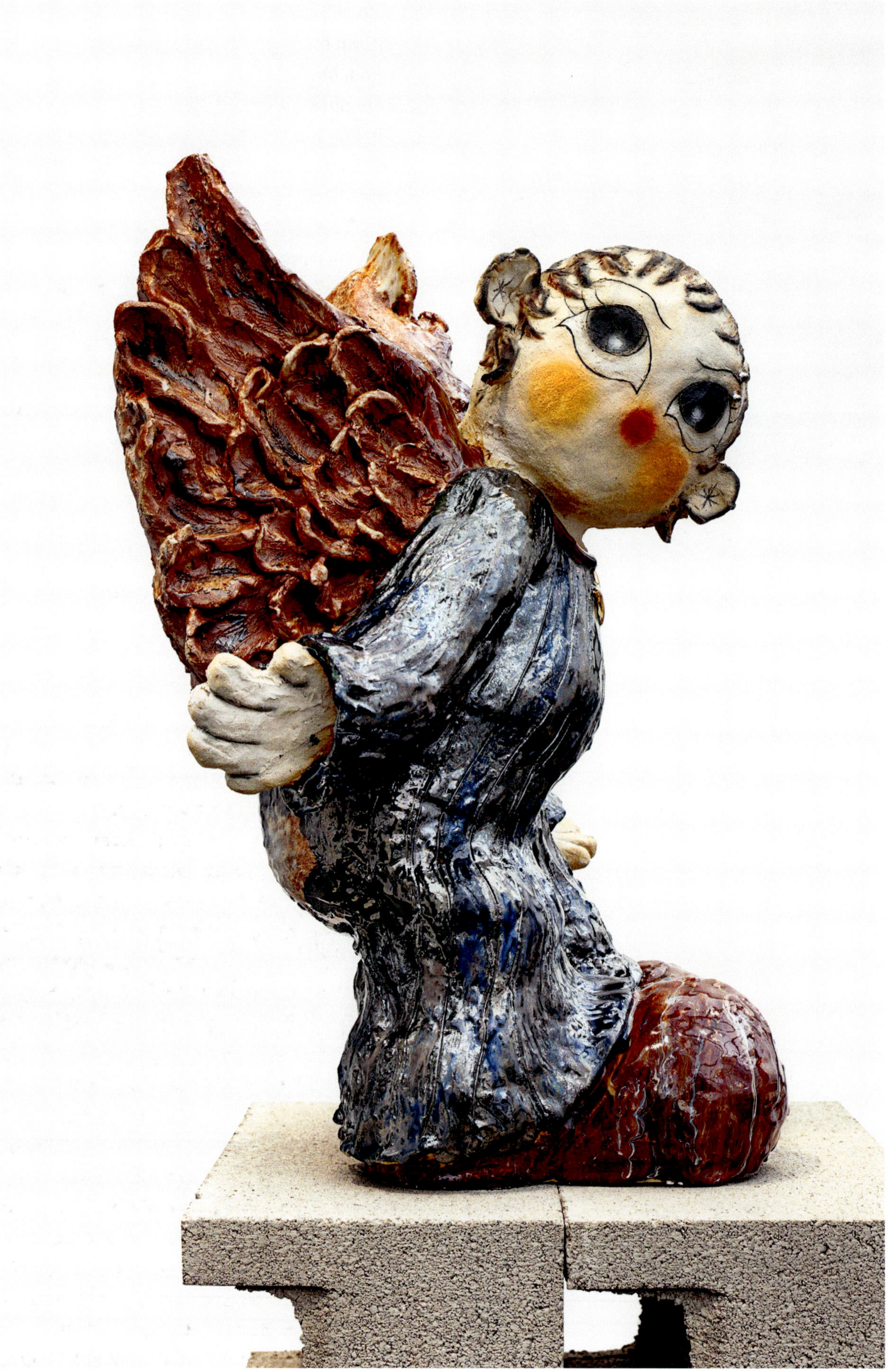

26 Diana Yesenia Alvarado, *Lista Para Volar*, 2022. Earthenware, glaze, underglaze, flocking, and luster, 22 × 18 × 12 in. (55.9 × 45.7 × 30.5 cm). Private collection

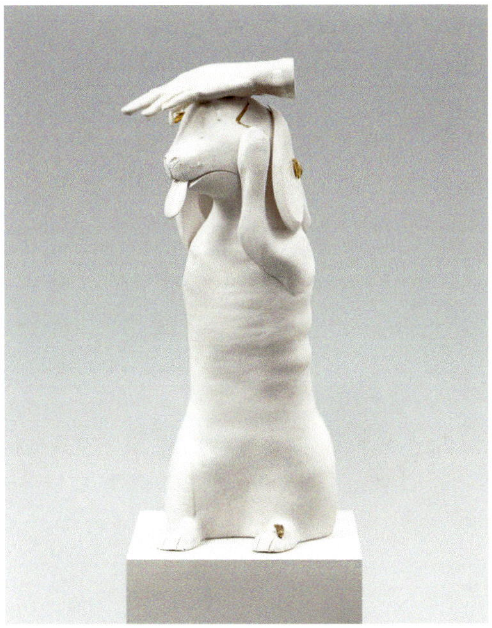

27 Alex Anderson, *Don't Touch My Hare*, 2019. Earthenware, glaze, and luster, 22 × 8 × 9 in. (55.9 × 20.3 × 22.9 cm). Museum of Arts and Design, New York; gift of the artist, 2022

therefore, the need for protection. However, Alvarado aims to establish a balance between vulnerability and strength that mirrors the inherent dichotomy of cuteness.[68] In *Lista Para Volar* (2022) [fig. 26], the angel is ready to "fly" or metaphorically pursue its dreams, but the figure's feet are comically large and heavy, grounding it. It conveys the complicated nature between the desire to do something and the ability to do it.

Anderson navigates his lived experiences as a Black and Japanese American gay man in his work through the juxtaposition of challenging subject matter with a lighthearted approach. *Don't Touch My Hare* (2020) [fig. 27] is a play on Solange Knowles's 2016 hit song "Don't Touch My Hair" which addresses the historical lack of respect for Black bodies. The sculpture depicts a disembodied white hand patting the head of a hare, which panics and sticks out its tongue in distress. Despite portraying a racially charged scenario, the humor "invite[s] grace to a subject historically contextualized as abject and other," Anderson explains.[69]

The oldest artist in *Funk You Too!*, with a career spanning over six decades, Los Angeles-based Magdalena Suarez Frimkess had her first solo show in 2014 at eighty-four.[70] She is best known for her collaborative work with her husband, Michael Frimkess, who would throw delicate pots that she then decorated. While Mr. Frimkess did everything possible to hide his hand, Suarez Frimkess's practice shows unrestrained freedom. Mickey and Minnie Mouse [fig. 28], the Chilean Condorito, and Betty Boop are just a few of the characters that Suarez Frimkess illustrates in her expressive sculptures. For her, "you can see the whole world through these cartoons,"[71] making them ideal proxies for the human condition.

In 1965 Arneson sought a more "serious" subject matter and began experimenting with figuration in *Self-Portrait of the Artist Losing His Marbles* (1965) [fig. 29]. It started as a conventional portrait bust but, dissatisfied with it, Arneson repeatedly glazed and fired it, causing a massive crack. Impulsively, he glued marbles inside the crevice and retitled it. The joke saved the sculpture and convinced him to stick to his satirical instincts. By the early 1970s, his likeness was a staple of his practice, eventually becoming his most iconic imagery. These were irreverently self-deprecating and often showed the artist behaving mischievously or in various states of psychic or physical turmoil. After all, he said, "If you're going to abuse someone, it better be yourself."[72] One example is the anthropomorphic *Portrait of the Artist as a Clever Old Dog* (1981) [fig. 30]. In it, he puts himself in the "doghouse" by transforming into a scruffy gray dog proudly smoking a cigar with a collection of colorful turds accompanying him.

Melvino Garretti developed his interest in ceramics as a resident at the Studio Watts Workshop in the 1960s—a program that served the neighborhood's African-American residents—and through a lasting friendship and professional collaboration with Michael Frimkess beginning in 1970.[73] The spontaneity of jazz and his social exploration as a self-described "urban and suburban anthropologist"[74] guide his practice. Despite their celebration in Black artistic circles, artists like Garretti or potter Doyle Lane have only received recognition by the broader art world in recent years. Garetti's introspective and self-

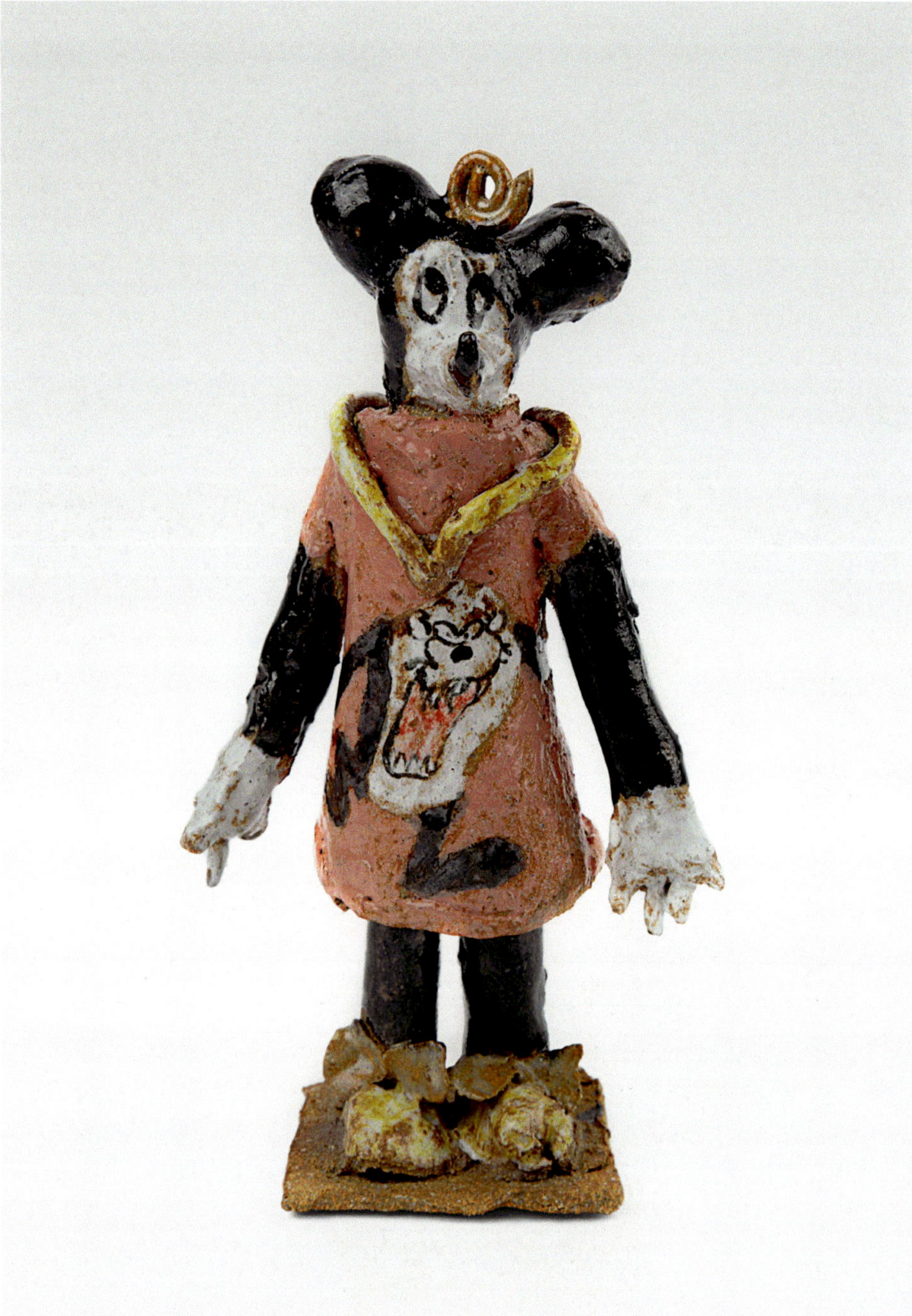

28 Magdalena Suarez Frimkess, *Untitled*, 2018. Ceramic and glaze, 9 × 5 × 3 in. (22.9 × 12.7 × 7.2 cm). Collection of KAWS

deprecating sense of humor comes through in sculptures like *I'm a Clown Just Horsin' Around* (2020) [fig. 31], a portrait of a clown-like head atop which, almost like a thought bubble, a miniature figure rides a hobby horse. The clown is a character who moves between jollity and misery by making others laugh at its own expense.

Sally Saul became immersed in the 1970s art scene through her husband, Peter Saul—an artist featured in *FUNK*, and at the Candy Store—but it was not until they moved to Texas a decade later that she began working in clay.[75] Naturally inclined to make narrative-based work, which she attributes to her background in literature, her charming sculptures of animals and people reflect on nature, art history, and the political landscape. Saul's *Transformed* (2020) [fig. 32] depicts a woman with a distorted face wearing a vibrant top and matching necklace. Despite the potential for the grotesque, her rendering,

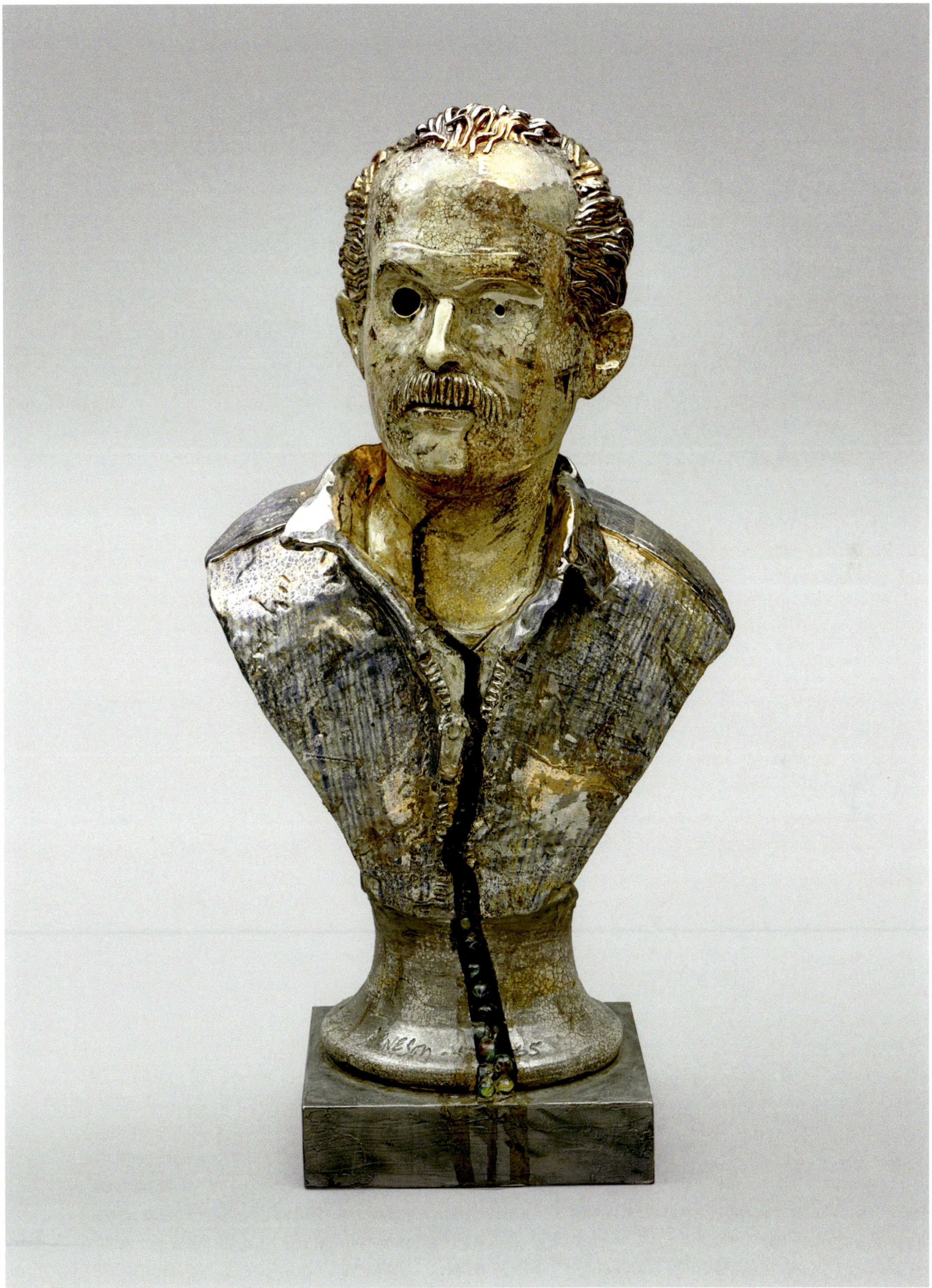

29 Robert Arneson, *Self-Portrait of the Artist Losing His Marbles*, 1965. Earthenware, luster glaze, pigments, and glass marbles, 31 × 17 ½ × 9.5 in. (78.7 × 44.5 × 24.1 cm). Museum of Arts and Design, New York; gift of the Johnson Wax Company, through the American Craft Council, 1977

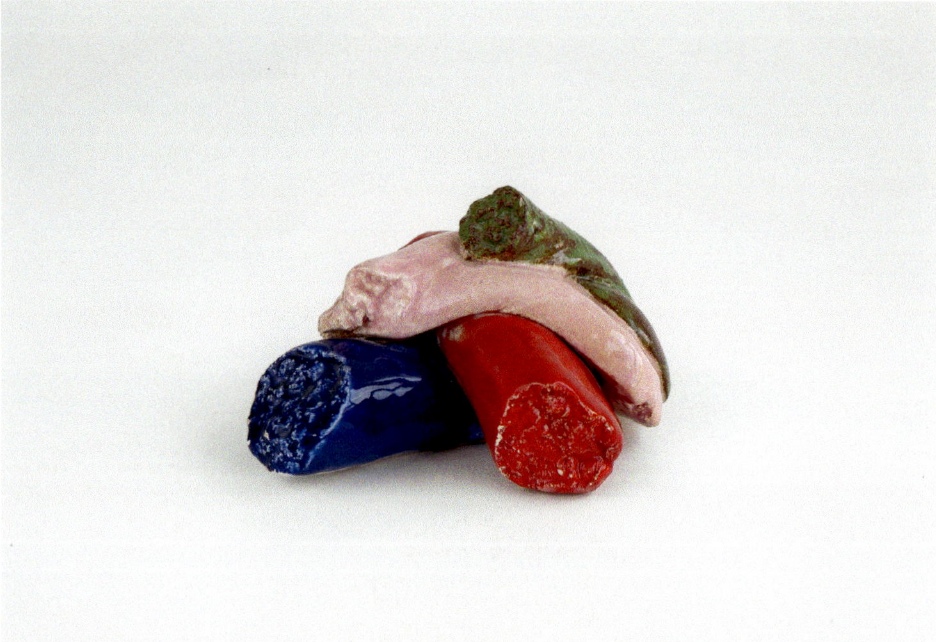

30 Detail of Robert Arneson, *Portrait of the Artist as a Clever Old Dog*, 1981

inspired by the abstract work of Asger Jorn, is a metaphor for the difficulty of personal transformation.

Chicago-based contemporary artist Salvador Jiménez-Flores has developed an eclectic style combining Indigenous, colonial, and postcolonial aesthetics to address issues affecting immigrants and people of color. In the ongoing "Rasquache Futurism"[76] series, catalyzed in 2016 by the incendiary comments made by Donald Trump about Latine people, the artist uses the cactus as a metaphor for how this community thrives despite systemic oppression [fig. 33]. Influenced by the models of 1920s Mexican Muralism and 1930s Taller de Gráfica Popular, which incorporated political messages into art to unify people and bring about social change, Jiménez-Flores aims to affect change through his work. Intentionally referencing the comedic self-portraits of Arneson, Jiménez-Flores's work features his mustached likeness sticking his tongue out. Through portraiture, Jiménez-Flores ensures the presence of Brown people in art for years to come.

Through confectionary aesthetics, Chicago-based contemporary artist Yvette Mayorga shares stories of immigration, her local community, and United States-Mexico border politics. With thickly piped acrylic paintings and chunky ceramics that resemble frosted cakes and sugar sculptures, she points to the gendered, and unappreciated, jobs carried on generationally by Latine immigrants in the United States, from construction to baking. Her work is reminiscent of Sandra Shannonhouse's candy sculptures [fig. 34]. As an undergraduate at Davis in the late 1960s she took Arneson's introductory glaze class, and created a form using what she describes as a "fondant kind of glaze."[77] She made a big box of pink and yellow candies. While living at Rainbow House after graduating, she continued making clay sculptures of desserts. However, she quickly became frustrated by the limitations of whiteware. Arneson gave her porcelain to try, which allowed her to craft thin boxes and delicate paper wrappers.[78] He also introduced Shannonhouse to McHugh, who made Shannonhouse's delectable sculptures the only candy sold at the Candy Store. Although she eventually stopped making bonbons, her ultra-feminine, domestic, and cute pursuit remains a flippant statement against the "macho" aesthetics that dominated the ceramics world.[79]

In the "Surveillance Locket Series" [fig. 35], Mayorga references 1990s Polly Pocket toys to

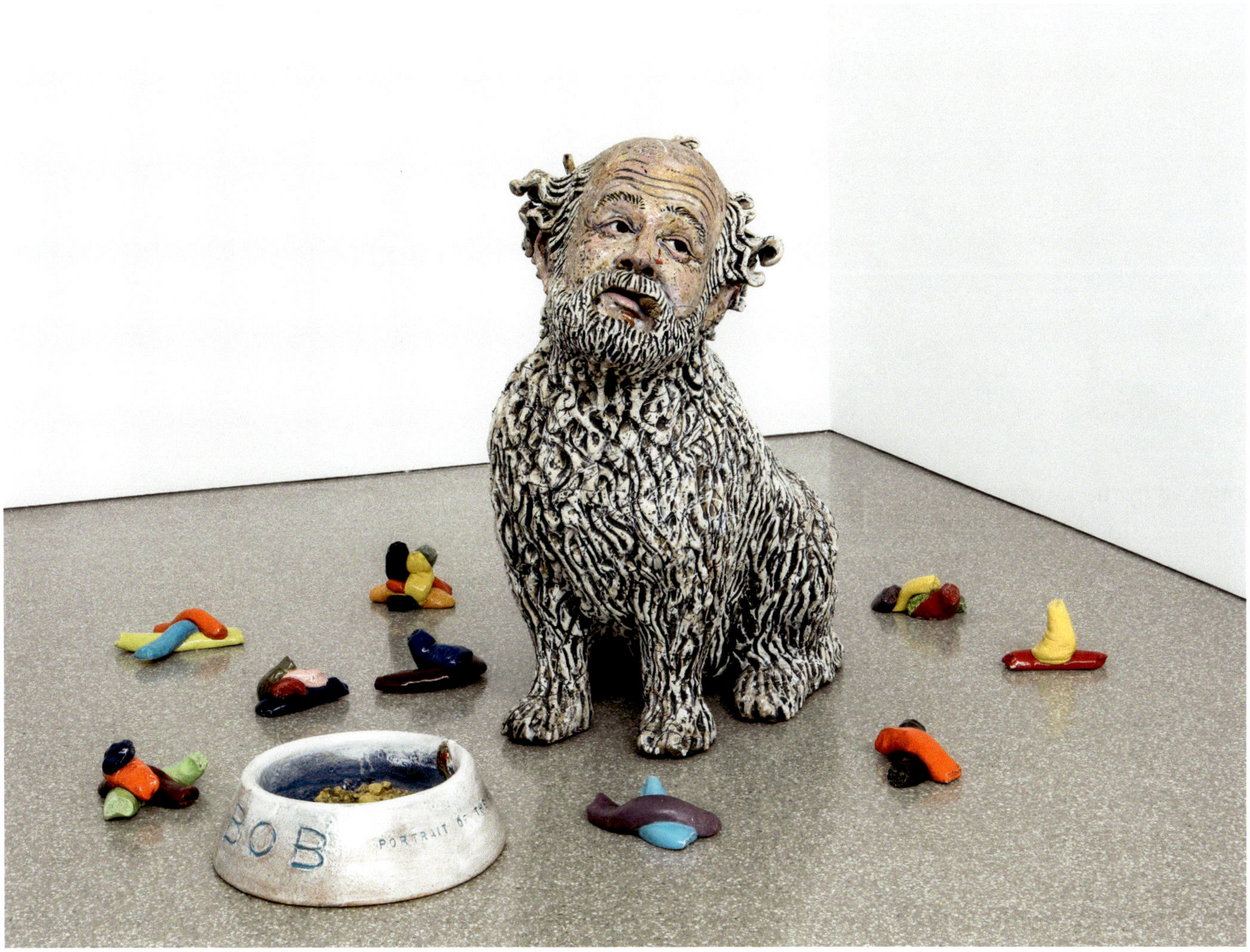

30 Robert Arneson, *Portrait of the Artist as a Clever Old Dog*, 1981. Stoneware and glaze, eleven parts, dog: 32 ⅜ × 18 × 30 ¼ in. (82.2 × 45.7 × 76.8 cm). Courtesy Michael Rosenfeld Gallery, New York

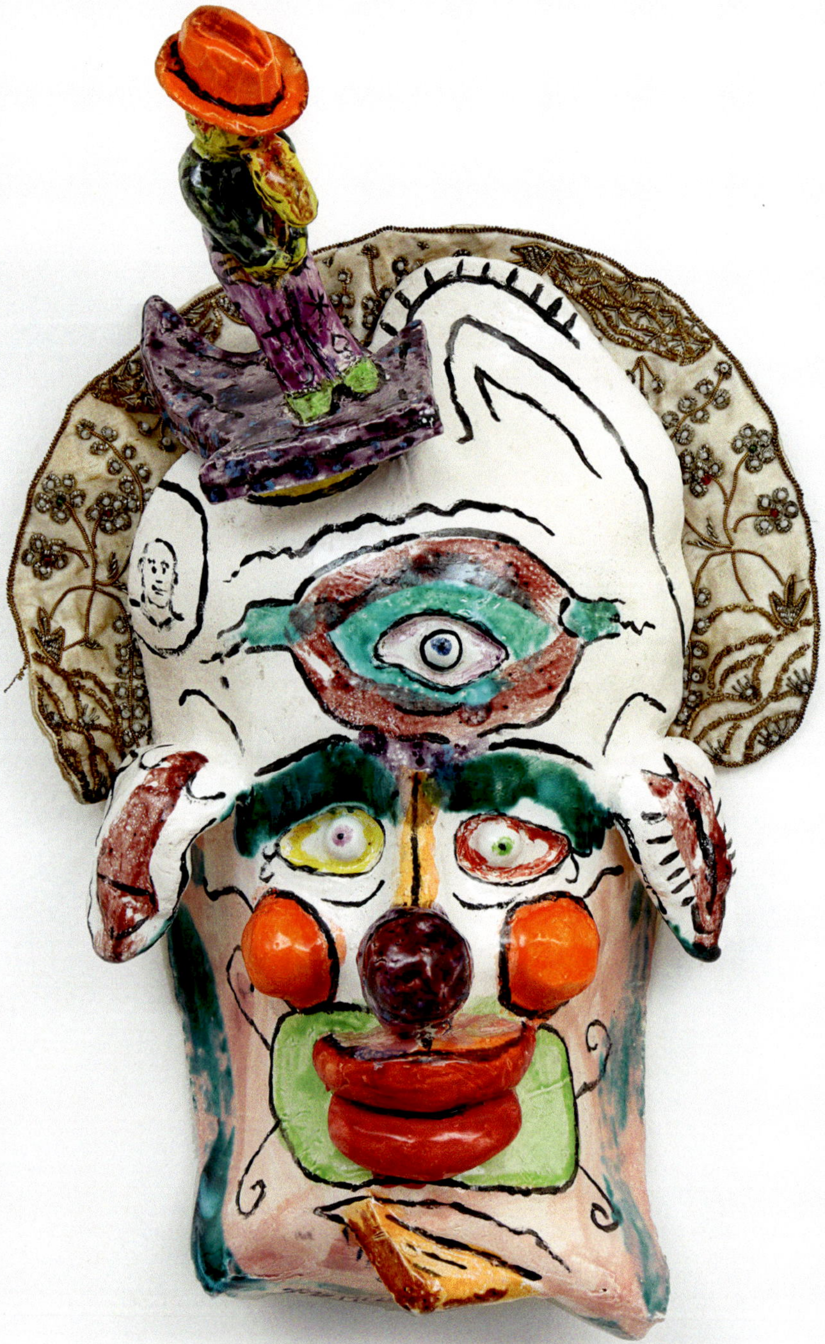

31 Melvino Garretti, *I'm a Clown Just Horsin' Around*, 2020. Earthenware, glaze, and vintage textile, 16 × 10 × 5 ¾ in. (40.6 × 25.4 × 14.6 cm). Courtesy the artist and Parker Gallery, Los Angeles

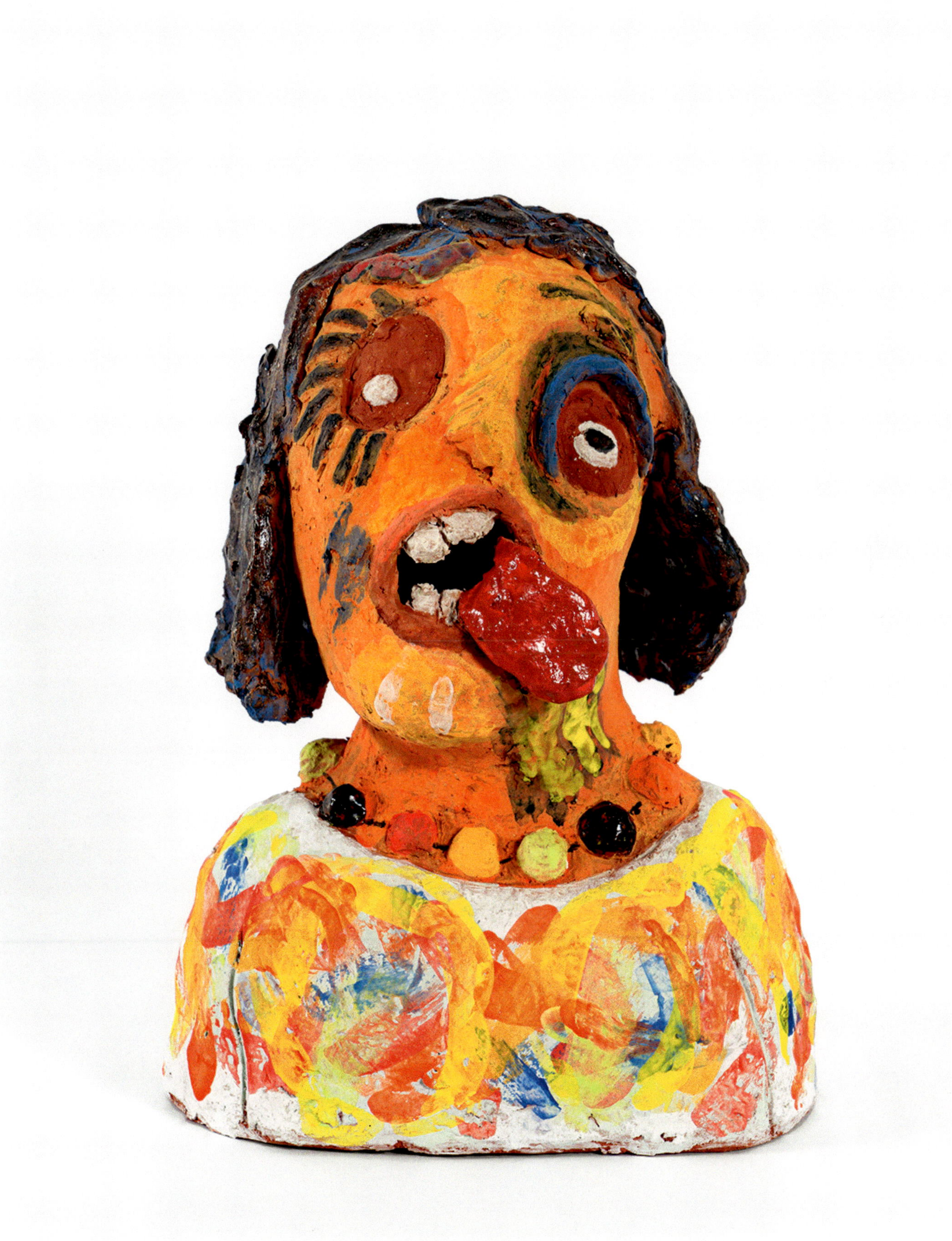

32 Sally Saul, *Transformed*, 2020. Ceramic and glaze, 11 × 8.5 × 6.5 in. (27.9 × 21.6 × 16.5 cm). Courtesy the artist and Venus Over Manhattan, New York © Sally Saul

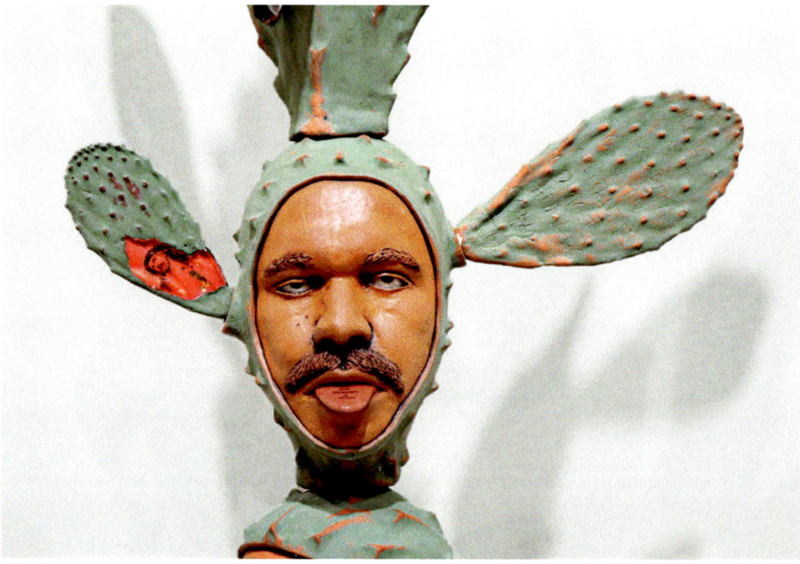

33 Detail of Salvador Jiménez-Flores, *The Resistance of the Hybrid Cacti*, 2017

celebrate her childhood and girlhood without abandoning her ongoing critique of consumerism. These "lockets" are contemporary takes on Rococo excess, with labyrinths of lavish interiors that, while playful and inviting, include watchful, sinister characters to address the surveillance of immigrants in the United States. Mayorga posits the United States as a consumerist Candyland and highlights the dichotomy between the romanticized American Dream and the less-than-ideal reality for many immigrants. Referencing sixteenth-century European banquet culture where sugar centerpieces incited conversation through subtle political messaging, the porcelain *Alligator Boots* (2018) [fig. 36] depicts an allegorical figure of the American Dream as a brown-skinned woman—an American flag draped over her shoulder, her feet clad in Indigenous tribal boots from Mexico—presiding over other figures. This iteration offers various perspectives on the journey of Latine immigrants crossing the border. One figure has drowned from the weight of their dreams, while others await the journey ahead. Mayorga achieves political subversiveness through vibrant colors and a childlike rendering that extends the Candyland metaphor into her three-dimensional practice.

Other artists who have criticized the American government and society in their ceramics include Los Angeles-based contemporary Sharif Farrag, along with Funk artists Arneson and Kottler. Farrag infuses his sculptures with the tension of growing up Muslim after 9/11, the effects of his father's health condition on his family, and the vibrancy of California skateboarding and graffiti, resulting in a conglomeration of melted textures, colors, and imagery that make up a nonsensical comic world. He created *Bouquet* (2020) [fig. 37] at the height of the 2020 Black Lives Matter protests. The base of the work is a conventional pot with a simplified American flag motif from which a set of cartoonish hands, wildflowers, and vines explode. They break free of existing systems, a notion magnified by the fantastical color palette at the top of the sculpture. The wristwatch on the arm points to five o'clock—the artist's lucky number, important in Egyptian mythology. The layered nature of the work reflects the complexities of identity for the artist.

Kottler became best known for his decalcomania work exploring queerness and denouncing American ideals. His "American Supperware" series (1969) [fig. 38], comprised of six interpretations of the American flag, was conceived in protest of the Vietnam war.[80] Some of the plates are *Exhausted Glory*, in which the flag becomes the exhaust of a race car, expressing fatigue over fighting wars, and *Hollow Dream*, which shows

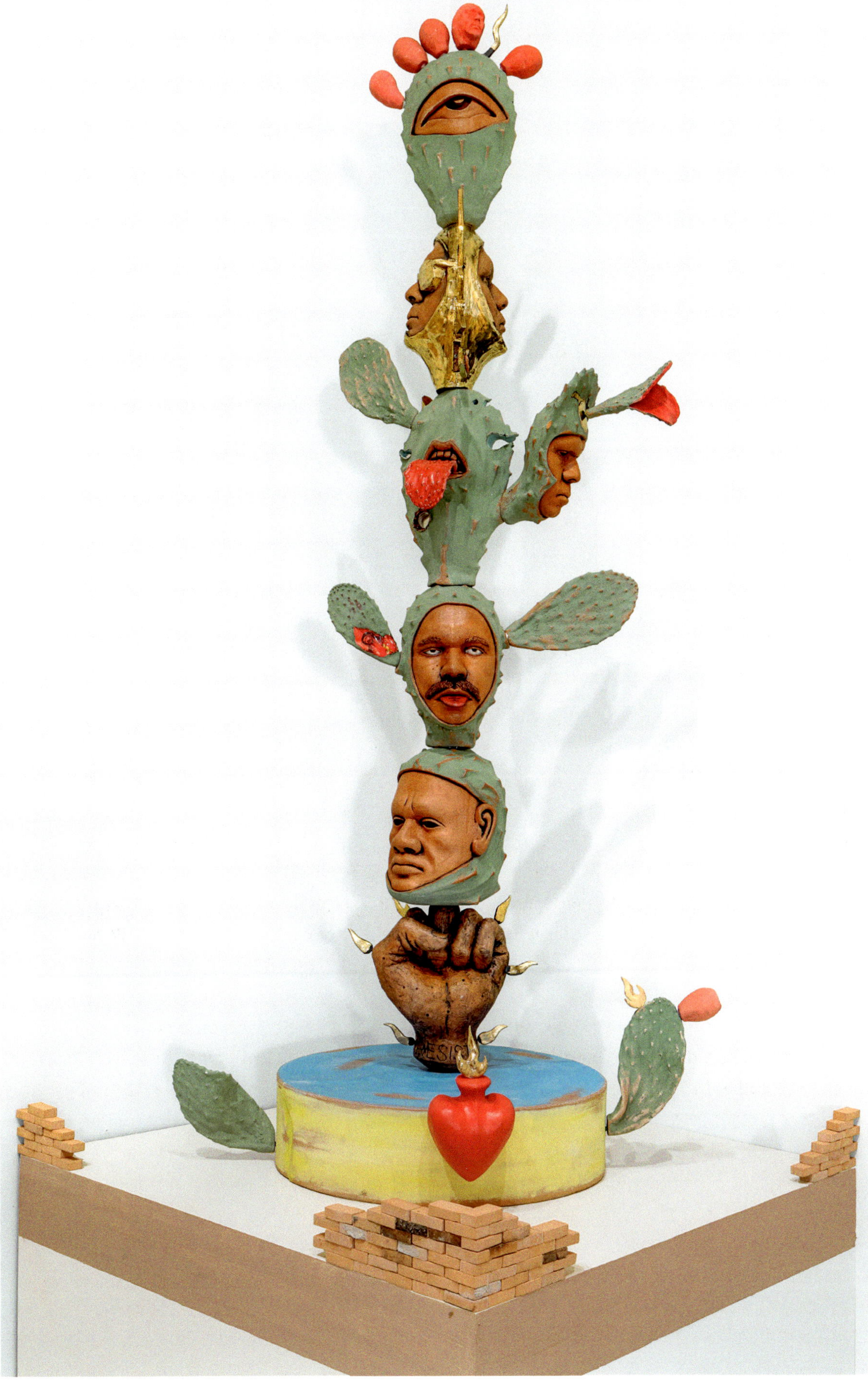

33 Salvador Jiménez-Flores, *The Resistance of the Hybrid Cacti*, 2017. Earthenware, underglaze, glaze, luster, and terracotta slip, 70 × 29.5 × 29.5 in. (177.8 × 74.9 × 74.9 cm). Courtesy the artist

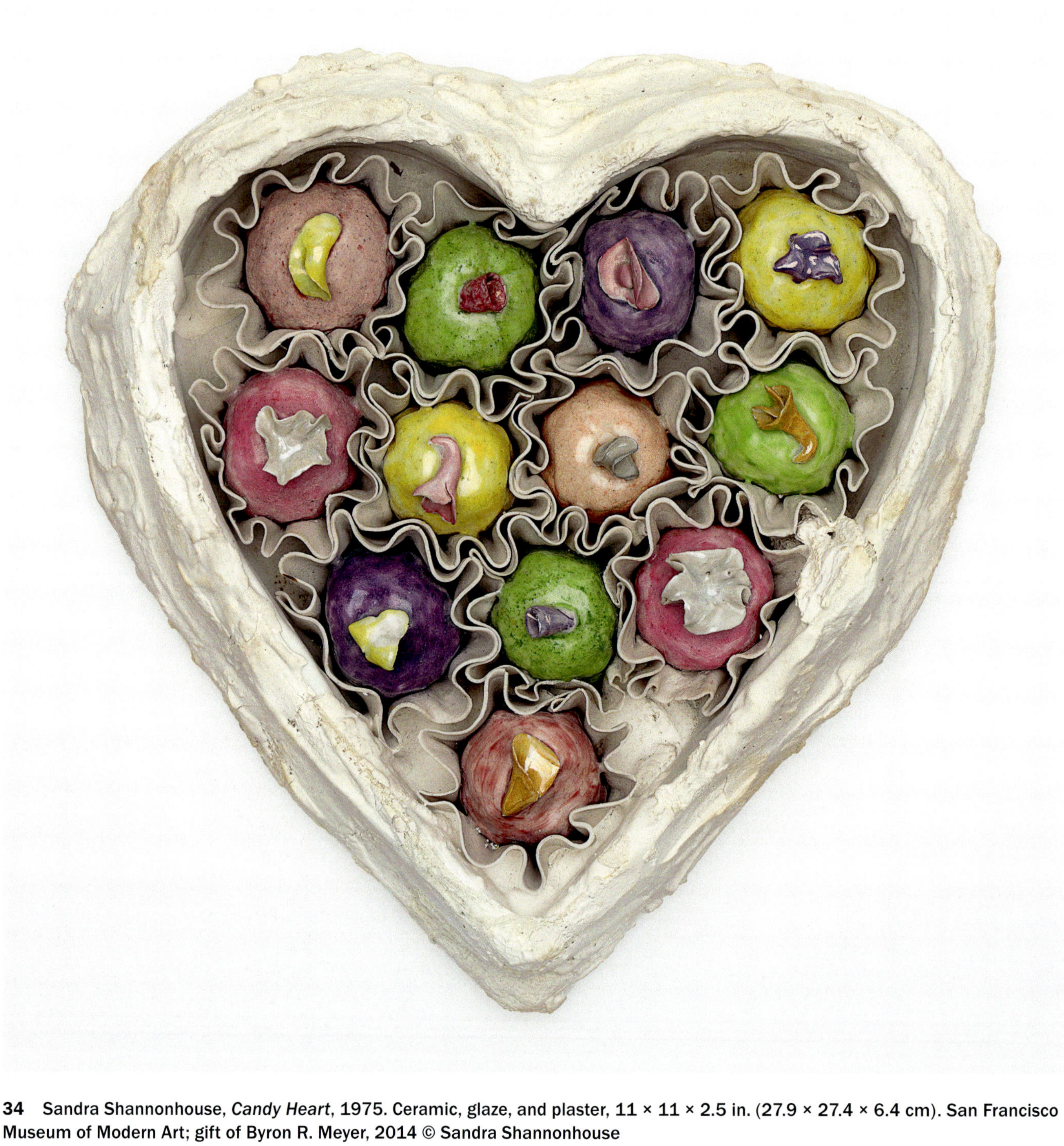

34 Sandra Shannonhouse, *Candy Heart*, 1975. Ceramic, glaze, and plaster, 11 × 11 × 2.5 in. (27.9 × 27.4 × 6.4 cm). San Francisco Museum of Modern Art; gift of Byron R. Meyer, 2014 © Sandra Shannonhouse

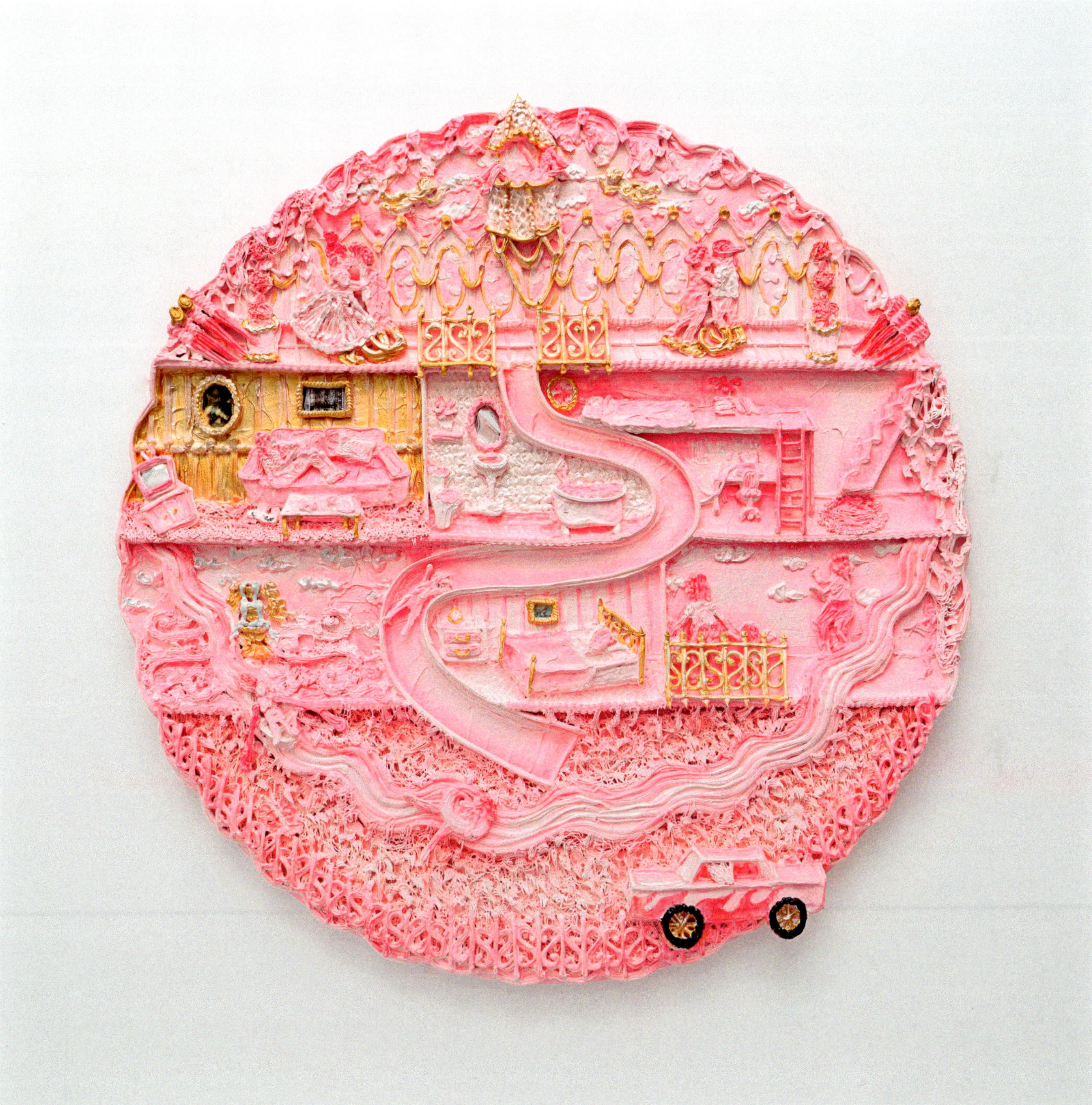

35 Yvette Mayorga, *Surveillance Locket 2*, 2021. Acrylic piping and collage on panel, 36 in. diameter (91.4 cm). Courtesy the artist

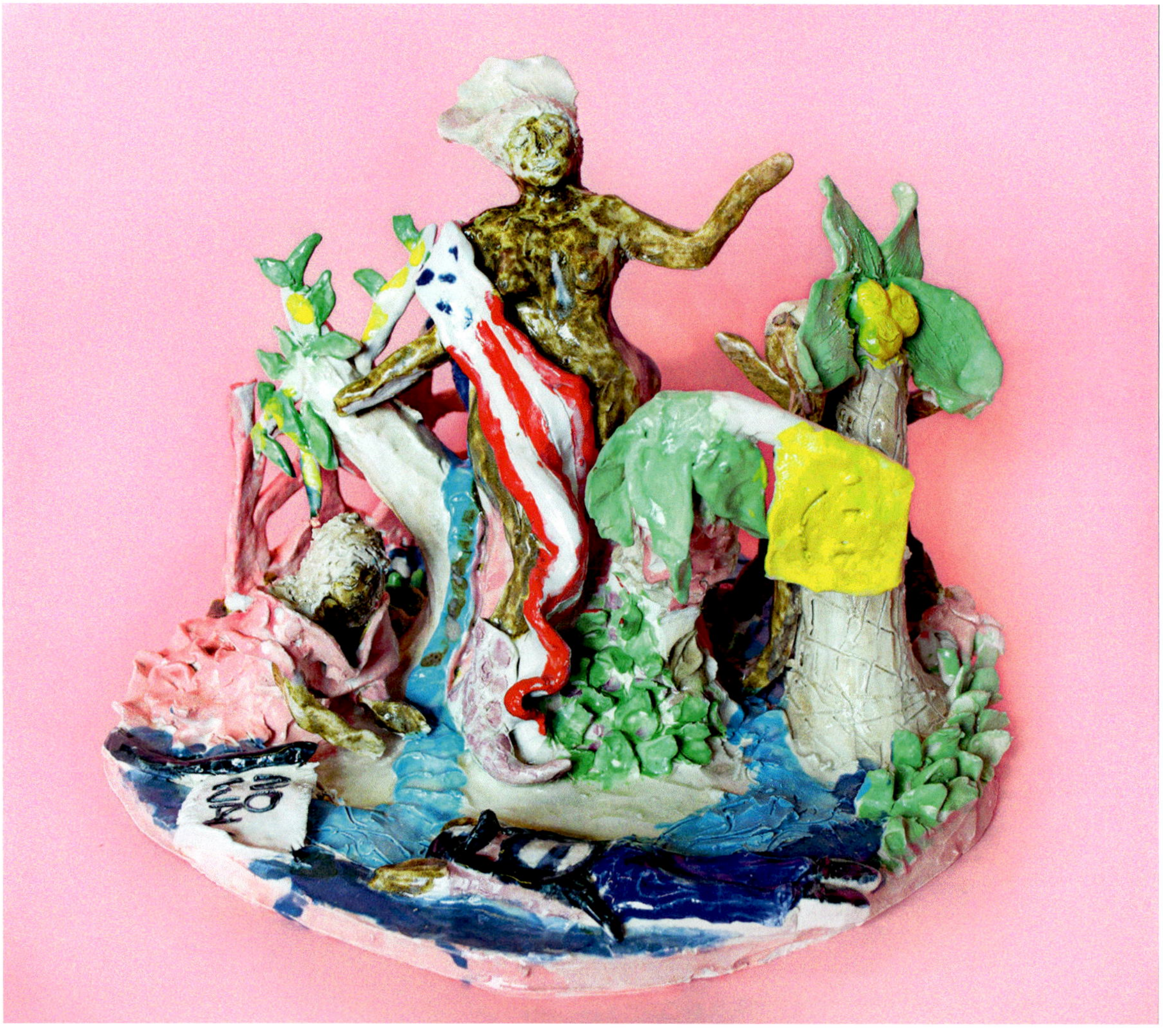

36 Yvette Mayorga, *Alligator Boots, After Lenardi, Giovanni Battista, Sugar Sculpture 16th Century*, 2018. Porcelain and glaze, 12 × 12 × 12 in. (30.5 × 30.5 × 30.5 cm). Courtesy the artist

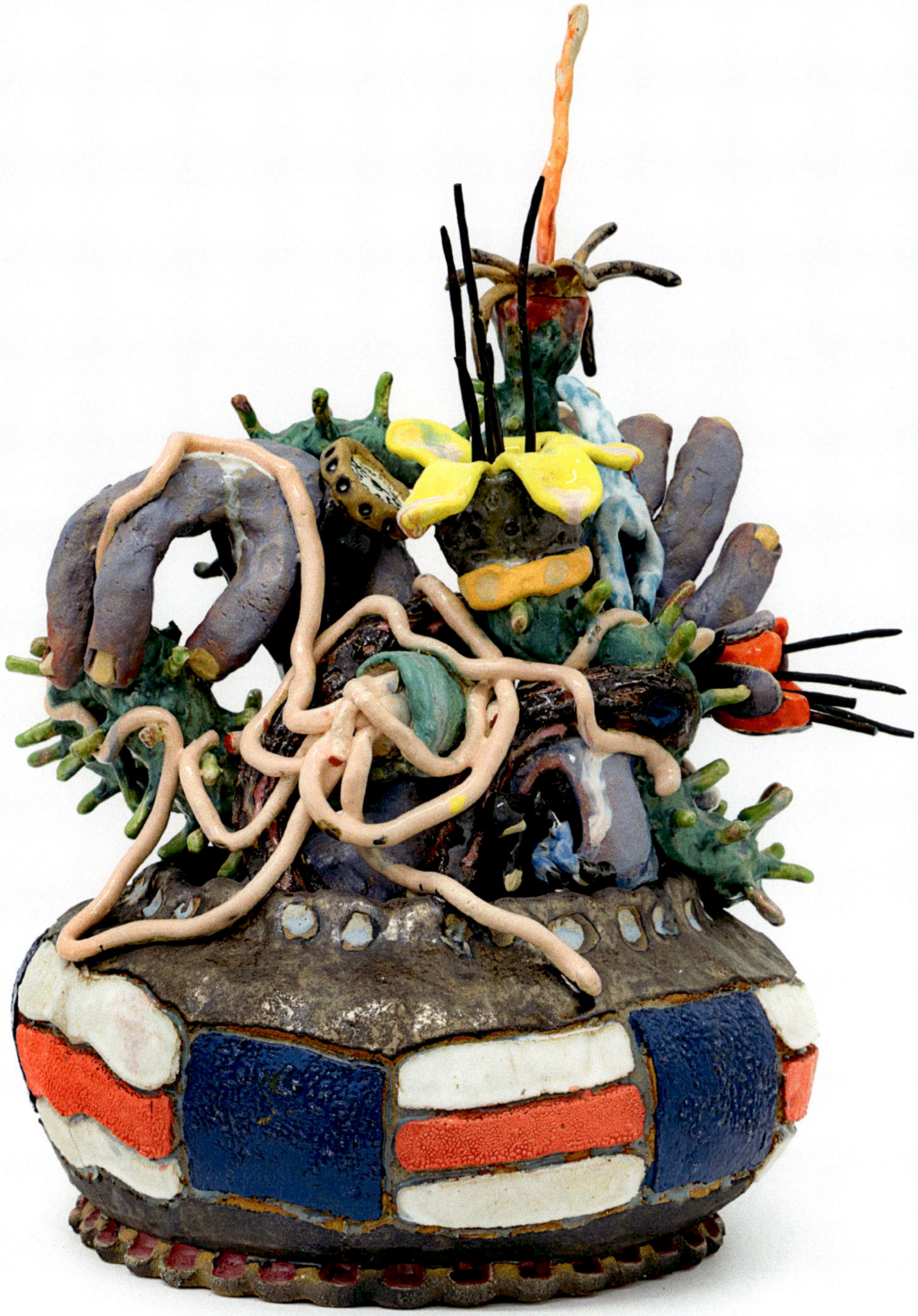

37 Sharif Farrag, *Bouquet*, 2020. Ceramic and glaze, 23 × 15 × 18 in. (58.4 × 38.1 × 45.7 cm). Museum of Arts and Design, New York; purchase with funds provided by the Kottler Fund, 2020

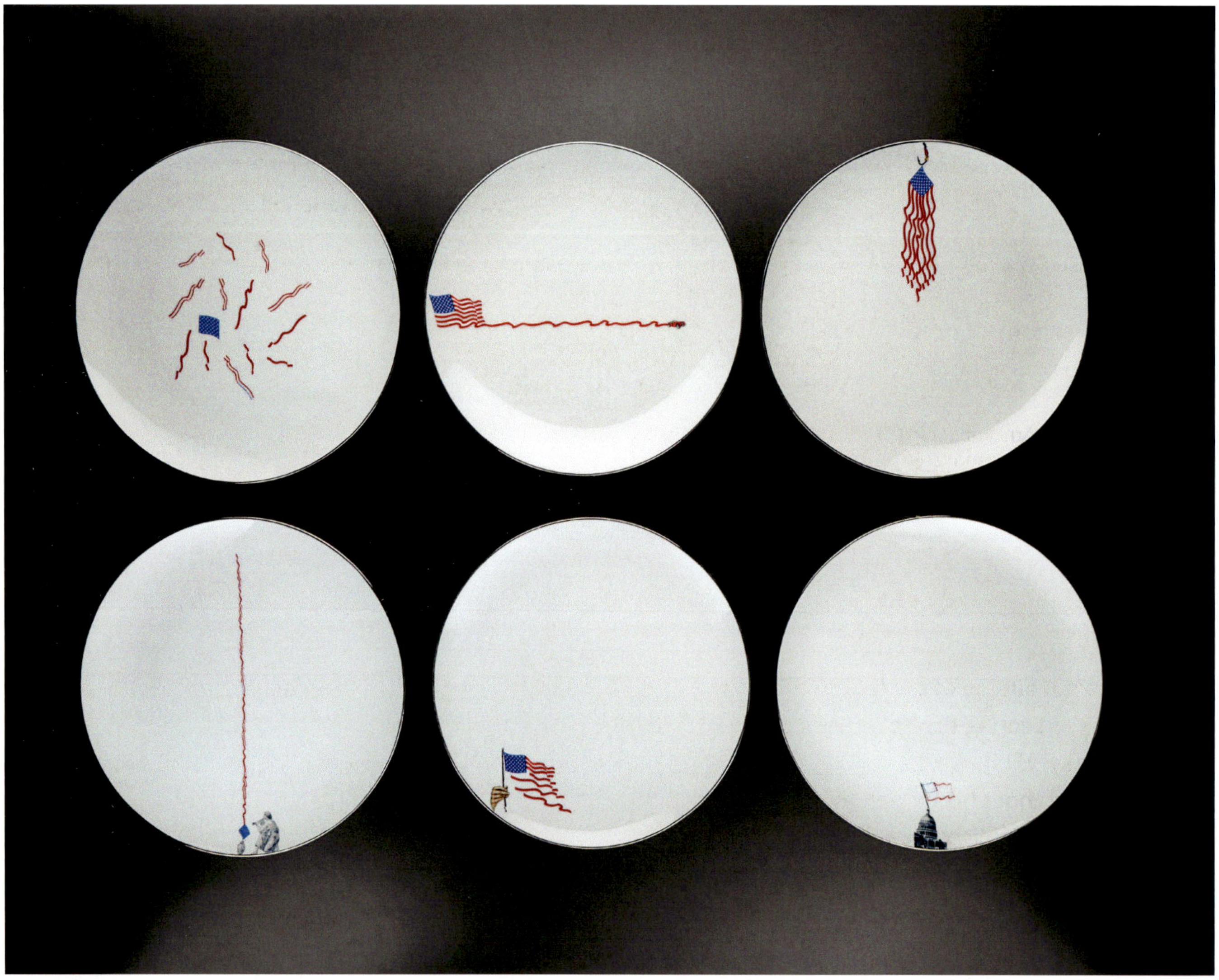

38 Howard Kottler, Clockwise from top left: *Flag Kit*, *Exhausted Glory*, *Drip Dry*, *Hollow Dream*, *Made in the USA*, and *Charming Lyre*, from the "American Supperware" series, 1969. Porcelain blanks, decals, and luster, variable dimensions. Museum of Arts and Design, New York; gift of the Howard Kottler Testamentary Trust, 1991

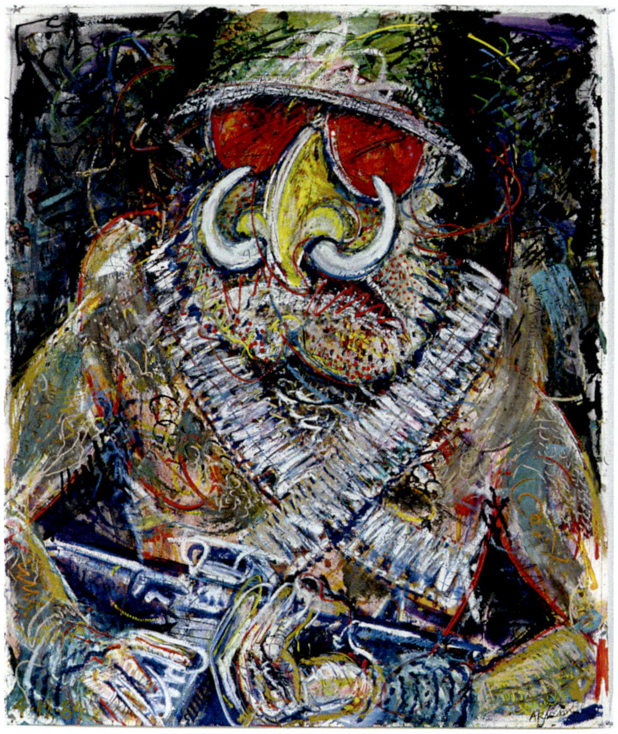

39 Robert Arneson, *I Ain't Your Mother*, c. 1985. Pastel, acrylic, oil, and graphite on paper, 58 × 50 in. (147.3 × 127 cm). Museum of Arts and Design, New York; gift of Alfred and Mary Shands, 2008

the blank outline of the flag at the Capitol Building underscoring the emptiness of American democracy.[81]

Throughout his career, Arneson was outspoken about his disapproval of wars and nuclear threats, which prompted a series of works depicting military generals as monsters resembling aboriginal masks from New Guinea [fig. 39]. He also expressed disdain for political figures such as President Ronald Reagan, whom he rendered in *Ronny Portable* (1986) [fig. 40] in the guise of a television set hinting at Reagan's former career as an actor. Near the end of his life, Arneson produced his most political and controversial body of work, "The Black Series," 1988–90. Through this series, based on the vilification of Black men by the American media and how it helped exacerbate stereotypes, Arneson sought to tackle racism in the United States. In a statement accompanying the work, he stated it was "hard looking—looking hard—confronting our perceptual awareness and attitudes toward the national dilemma. Racism." He also shared that it was "intended for the white walls of a white institution, in a white world" [fig. 41].

In works like *Chief Executive Officer* and *Rapist & Drug Dealer* (1989) [fig. 42], Arneson directly confronts racial stereotyping and profiling, issues still relevant today. *Chief Executive Officer* depicts a Black man in earthenware while *Rapist & Drug Dealer*, glazed in white, represents a white man. While this scenario is entirely plausible, many would have guffawed at it in the past, betraying implicit bias. Nevertheless, the series was not without missteps. A provocateur at heart, in 1991, Arneson stated: "If people like

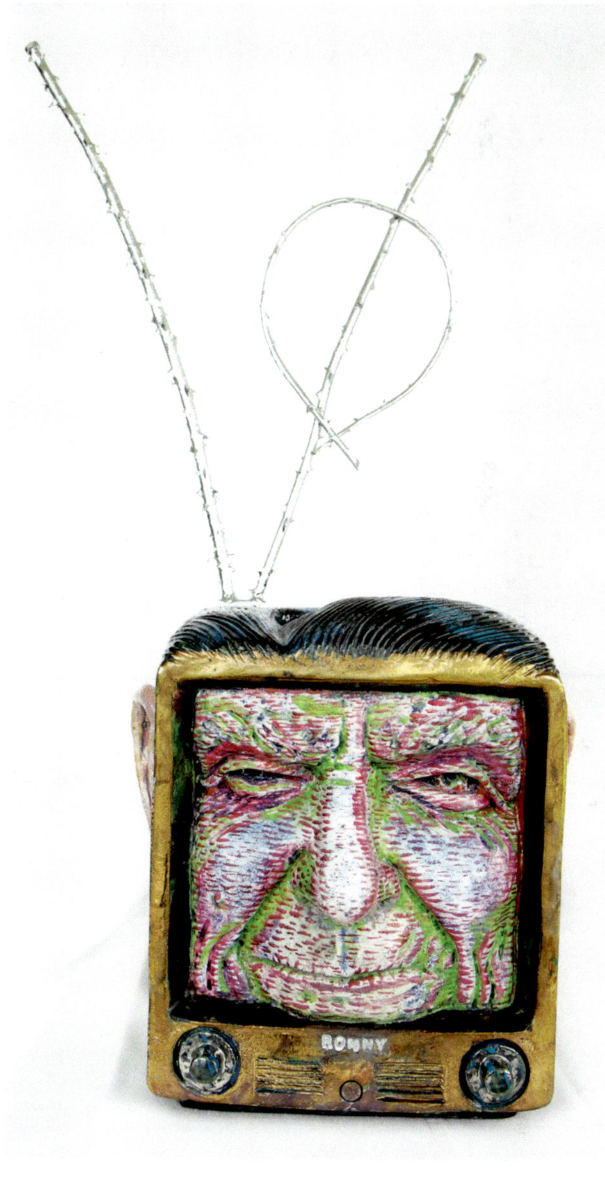

40 Robert Arneson, *Ronny Portable*, 1986. Ceramic, glaze, and bronze, 35 ½ × 21 ½ × 14 in. (90.2 × 54.6 × 25.6 cm). Collection of Judie and Howard Ganek, courtesy George Adams Gallery, New York

STUDIO AS
430 First Street
Benicia, CA 94510
707/745-8413

My recent images of Black Americans in black and white about white and black, are hard looking - looking hard - confronting our perceptual awareness and attitudes toward the national dilemna - racism.

They are intended for the white walls of a white institution in a white art world, hopefully to be acquired by a corporate headquarters to replace interior designs by Roy Lichtenstein.

Robert Arneson

Feb. 1990

41 Robert Arneson, “The Black Series” statement, 1990

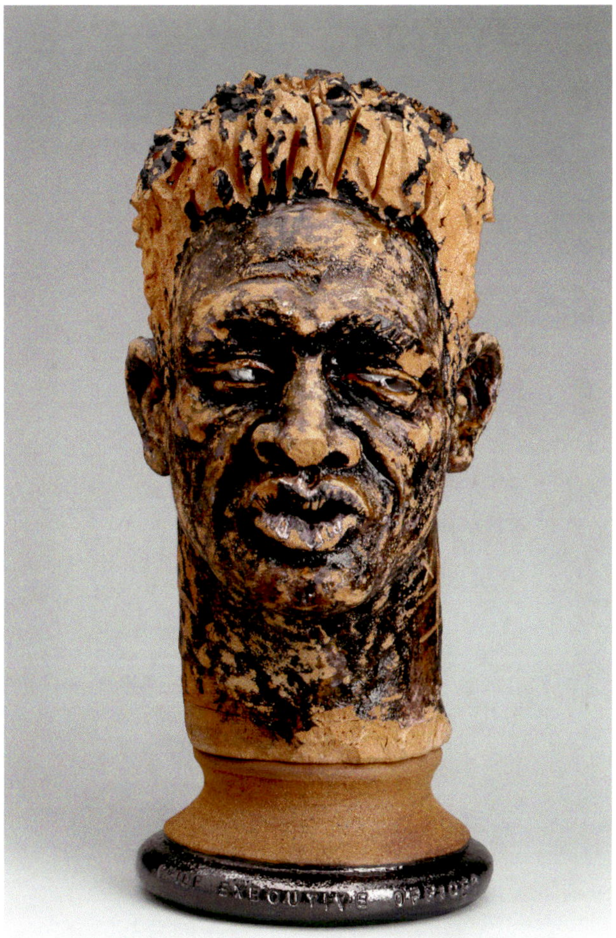

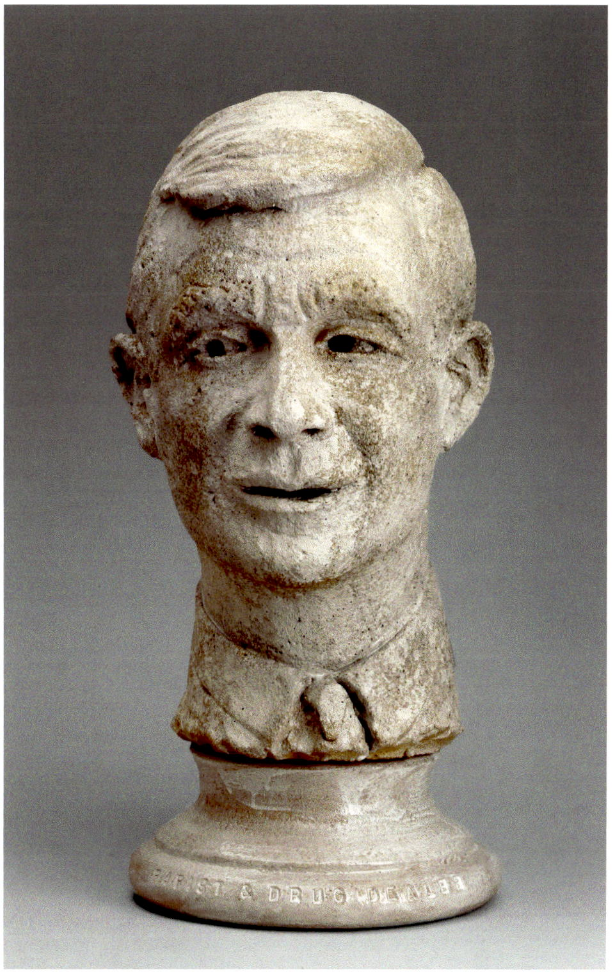

42 Robert Arneson, *Chief Executive Officer* and *Drug Dealer & Rapist*, 1989. Ceramic and glaze, 25 × 12 × 12 in. (63.5 × 30.5 × 30.5 cm.) each. Estate of Robert Arneson, courtesy George Adams Gallery, New York

what you're doing, you're in trouble. You've got to keep it edgy, keep pushing until it's not quite likable, until it's troublesome—particularly troublesome to the artist. I can remember when my early works were so troubling that I just couldn't get them out of my mind—they bothered me. Making a toilet sculpture was shocking to me."[82] Most disquieting were a drawing and a sculpture of Arneson's likeness in blackface. The drawing featured Arneson's winking face with a bellhop hat decorated with the words "yas-suh!" The sculpture was glazed in black except for pure white circles around wide eyes and grimacing mouth. Arneson joked that he was his "own cheapest model"[83] and likely used his face only to make a point about the history of such imagery in the United States. This series was also a personal reckoning[84] and while Arneson had genuine intentions to hold himself and others accountable, the work is inflammatory.[85] It would be unfathomable to produce work like this in today's political climate, yet Arneson's "The Black Series" is an important case study on problematic depictions of Blackness by non-Black artists.

In her sculptures, Natalia Arbelaez, a New York-based contemporary artist, shares stories of Amerindian identity, women of color, immigration, and colonization through quirky sharp-toothed grimacing figures inspired by Indigenous pottery from Latin America. Arbelaez conveys these narratives materially by juxtaposing terracotta—the clay used by her Indigenous ancestors—with a white majolica or tin glaze. The latter was brought to Latin America by the Spanish conquistadors from Europe, where it was used to imitate Chinese porcelain. In *Mestizo Arbelaez* (2020) [fig. 43], the colonizer is identifiable through the glossy white surface while slain bodies of Native people are depicted in reddish brown, as is the personified Indigenous land, wincing as the horse steps on it. Expanding her practice into video and performance in *Culebra Portal* and *Mach'aqway Tusuy* (2022) [fig. 44], the artist envisions a time machine to connect with her ancestors, composed of two ceramic pillars adorned with motifs borrowed from different Indigenous cultures. In the video, Arbelaez reinterprets Muisca (Indigenous people of Colombia) ceremonial practices by donning a fringy costume, gold-painted skin, and a golden ceramic mask. Arbelaez playfully remixes her heritage and American identity as she dances to a catchy beat wearing a stuffed snake across her neck—a reference to Britney Spears's iconic performance of "I'm a Slave 4 U" at the 2001 MTV Video Music Awards. The result is a hypnotizing montage of colors and celestial imagery that suggests a cosmic connection that defies time and space.

Maryam Yousif fuses the past and present to create hybrid objects that parallel the complexity of her identity. In her practice, the contemporary artist brings together Iraq's long tradition of ceramic-making and the modern history of Funk, which she became familiar with living in San Francisco. Yousif developed an archetype of a woman in her work that, while not a self-portrait, very much resembles her. It is an homage to Yousif's empowering female role models throughout time, from Sumerian queen Puabi to her grandmother, mother, and Pan-Arab pop stars. She cheekily recontextualizes these figures as pop stars or fashion models [fig. 45], professions coveted and desired in American society, and reinterprets historical artifacts as purses [fig. 46] to return attention to the beauty of Iraq, a country tarnished by war and American military occupation.

Yousif's interest in showing strong female figures builds upon the examples of Los Angeles-based contemporary artist Ruby Neri and Funk contemporary Frey, who moved to the Bay Area in 1960. Frey's work seamlessly blends Abstract Expressionism, Pop Art, and Funk. Best known for her larger-than-life figurative sculptures [fig. 47], which she began making in the 1970s, her preferred scale was subversive and audacious. Frey's sculptures towered over most at a time when male artists were trying to build bigger as a demonstration of their virility and power. She triumphed by creating an army of women and men in 1950s clothing with dramatic physical poses and facial expressions, using a technicolor array of glazes.

Neri was born into the Funk community. Her father, Manuel Neri's abstract ceramic sculptures were part of *FUNK*. Much like Frey, Neri is well-known for her large sculptures of women. The coil-built figures and vessels are intimate portrayals of daily life that she sees as "self-referential" but not "autobiographical."[86] Neri's imagery of "bombshells" is pervasive, multiplying over surfaces and forms with joyful exuberance. Her airbrush technique, which looks like graffiti, heightens the figures' cartoonish aesthetic.[87] *Mamma* (2020) [fig. 47], a large archetypical woman, sits down blowing a kiss to a smaller version of herself while cradling another in her arms—a depiction of dual identities as mother and daughter, as well as self-love. The nude women are free and in command of their bodies, turning on its head the male gaze that defined the reclining nudes of art history's past.

Many of the Funk ceramicists were caught in limbo: too wild for the traditional potters, and too crafty for the fine art establishment. Today, ceramic sculpture is part of the mainstream art world, and the newer generation of artists featured in *Funk You Too!* represents an important strand of contemporary artistic practice. Over fifty years ago, Funk ceramicists used humor to address the marginalization of ceramics in the art world by mocking elite forms of taste and found that this strategy could be applied to share compelling personal and political narratives. Their legacy continues in the work of this younger cohort who have reenergized the field to address a wider range of concerns plaguing the United States through humor to affect social change.

Angelik Vizcarrondo-Laboy, Curator

1 The exhibition title for the 1967 exhibition will be stylized as *FUNK* in this catalog to avoid confusion with Funk art.

2 Paul J. Karlstrom, *Peter Selz: Sketches of a Life in Art*, (Berkeley: University of California Press, 2012), 110.

3 Peter Selz, "Acknowledgements" in *Funk*, exh. cat. (Berkeley: Berkeley Museum of Art, 1967), 2.

4 Selz, "Notes on Funk" in *Funk*, 5. RPBA was an art collective.

5 Ibid., 3.

6 James Monte, "'Making It' Funk," *Art Forum*, Vol. 5, No. 10 (1967), 56.

7 Peter Selz, Mowry Gaden, Joan Brown, Bruce Conner, Manuel Neri, James Melchert, and Peter Voulkos, *Funk Symposium*, April 28, 1967. Peter Selz papers, 1929–2014. Archives of American Art, Smithsonian Institution, and *Funk Surveys*, 1966–67, Archives of the Berkeley Art Museum and Pacific Film Archive. Conner and Brown were among the loudest critics, taking Selz to task for not curating a comprehensive show that accounted for the previous ten years and included other members of their art collective, such as Wally Hendrick and Jay DeFeo.

8 Monte 1967, 56.

9 Harold Paris, "Sweet Land of Funk," *Art in America* 55 (March 1967), 95.

10 Selz et al., *Funk Symposium*, and Nicole Rudick, "Funk," in *What Nerve! Alternative Figures in American Art, 1960 to the Present* (Rhode Island: RISD Museum), 128.

11 Karlstrom, *Peter Selz: Sketches of a Life in Art*, 115. Selz openly speaks of his collaboration with Paris on "Sweet Land of Funk" in the "Acknowledgements" of the *FUNK* exhibition catalog. This article was unlike anything Paris had worked on before.

12 Ibid., and Miriam Dungan Cross, "Four-Letter Art in U.C. Exhibit," *Oakland Tribune*, May 14, 1967, 29.

13 Selz was notoriously outspoken about his distaste for Pop Art, a movement that gained prominence in New York in the years prior to of his departure.

14 Selz, "Notes on Funk," 3.

15 Ibid.

16 Ibid.

17 Monte 1967, 57.

18 Karlstrom, Peter Selz: *Sketches of a Life in Art*, 114.

19 Selz, "Notes on Funk," 5.

20 Ibid., 6.

21 Ibid., 3.

22 Selz, "Acknowledgements," 2.

23 Monte 1967, 56.

24 Robert Arneson, *Non Statement Or Thoughts To Go By.....By*, 1970.

25 Selz, "Notes on Funk," 3.

26 Karlstrom, Peter Selz: *Sketches of a Life in Art*, 116.

27 John Natsoulas, "Funk," in *Humor, Irony, and Wit: Ceramic Funk from the Sixties and Beyond*, exh. cat. (Phoenix: Arizona State University Art Museum, 2004), 5. Another popular story from the RBPA is that of Wally Hendrick describing his ex-wife, Jay DeFeo's penchant for putting dirty underwear in a fridge as the epitome of Funk.

28 Rickey Vincent, "Introduction to Funk: The Bomb," in *Funk: The Music, The People, and The Rhythm of the One* (New York: St. Martin's Griffin, 1996), 3.

29 Neri was the only exception. His parents were Mexican immigrants.

30 Mona Lisa Saloy, "Black Beats and Black Issues," in *Beat Culture and the New America*, 1950–1965, exh. cat. (New York: Whitney Museum of American Art and Flammarion, 1996), 155–59.

31 Ibid., 155.

32 Ibid., 156.

33 Glenn Adamson, "Chapter 5: Amateur," in *Thinking through Craft* (London: Bloomsbury Academic, 2007), 147–48.

34 Karlstrom, Peter Selz: *Sketches of a Life in Art*, 114.

35 Selz, after all, had a background in European Modernism and, by that point, had worked most of his career with white male artists. However, that changed significantly throughout the years as his curatorial practice evolved, and it is most evident in his 2006 book *Art of Engagement: Visual Politics in California and Beyond*, which goes in-depth into work by artists of color and women.

36 Scott A. Shields, "The Candy Store Gallery," in *The Candy Store: Funk, Nut, & Other Art with a Kick*, exh. cat. (Munich: Hirmer Publishers; Sacramento: Crocker Art Museum, 2022), 16.

37 Ibid., 18, and Mady Jones, *Oral History Interview With Robert Arneson* (transcript), August 14–15, 1981, Archives of American Art, Smithsonian Institution.

38 Marilyn Mantay, "First Lady of Funk," *Stuttertown*, Vol. VII, No. 20, 1981, and Candy Store Gallery records, 1968–2004, Archives of American Art, Smithsonian Institution. Records from the gallery show extensive correspondence via postcards, letters, and handmade cards to McHugh from her artists.

39 The Crocker's exhibitions include *Welcome to the Candy Store* in 1981 and more recently in 2022, *The Candy Store: Funk, Nut, & Other Art with a Kick.*

40 Ralph (Doggy) Dinsmore AKA Roy De Forest, "Statement," in *Nut Art*, exh. cat. (Hayward: California State University, Hayward Gallery, 1972). Peeples-Bright's Rainbow House was featured in multiple publications in its prime. Unfortunately, the house was repainted once it changed owners.

41 Shannonhouse, VandenBerge, and Warashina have changed their aesthetic significantly. The latter two remained humorous in their approach.

42 In part, this is a result of the Servicemen's Readjustment Act of 1944 or GI Bill. Many returning veterans chose to study art, and art departments in this period experienced exponential growth as they expanded to accommodate the new students. Jim Crow laws made attending college difficult or limited majors for African-Americans. However, the movement was not exclusively white, as there were prominent Asian artists.

43 This is the hook of the song "Spoonful of Sugar" performed by Julie Andrews in the titular role of Disney's *Mary Poppins* from 1964.

44 Ken Kelley, "Arneson in His Studio," *Style* (October 1987), 42.

45 See Arneson's *FUNK* survey.

46 Adamson, *Thinking Through Craft,* 144, and Paul J. Smith, *Clayworks: Twenty Americans* (New York, Museum of Contemporary Crafts, 1971, n.p. Arneson was represented by multiple galleries and had many retrospective exhibitions including at the Institute of Contemporary Art in Chicago and the San Francisco Museum of Modern Art in 1974, the Hirshhorn Museum in 1986, and in 1992 at the Institute of Contemporary Art in Philadelphia, months before his death. He was also widely collected nationally and internationally.

47 Patricia Falling, *Howard Kottler: Face to Face,* (Seattle: University of Washington Press, 1995), 3.

48 Ibid., 30–48.

49 John Natsoulas and Bruce Nixon, *Thirty Years of TB-9: A Tribute to Robert Arneson* (Davis: John Natsoulas Gallery, 1991), 17. However, Shannonhouse argues that when she took classes with Arneson there were "mostly women" in them.

50 Casey Lesser, "Genesis Belanger's Uncanny Ceramics Help Us Cope with the Present," *Artsy,* October 1, 2020. https://www.artsy.net/article/artsy-editorial-genesis-belangers-uncanny-ceramics-help-cope

51 Angelik Vizcarrondo-Laboy, Alex Anderson, and Didi Rojas, "This is Not a Shoe with Didi Rojas," *Clay in Color*, podcast, October 19, 2021.

52 Glen Helfand, "Artist Woody De Othello's Oversize Ceramic Sculptures Distort Household Furniture and Appliances," *W Magazine*, November 14, 2019. https://www.wmagazine.com/story/woody-de-othello-artist-interview/

53 Anna Furman, "Woody De Othello's Extraordinary Monuments to the Mundane," *T Magazine*, March 17, 2022. https://www.nytimes.com/2022/03/17/t-magazine/woody-de-othello-art.html

54 Ibid.

55 Diana L. Daniels, "What If...?," *Clayton Bailey's World of Wonders*, exh. cat. (Sacramento: Crocker Art Museum, 2011), 19.

56 Ibid., 24.

57 Ibid., 11–12.

58 Kenneth Baker, Tony Williams, John Natsoulas, and Terry Ann Tafoya, "Formative Years," *David Gilhooly* (Davis: John Natsoulas Gallery, 1992), 16–17.

59 Ibid., "More Is Not Enough," 53–54.

60 John Natsoulas, *Interview with Peter Vandenberge*, December 1990.

61 Ibid.

62 Other names for the artist include Maija Gegeris, Maija Zack, and Maija Woof. The latter she adopted after her beloved pet passed away.

63 Catherine Wagley, "Maija Peeples-Bright's Anti-hierarchical Utopias and the Art of World Building," *Carla* 22 (November 1, 2020).

64 Cuteness has been used by Japanese artists such as Yoshitomo Nara and Takashi Murakami for decades, and it is an important element of Kawaii culture in the Japanese market.

65 Sianne Ngai, *Our Aesthetic Categories: Zany, Cute, Interesting*, (Cambridge: Harvard University Press, 2012), 3–4.

66 Alake Shilling, "Artist Bio," *Salon 94*. https://salon94.com/artists/alake-shilling/

67 Ngai, Our Aesthetic Categories: *Zany, Cute, Interesting*, 24.

68 Angelik Vizcarrondo-Laboy, "Seriously Cute: Six Artists Harnessing the Power Dichotomy of Cuteness," *Cultured*, November 17, 2020. https://www.cultured-mag.com/article/2020/11/17/cute-contemporary-art

69 Ibid.

70 Francesca Kaufmann, "Magdalena Suarez Frimkess: The Freedom in her Ceramics," *Harper's Bazaar*, October 1, 2020.

71 Ibid.

72 Robert Arneson, "Guardians: The Spirit of the Work," *Ceramics Monthly* 39 (April 1991), 52.

73 Ezennwa Ukwouma, "The Search for Melvino Garretti," *Black Renaissance Noire* (Winter 2017), 107–109.

74 Ibid.

75 Based on phone conversation between author and artist, July 2022.

76 Rasquache art is a vernacular art movement associated with the Mexican population of Chicago characterized by the customization of found objects.

77 Mija Riedel, *Oral Interview with Sandra Shannonhouse* (transcript), July 22–23, 2015, Archives of American Art, Smithsonian Institution.

78 Ibid.

79 Arneson played a significant role in Shannonhouse's career and life. After a few tumultuous domestic years, Arneson divorced his first wife and married Shannonhouse in 1972. They were married until his death.

80 Judy S. Schwartz, *Confrontational Ceramics: The Artist as Social Critic*, (London: A&C Black; Philadelphia: University of Pennsylvania Press, 2008), 28.

81 Ibid.

82 Arneson 1991, 54.

83 Kelley 1987, 44.

84 Jonathan Fineberg, "Chapter 5: Parsing Desire, 1987–1992," in A *Troublesome Subject: The Art of Robert Arneson*, (Berkeley: University of California Press, 2013) 193–97. As progressive as Arneson's position seems in this series his relationship to race is contradictory. The series was born out of an incident in which African-American friend, artist, and fellow UC Davis professor, Mike Henderson whom Arneson depicted in bust *Mike* (1975)—glazed in blue to represent Henderson's love of blues music—accused Arneson of being racist. Henderson filed an official complaint with the school against Arneson in 1988 for his repeated use of "Yas suh," a slang of "yes sir" associated with enslaved African-Americans. Arneson, who was hard-of-hearing and wore a hearing aid, often replied with the phrase when anyone would yell to get his attention. Arneson and Henderson reconciled on Arneson's deathbed.

85 There are no known statements from Arneson directly addressing his use of blackface.

86 Ruby Neri, "Artist Bio," *Salon 94*. https://salon94.com/artists/ruby-neri/

87 This technique calls back to the Mission School movement in San Francisco of which Neri was a part of in the 1990s focusing on murals, graffiti, and street art.

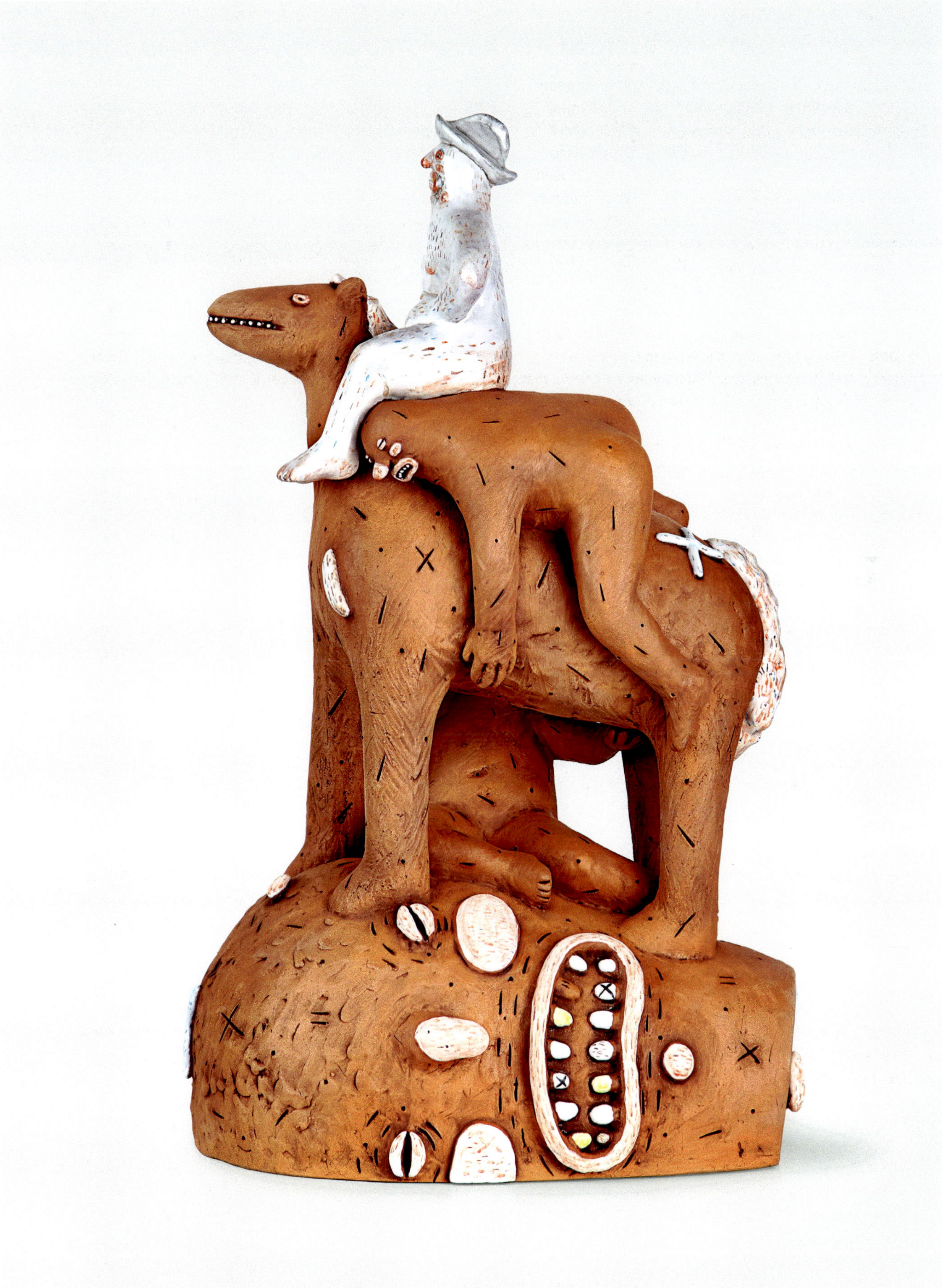

43 Natalia Arbelaez, *Mestizo Arbelaez*, 2020. Terracotta and majolica, 22 × 15 × 9 in. (55.9 × 38.1 × 22.9 cm). Museum of Arts and Design, New York; purchase with funds provided by the Kottler Fund, 2020

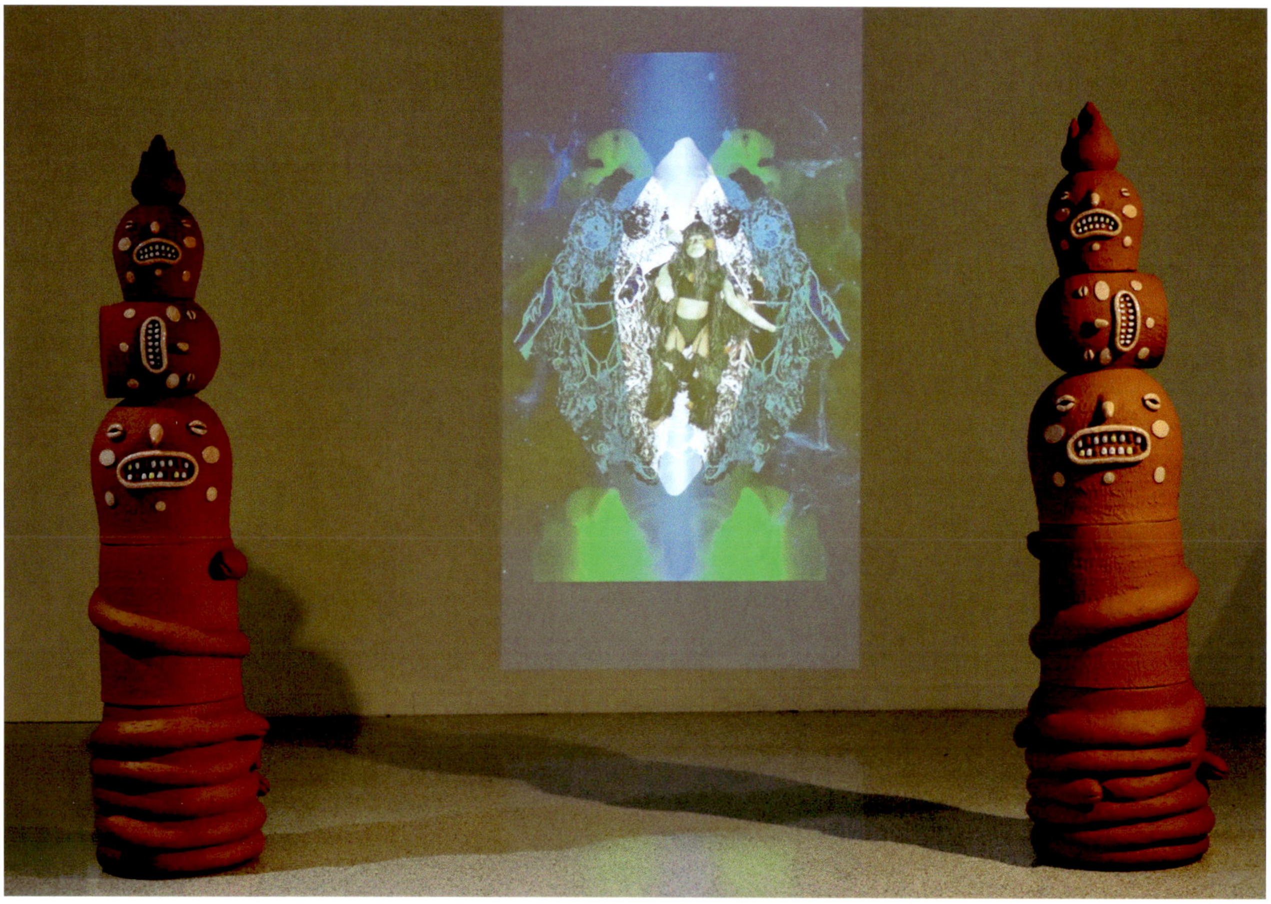

44 Natalia Arbelaez, *Culebra Portal* and *Mach'aqway Tusuy*, 2021. Terracotta and video, variable dimensions. Courtesy the artist and Mindy Solomon Gallery, Miami

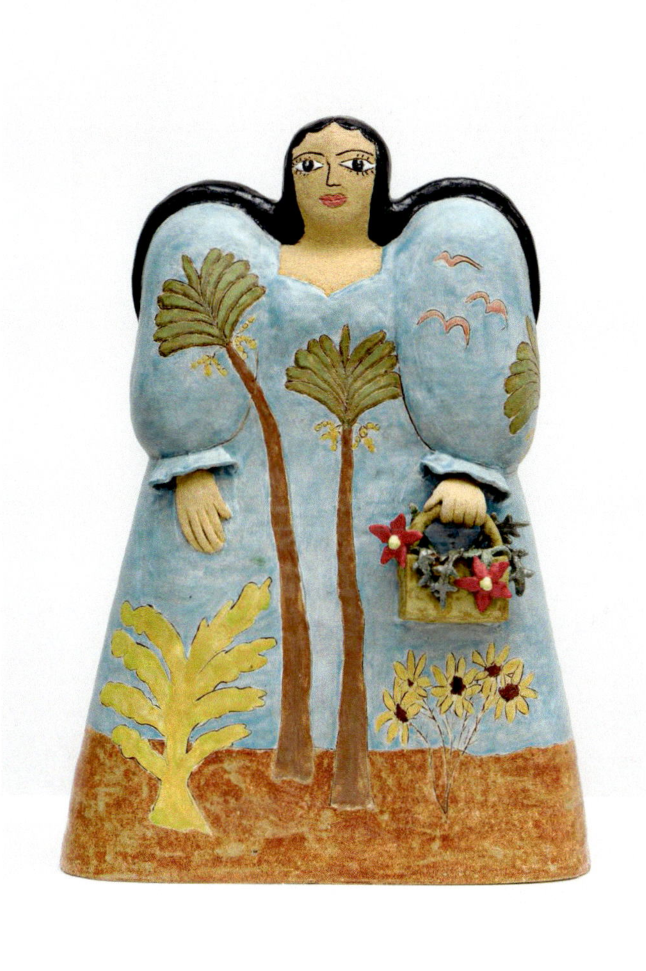

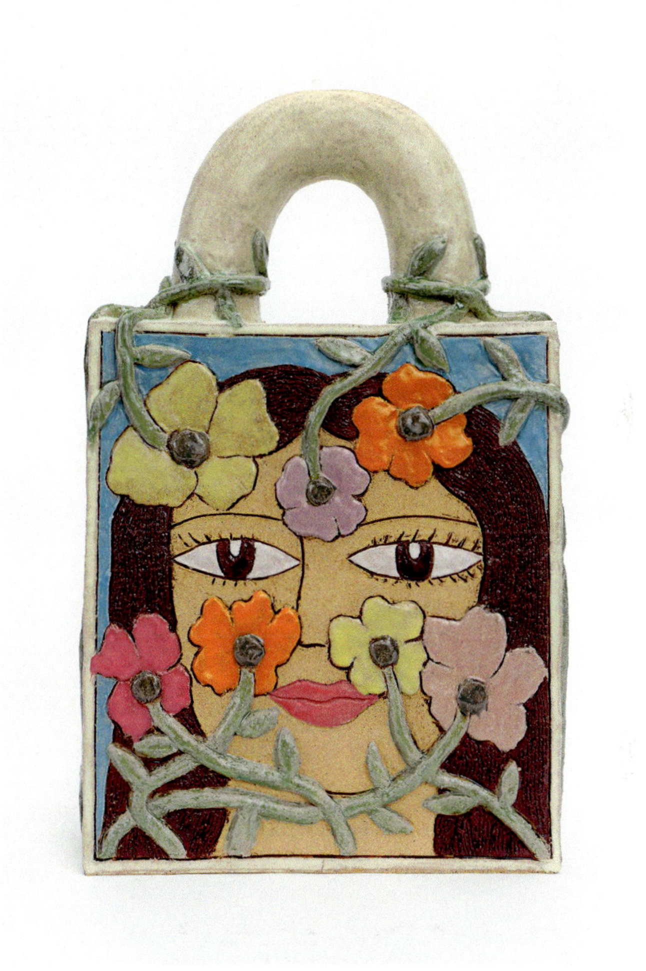

45 Maryam Yousif, *Fashion Show Model with Landscape Dress*, 2021. Stoneware and glaze, 22.5 × 16 × 5 in. (57.2 × 40.6 × 12.7 cm). Museum of Arts and Design, New York; purchase with funds provided by the Kottler Fund, 2021

46 Maryam Yousif, *Cosmic Handbag: Seeing Through Wild Flowers*, 2022. Stoneware and glaze, 18.5 × 12 × 4 in. (47 × 30.5 × 10.2 cm). Courtesy the artist and The Pit, Los Angeles

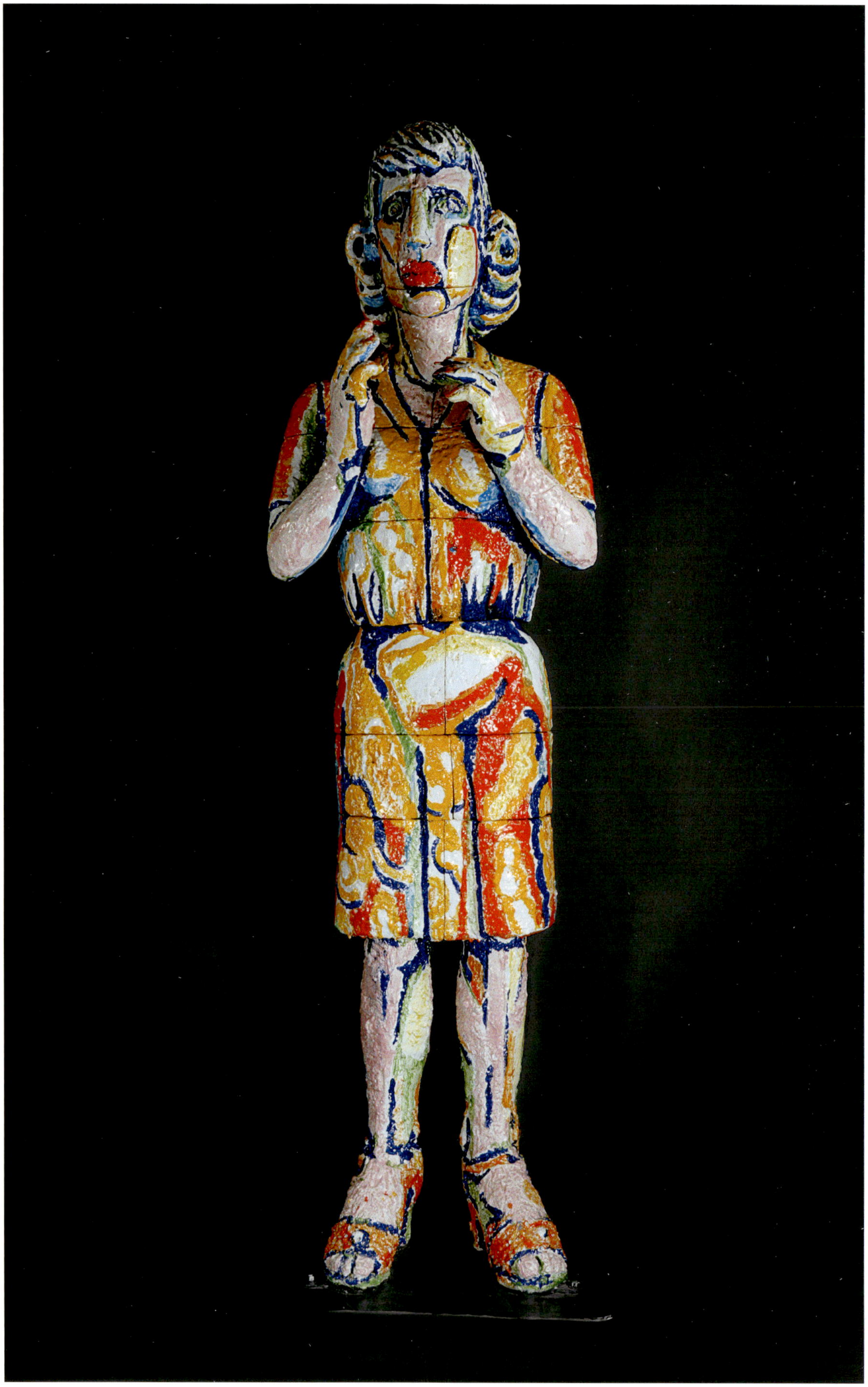

47 Viola Frey, *Group Series: Questioning Woman 1*, 1988. Ceramic and glaze, 108 × 33 × 28 in. (274.3 × 83.8 × 71.1 cm). Museum of Arts and Design, New York; purchase with funds provided by the National Endowment for the Arts, matching funds from the Associates of the American Craft Museum, and contributions from the general public, 1991

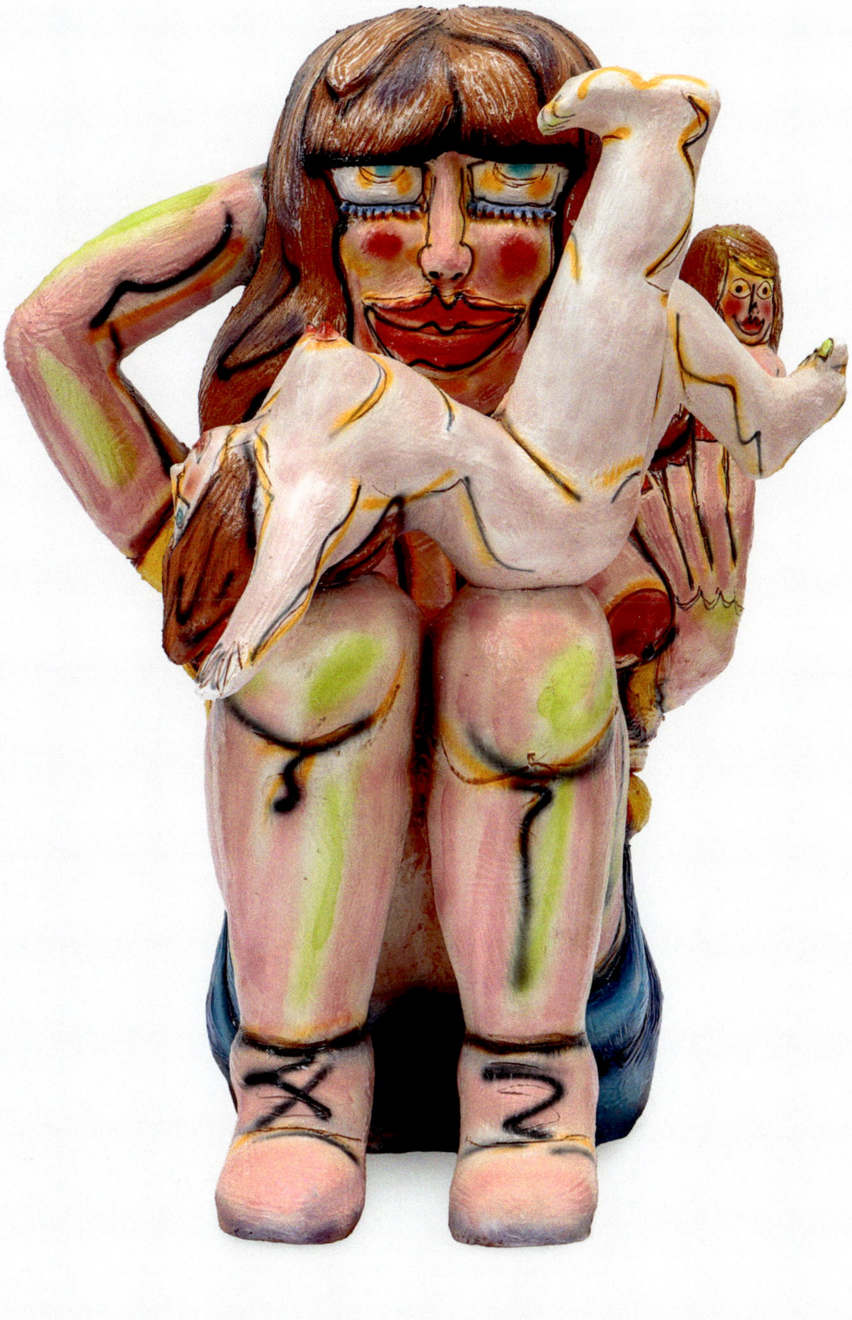

48 Ruby Neri, *Mamma*, 2021. Ceramic and glaze, 55 × 46 × 39 in. (139.7 × 116.8 × 99.1 cm). Courtesy the artist and LGDR, New York © Ruby Neri

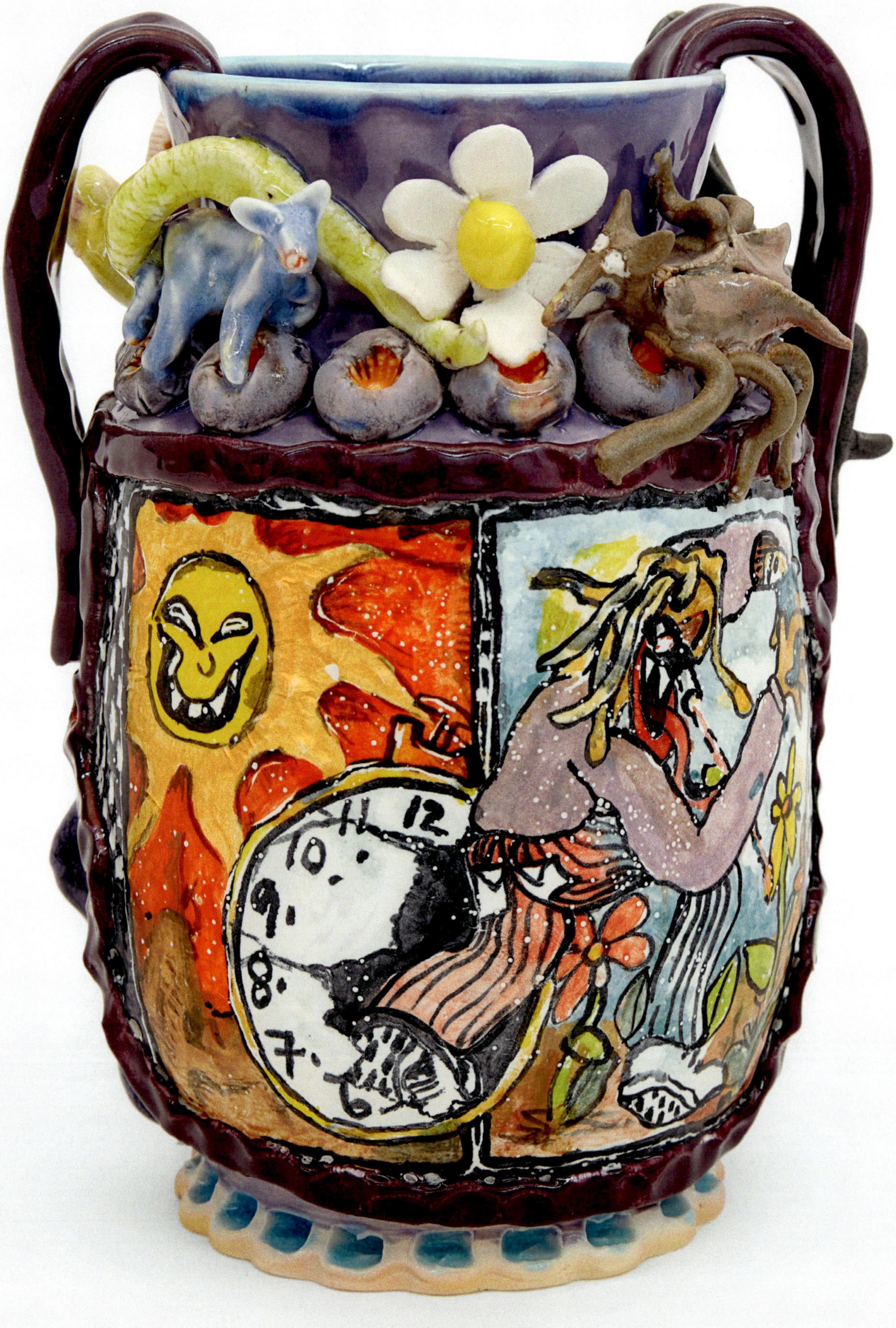

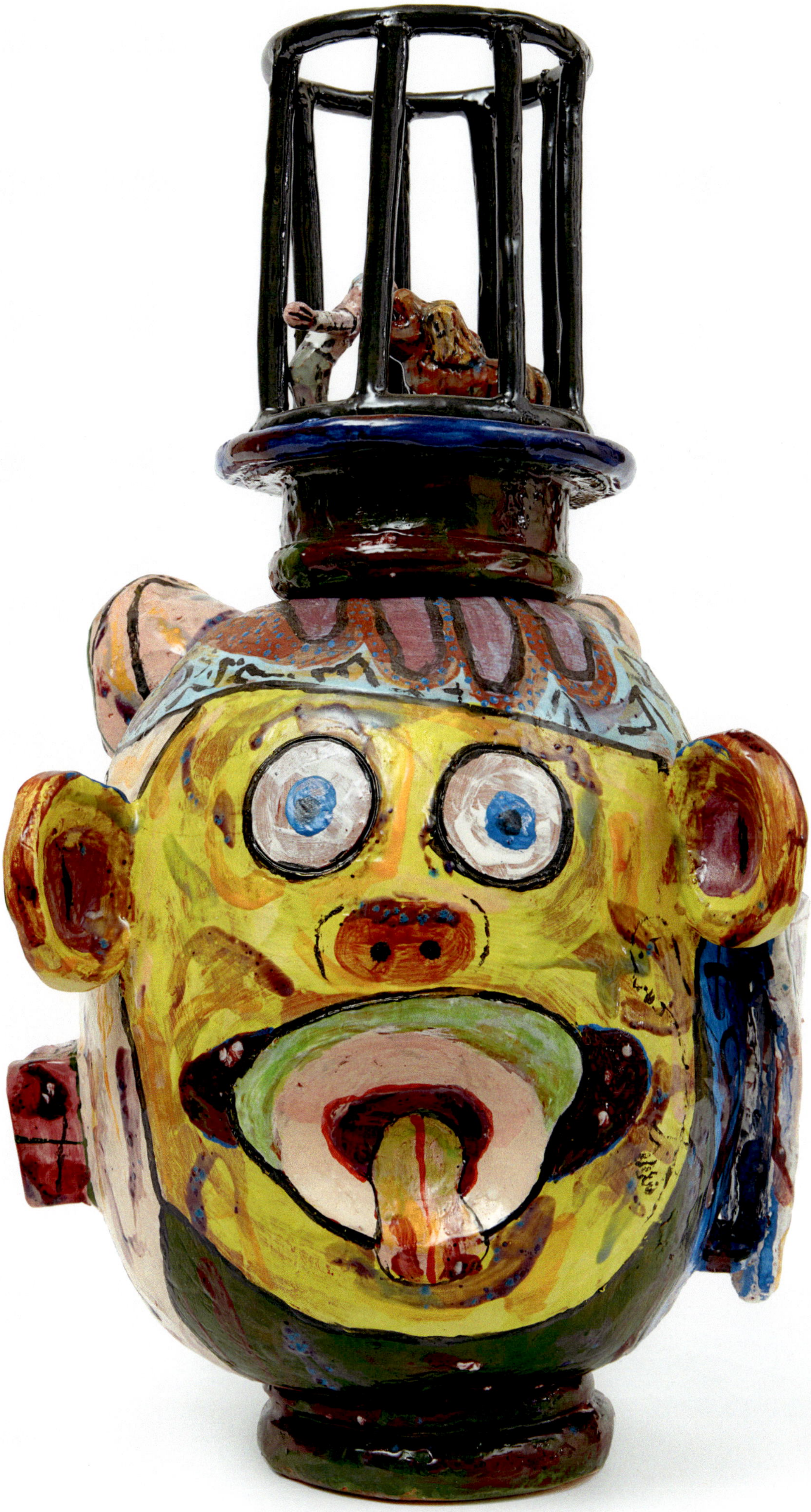

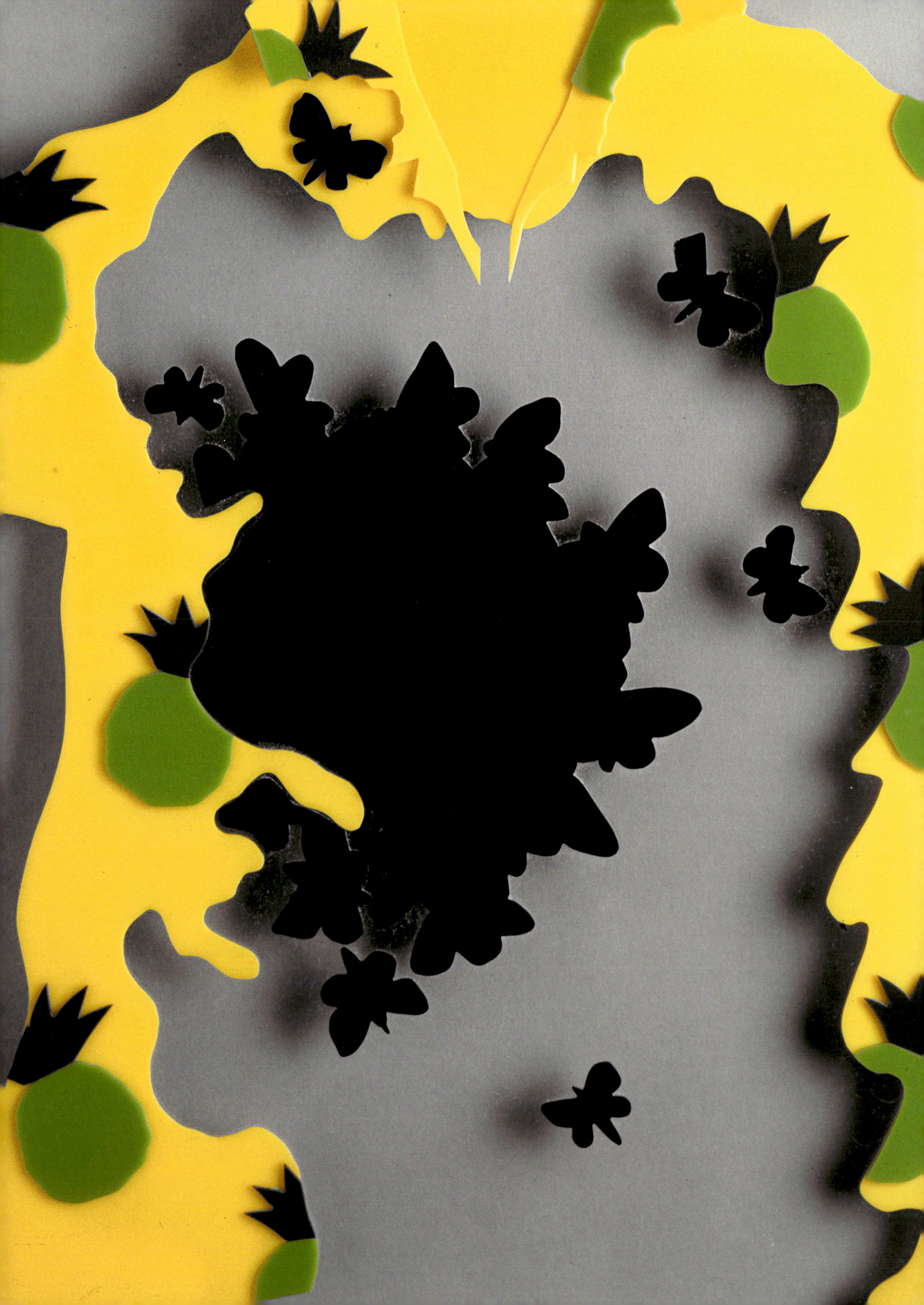

Finding Funk

In his catalog essay for the original *FUNK* exhibition at the Berkeley Art Museum in 1967, curator Peter Selz spends much of his essay on the squishy semiotics of the word "funk," poking at it, twisting it, and smearing it around like a wad of clay. Many of the artists in the exhibition chafed at being labeled as "Funk," and for the artists who worked in media outside of clay, the label simply dissipated after the exhibition ended. For most of the ceramicists, though, the term clung like the lingering stench implied by the word. In fact, Funk spread like a virus, taking root in the fertile soil of the Midwest, and even reaching internationally—to destinations as unlikely as Saskatchewan, Canada, and Australia.

The main reason that Funk resonated with ceramics is that it gave a name to a development that was already well underway. The aesthetic side of Funk can be traced back to the mid-1950s—to a way of exploring clay that was examined in depth in Rose Slivka's 1960 "New Ceramic Presence" essay in *Craft Horizons* magazine.[1] Its philosophical underpinnings are harder to trace but can be understood more broadly as a manifestation of the irreverence and mistrust of authority that fueled 1960s counterculture.

Because ceramics were largely ignored by art historians and critics, the field became ripe for homespun mythmaking and overwrought origin stories. Writers like Slivka who were paying attention to the crafts were able to virtually set their own narratives and biases in stone.[2] One foundational story from this period is the creation of Peter Voulkos's sculpture *Rocking Pot* [fig. 1] in 1956. With this piece, the World War II veteran trained by Montana potter Frances Senska, who found tremendous acclaim in the early 1950s for his vibrant, highly symmetrical functional pots, began slashing and disassembling his pots into nonfunctional sculptures.

Voulkos is often credited with singlehandedly inventing Abstract Expressionist ceramics, and *Rocking Pot* certainly captured the imagination of the field, but the truth is that Voulkos was far from alone in exploring new surfaces and pushing the sculptural possibilities of clay. I have the good fortune of being the curator overseeing the ceramics collection of the Everson Museum of Art in Syracuse. From 1932–72, the Everson (originally the Syracuse Museum of Fine Arts) hosted the oldest juried national exhibition of ceramics. It is an understatement to say that the *Ceramic Nationals*, as the exhibitions came to be known, were the most important of their time for the field of ceramics.[3]

Because the *Ceramic Nationals* jurors had a mandate to promote new talent and experimental work, the Everson's collection of close to three hundred purchase awards, along with the exhibition catalogs, provide a vital window into the dissemination of new ideas and techniques. Decades before Funk took root, American ceramic sculptors like Russell Barnett Aitken [fig. 2], Edris Eckhardt, and Viktor Schreckengost all explored satire and humor in their work, and even played with dripping, colorful glazes and lightly

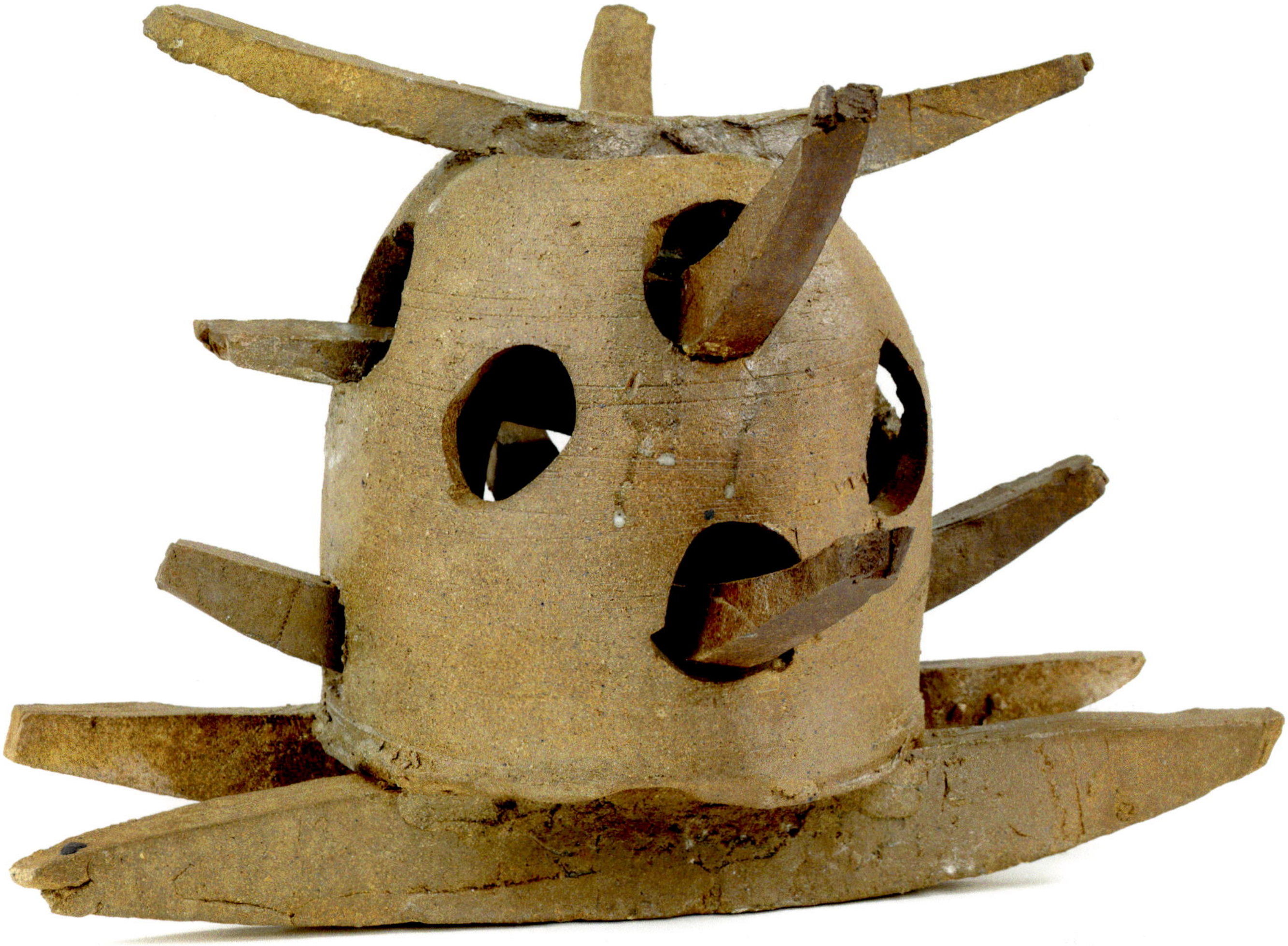

1 Peter Voulkos, *Rocking Pot*, 1956. Stoneware and colemanite wash, 13 ⅝ × 21 × 17 ½ in. (34.6 × 53.3 × 44.5 cm). Smithsonian American Art Museum, Renwick Gallery, Washington, D.C.; gift of the James Renwick Alliance and various donors and museum purchase, 1983

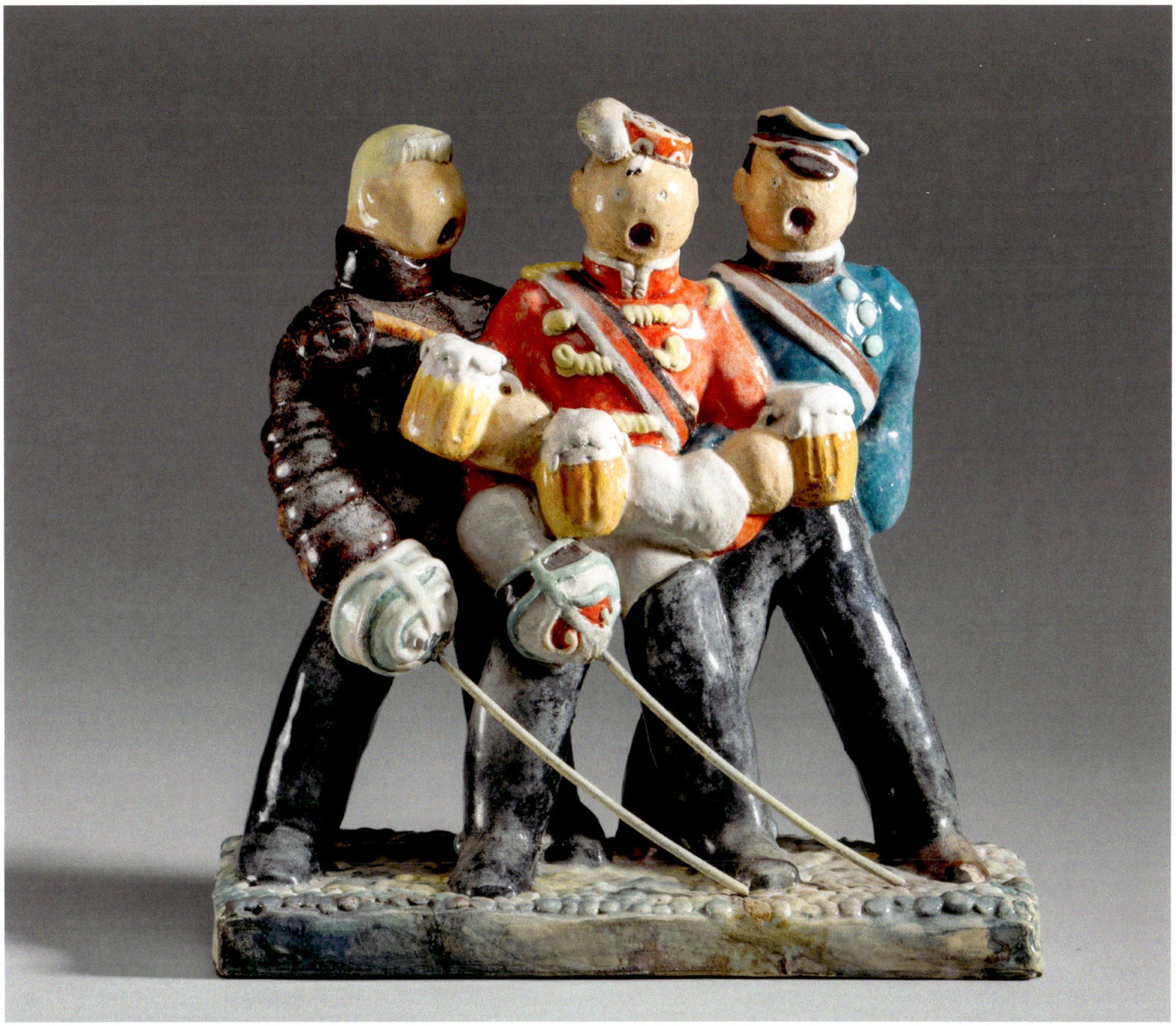

2 Russell Barnett Aitken, *Student Singers*, 1933. Ceramic and glaze, 12 × 12 × 5.5 in. (30.5 × 30.5 × 14 cm). Everson Museum of Art, Syracuse, NY; gift of the artist, 5th *Ceramic National*, 1936

mottled surfaces that would seem familiar to their Funk counterparts.

It is important to trace the evolution of sculptural surfaces in ceramics. With very few exceptions, ceramicists prior to the mid-1950s stayed in their lane. Sculptors created surfaces that highlighted the quality of their clay, such as "Chamotte," a clay characterized by rough particles of grog to add stability. Those using finer clay like terra cotta were able to get a smooth surface, sometimes accenting the clay body with colored slips. A handful of them glazed their work—mainly sticking to the same types of glazes that would be applied to pottery.

IN SEARCH OF SQUISH

Art critic Philip Rawson, who wrote *Ceramics* (1971), the definitive formal guide to writing about clay, begins the section of his book devoted to forming clay with this visceral description, which emphasizes the primacy of squishing clay:

> By squeezing clay one can, of course, make almost any shape one likes; though solid-modelled forms often tend towards those slightly rounded bun or button shapes which result naturally from contact between the soft flesh pads of the hands and the yielding

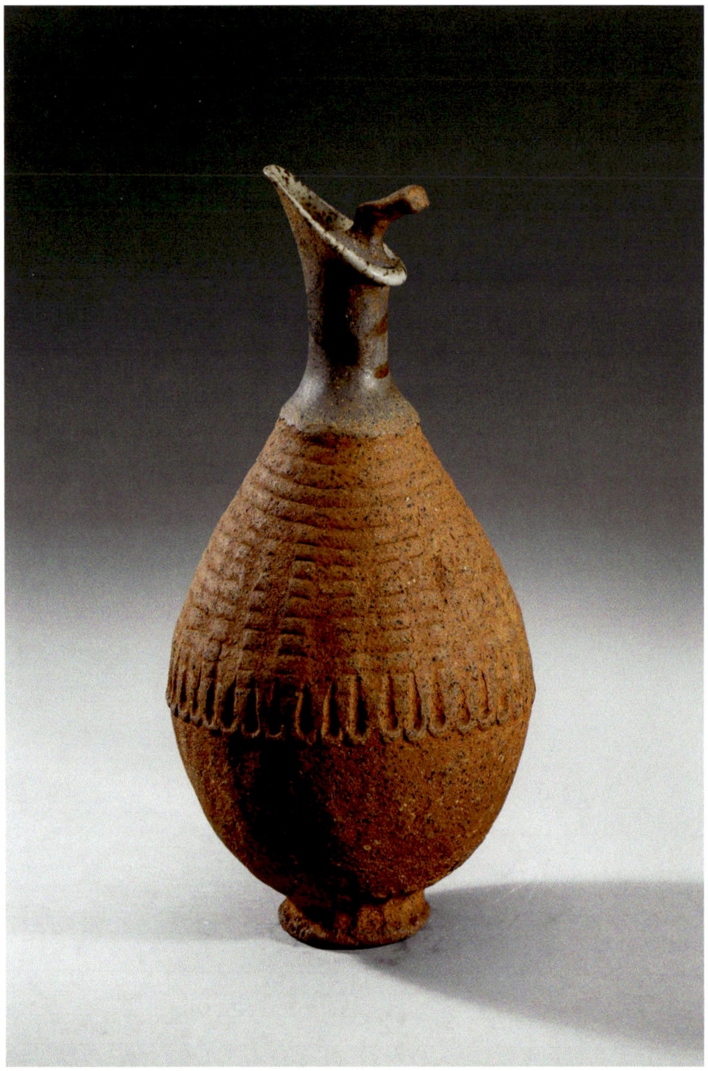

3 Theodore A. Randall, *Wine Bottle*, 1952. Ceramic, 11 3/5 × 5 3/5 in. (29.5 × 14.2 cm). Everson Museum of Art, Syracuse, NY; Purchase Prize given by Onondaga Pottery Company, 17th *Ceramic National*, 1952

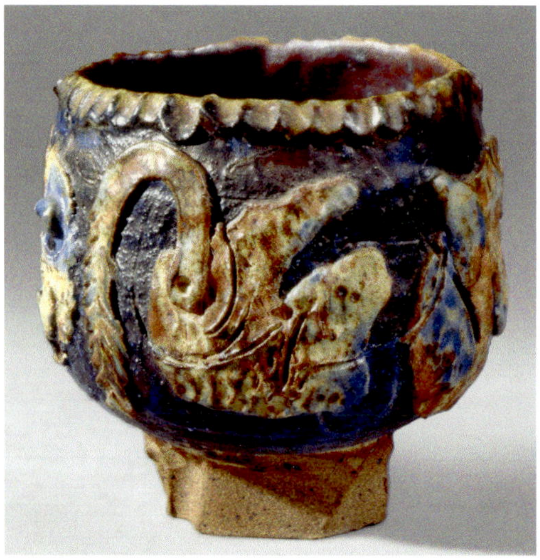

4 Robert Arneson, *Footed Bowl with Appliqué*, 1955. Stoneware, glazed, 7 × 7 × 7 in. (17.8 × 17.8 × 17.8 cm). Collection of Scripps College, Claremont, CA; gift of Mr. and Mrs. Fred Marer, 1981

> substance of clay. Many primitive figurines—icons, toys, and offerings—have been made by squeezing and pinching solid clay.[4]

It may sound shocking, but for the first half of the twentieth century, "squishing" clay was almost completely absent from the lexicon of surface techniques used by both potters and sculptors. One might find a fingerprint here or there in a sculpture, or perhaps a part of a handle pressed into a pot, but wiping, pressing, and squeezing clay was a signifier of amateur art. The earliest piece that I can find in the *Ceramic Nationals* collection that uses squishing as a strategy is a wine bottle by Alfred University professor Theodore "Ted" Randall made in 1952 [fig. 3]. The bottle, whose swelling form was made by coiling rather than throwing, is accented at the middle point of its belly by a row of marks made by dragging a tool through the still wet clay.

Alfred was hardly a hotbed of revolutionary clay-making at the time, but Randall was joined on the faculty by Robert Turner, who established the Pot Shop at Black Mountain College, as well as Daniel Rhodes, who became something of an evangelist for new modes of surface exploration. In Europe, squishing clay was the purview of fine artists working with clay. Miró and Picasso were both actively working in clay and, in 1953, CoBrA artist Asger Jorn began working in the Italian pottery village of Albisola.[5] On the West Coast, Beatrice Wood was beginning to settle into her studio in Ojai, which she had built in 1948. By 1952, she was experimenting with the lusters that would become her signature, but also applying bits of squishy clay to the surface of her pots.[6] Robert Arneson also demonstrated that he was slightly ahead of the curve when it came to the surface of his pots. A 1955 footed bowl in the Marer collection at Scripps is full of squishy, abstract sprigs, surface carving, and perhaps most boldly, a rim fluted in the style of a pie crust [fig. 4].[7]

To give credit where credit is due, when Voulkos began to cut and collage his pots in 1956, he also experimented with every conceivable mode of construction and surface decoration. By this point, Voulkos was settling into his role as an educational provocateur. Instead of drilling his students in the prime rule of throwing—that pots contain "life and lift," he instead advocated a philosophy of "dump and death," where gravity and entropy ruled the day.[8] In *Sculpture (Hobgoblin)* (1956) [fig. 5], he cuts and stacks thrown forms, then augments them with cut slabs. Most strikingly, Voulkos exaggerates the

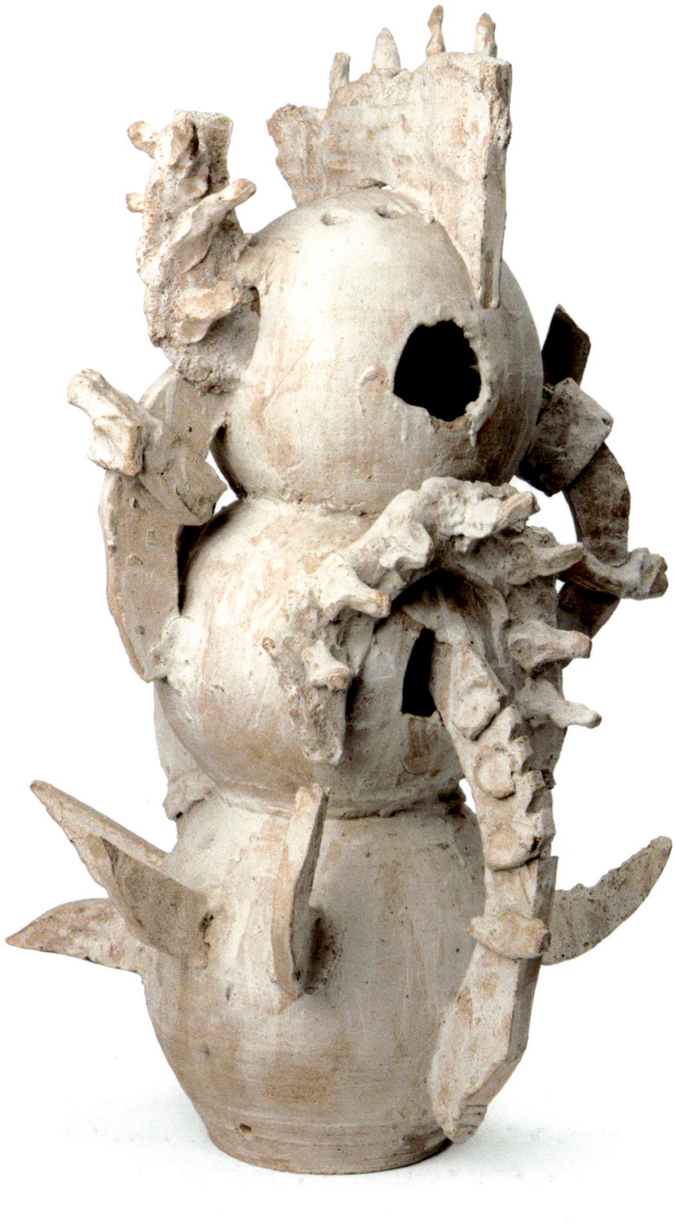

5 Peter Voulkos, *Sculpture (Hobgoblin)*, 1956. Stoneware, 35 × 21 × 21 in. (88.9 × 53.3 × 53.3 cm). Collection of Scripps College, Claremont, CA; gift of Mr. and Mrs. Fred Marer, 1982

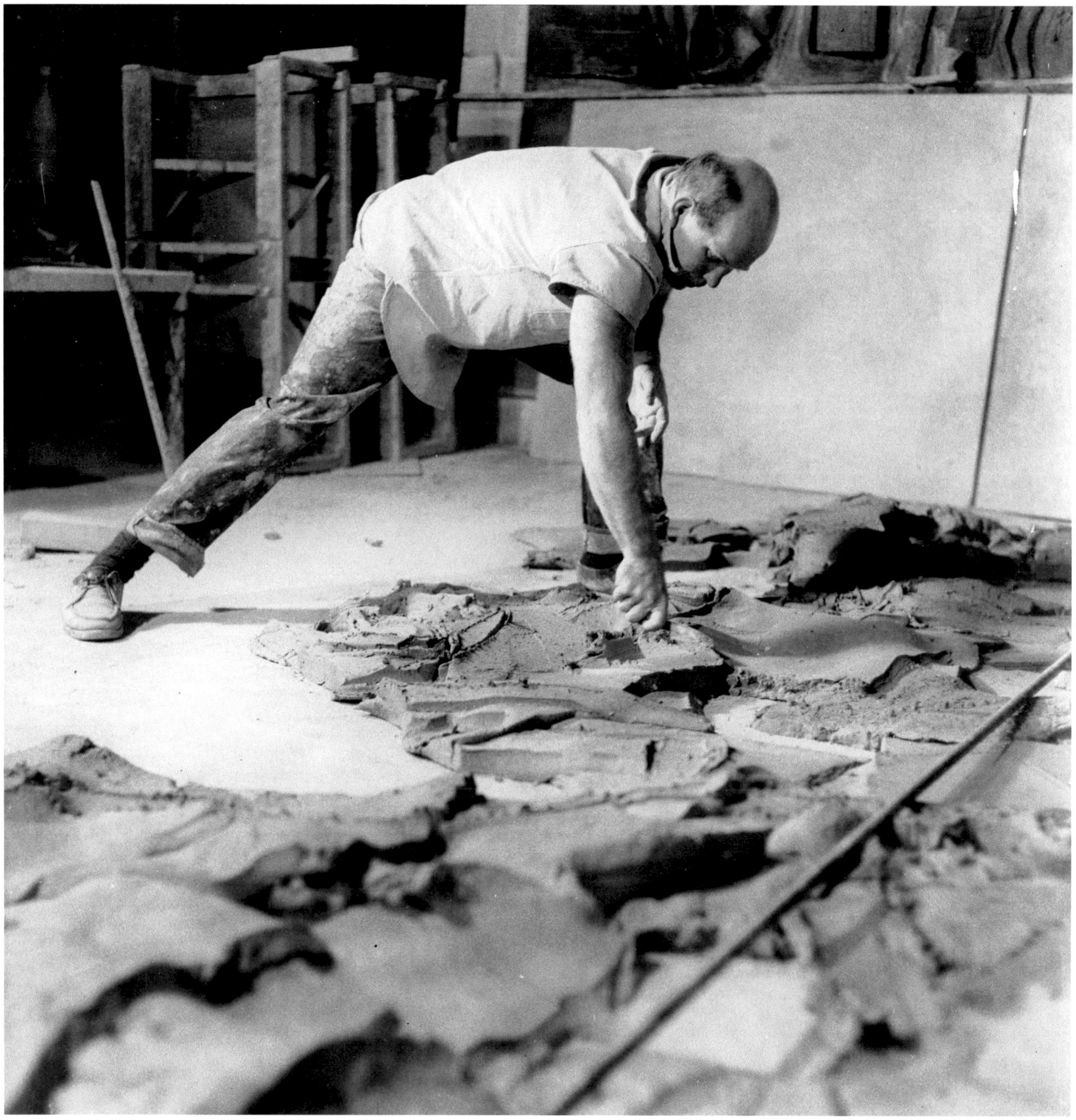

6 John Mason with *Blue Wall* in process, 1959

form with all manner of protuberances that he has squeezed with his hands. He also leaves finger marks in the soft clay and makes little effort to disguise the joints between his parts. By 1957, Voulkos had largely abandoned his squeezed forms, but still found ways to poke and prod his clay in more forceful ways.[9]

It is Voulkos's studio mate John Mason [fig. 6] who most fully picks up the gesture of "squish." His wall sculptures of the late 1950s shatter conventions of gesture, scale, and negative space. Similarly, his tall vertical sculptures, made possible by the industrial-sized kiln he shared with Voulkos, exhibit a wide visual vocabulary including but not limited to poking, folding, smearing, stretching, pressing, compressing, scratching, tearing, and, of course, squishing.[10] Whether Mason and Voulkos were merely riding a wave of impending squish or launching a revolution, it is clear that once the flood gates were opened, the entire field of ceramics—from new students to established masters—threw caution to the wind, and began exploring a virtually unlimited range of surface techniques.

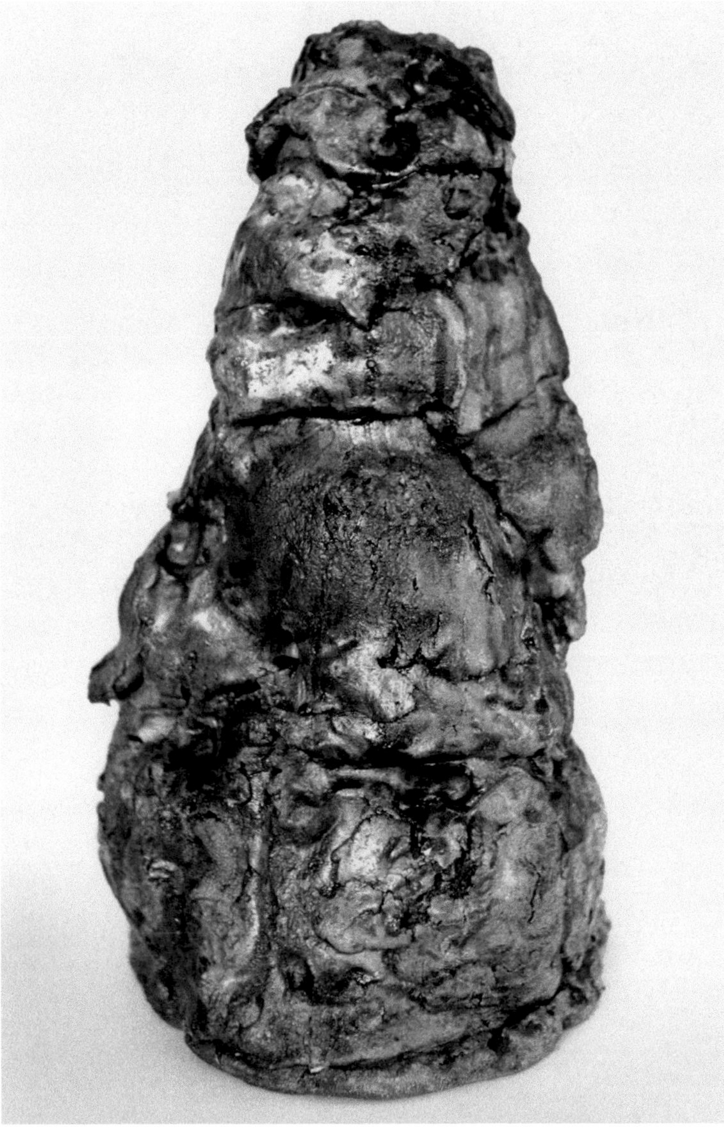

7 Harold Myers, *Big Pile*, 1960. Stoneware, 18 in. (45.7 cm)

By the 1960 *Ceramic National*, signature sculptures by Mason and Voulkos are matched by audacious works by Paul E. Nelsen, Win Ng, and Betty Feves. Potters can also be seen stepping into the fray. Robert Sperry, Dorothy Perkins, E. Ruth Laird, and Ernie Kim all show some level of "squish," although their pots remain resolutely symmetrical.[11] 1960 was also the year that Slivka wrote "The New Ceramic Presence," which included Ng, Voulkos, and Mason, but curiously omitted Feves (and all other women). The works singled out by Slivka for the article range from conventionally muscular compositions by Voulkos and his student Malcom McClain to a few sculptures that take Voulkos's "dump and death" mantra to the next level, notably the aptly named *Big Pile* by Harold Myers [fig. 7], which drew the ire of Minnesota potter Warren MacKenzie, who inveighed:

> For the longest time, we had thought that the 'Big Pile' in our neighbor's cow pasture was good only for enriching the fields. Now we find that if you can pile it high enough with the written word, or in the visual fields, it can pass for art. In the future, we will give up any attempt to make functional ceramics as an expressive form since, apparently, 'Containers ... make almost no demands on our sensibilities, leaving us free'—free to concentrate on getting the cows to cooperate for higher and larger works of 'ART.'[12]

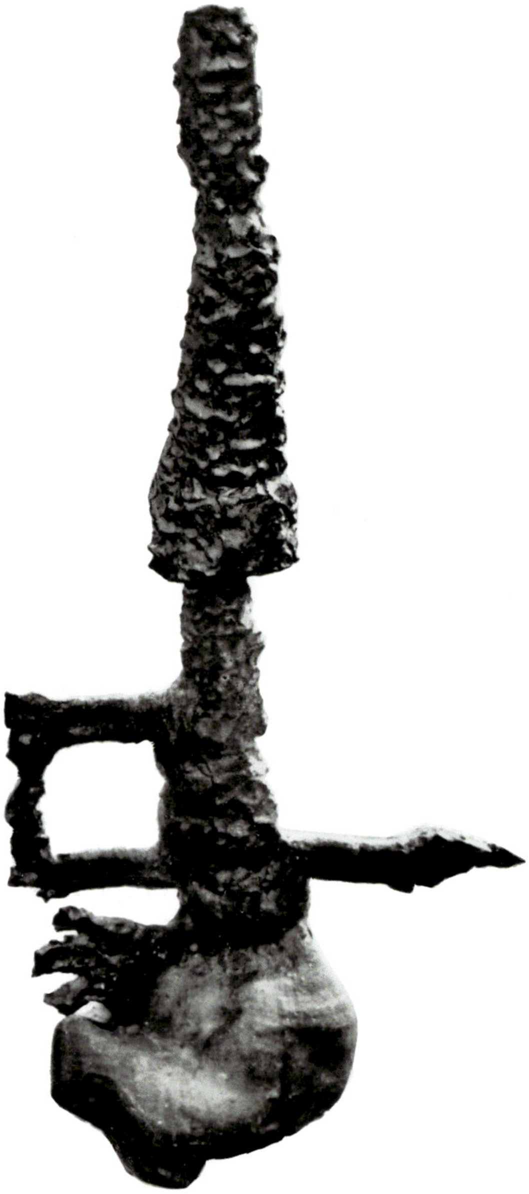

8 Jeff Schlanger, *Sculpture*, c. 1961. Ceramic, 42 in. (106.7 cm)

The most boundary-pushing work from Slivka's article is New York-based artist Jeff Schlanger's *Sculpture* [fig. 8], which would have been right at home in the original *FUNK* exhibition. At forty-two inches high, *Sculpture* is spindly and ungainly; instead of smoothing the clay coils during construction, Schlanger pinched and prodded them with his fingers. If you squint, the sculpture could maybe be a post-apocalyptic teapot, melted here, stretched there. The overall effect shares DNA with the scuzzy, provocative sculptures that Bruce Conner and his Rat Bastard Protective Association (RBPA) cohorts like Joan Brown were exploring in the Bay Area.

WE WANT THE FUNK

The first work of ceramics labeled as "Funk" is generally agreed to be Robert Arneson's *No Deposit, No Return*, a wheel-thrown bottle of beer with a bottle cap on top that he made in 1961 while demonstrating for the public at the California State Fair. Arneson has acknowledged a debt to Jasper Johns, whose own bronze cans of Ballantine ale were created the previous year. Arneson's bottle was shown in 1962 at a two-person exhibition at the De Young Museum in San Francisco and was eventually acquired by LACMA.[13] *No Deposit, No Return* was largely panned by critics, including *Craft Horizons* writer Alan Meisel, who wrote that "If the purpose of including this in the exhibition is to irritate reviewers, it did."[14]

I would like to propose a different origin story for Funk ceramics. It is clear that Funk as an attitude thrives in the absence of a burgeoning commercial art scene. From the 1950s through the 1970s, offbeat humor and the grotesque flourished in such disparate locations as the Bay Area (RBPA), Chicago (The Hairy Who), and Detroit (Destroy All Monsters). In all these cases, the artists had to create their own scenes and organize their own exhibitions. Provocation went hand in hand with powerlessness.

In the early 1960s, Madison, Wisconsin was the birthplace of the Studio Glass movement under pioneering educator Harvey Littleton, who was originally hired to teach ceramics. Wisconsin native Clayton Bailey was a student of Littleton's who arrived in Madison with a worldview shaped by his love of hot rods and *MAD* magazine. During his time in Madison, Bailey got to attend workshops with both Peter Voulkos and British potter Bernard Leach. He also studied with Toshiko Takaezu in the summer of 1959. Determined to carve his own path and not be seen as a Littleton acolyte, Bailey began making unique pinch pots and "critters" that were no less radical than the work of artists championed by Slivka in "The New Ceramic Presence."

Bailey recalls his first "critter" being a freshly thrown pot that he dropped on the floor, then added eyes, nose, and teeth to, and used as an ashtray.[15] Bailey's "Critters" emerged a full year before Arneson's beer bottle and have all the hallmarks of what would later be labeled as Funk. To use Selz's own criteria, "If these artists express anything at all, it is senselessness, absurdity, and fun. They find delight in nonsense, they abandon all of the strait jackets of rationality, and with an intuitive sense of humor they present their own elemental feelings and visceral processes."[16] Like Arneson, Bailey proudly weathered attacks by local critics, a rite of passage for Funk artists. During a 1962 exhibition in St. Louis, where he was teaching at the People's Art Center, the St. Louis *Post-Dispatch* labeled his work as "tasteless and obscene."[17]

Of course, the *Post-Dispatch* probably had a point. By 1963, Bailey had created his first *Critter Stool* [fig. 9], a coil-built garden stool emblazoned with male genitalia on the front—so the person sitting on the stool would appear to be exposing themselves. Like Arneson, who began teaching at the University of California, Davis in 1962, Bailey was also entrusted with teaching college students, first during visiting stints at the University of Iowa, and then at Whitewater State University in Wisconsin, where he taught his students to "search for the new and unusual, and not strive for beauty." One of his students crystalized this philosophy into the slogan "think ugly," which was painted on the wall of the ceramic shop.[18]

Despite his subject matter, notoriety came quickly for Bailey. In 1962, his work was accepted into the prestigious *Young Americans* exhibition at the Museum of Contemporary Crafts (now the Museum of Arts and Design) in New York. This show led to *Critter*s, a solo exhibition at the same museum in 1964, which coincidentally overlapped with Robert Arneson's debut exhibition at the Allan Stone Gallery. In the exhibition's modest catalog, artist Bruce Breckenridge emphasized the primacy and novelty of Bailey's construction methods over his outré subject matter:

> Taking moist movable clay, Bailey begins to knead and squeeze, forcing clay under pressure to almost explode between his fingers. Noses, ears, faces and bodies formed in this action are joined to hand rolled or slab constructions with the decorative and structural pinch marks that are characteristic of Bailey's work. For Bailey, the hand has replaced the potter's wheel as the tool that can best define his basic ceramic form; even large vases are primarily slab-constructed.[19]

Bailey may have developed his "Critters" before news of what Arneson was brewing in California had reached him in Wisconsin, but a direct bridge to Funk was built in 1963 when Arneson's friend Wayne Taylor joined the faculty at UW-Madison as the new instructor of painting, sculpture, and ceramics. Taylor had been at the State Fair when Arneson created *No Deposit, No Return*, and was making his current work out of low-fire clay and commercial glazes.[20]

The World's Most Fascinating Hobby

In every article about Funk ceramics, there is usually a passing reference to the adaptation of hobby glazes and low-fire clay bodies by Bay Area artists. Unless you are an artist who has experience with whiteware clay or have gotten to touch and experience a piece of 1960s Funk ceramics, it is difficult to understand the magnitude of Funk's tectonic shift in the ceramic realm. To go back to the history of twentieth-century American studio ceramics, before Funk, the clay body that artists worked with mattered. In the 1930s and 1940s, Glen Lukens dug native clay and experimented with alkaline metals that he found in the Mojave Desert. Before the founding of commercial clay manufacturing, many artists knew how to read US Geological Survey maps to find clay deposits. Even as the "New Ceramic Presence" era dawned in the late 1950s, most ceramic artists still used brick clay or stoneware, which had its own kind of beauty and integrity.

Speaking from first-hand experience, whiteware is objectively disgusting, and can even be thought of as an "anti-material." In the years following the Great Depression and World War II, the hobby ceramics industry developed as a discipline mainly aimed at housewives who had (supposedly) gained newfound leisure time due to advances in appliances and consumer products.

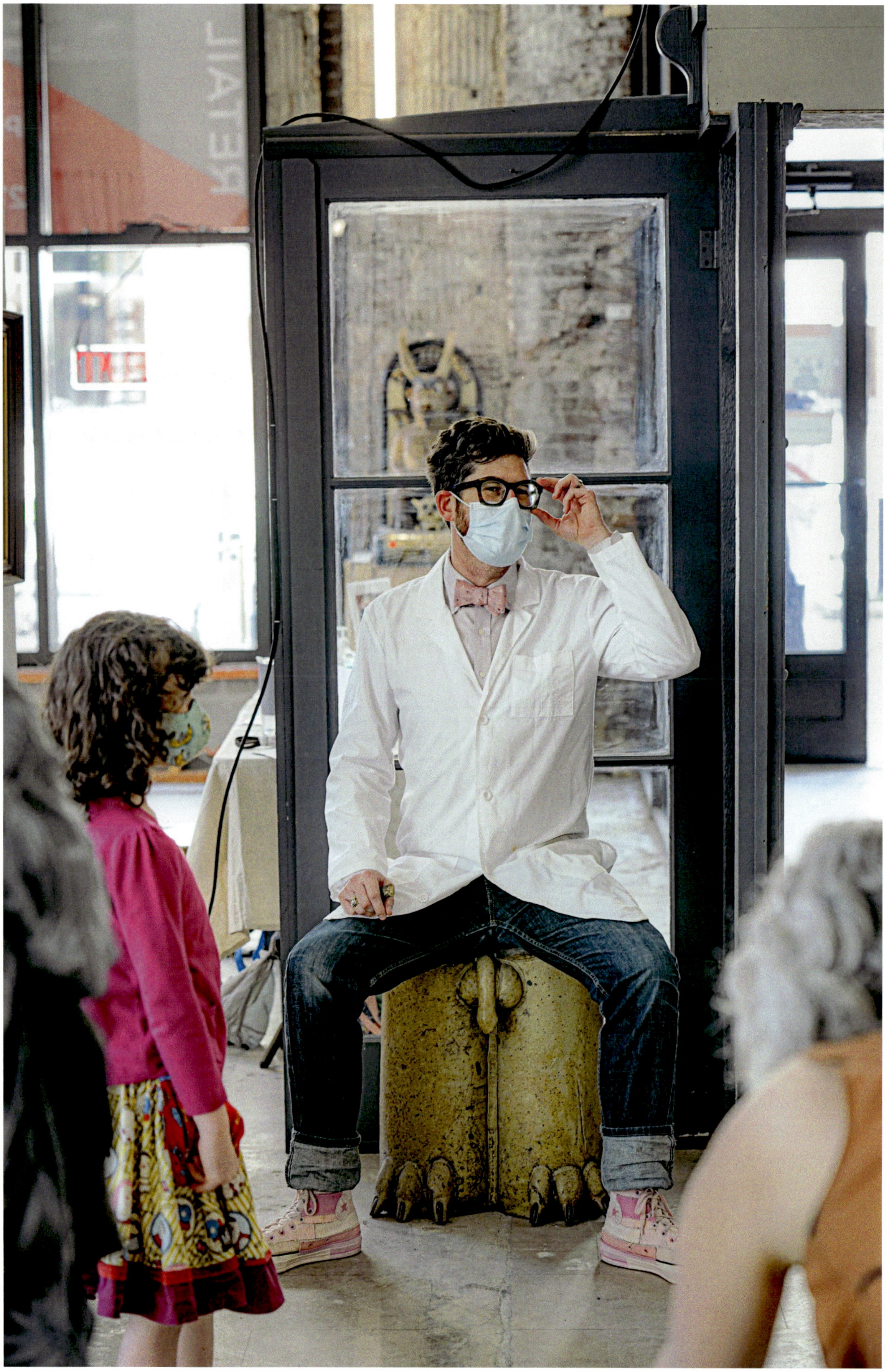

9 Clayton Bailey, *Critter Stool*, 1963. Stoneware and salt glaze, 20 × 20 × 20 in. (50.8 × 50.8 × 50.8 cm). Estate of Clayton Bailey

Hobby shops sold unfired ceramic knick-knacks cast from an inexpensive clay body made from equal parts talc and ball clay. The hobbyist would clean up the residual casting lines, then color the piece by applying layers of colorful glazes and underglazes. These shops mainly died out in the 1980s but have been reborn as "paint your own pottery" businesses that operate in much the same way, but with a "date night" twist in recent years.

Where stoneware is vitreous and when fired in a reduction atmosphere, toasty and inviting, whiteware is chalky and fragile. Countless broken pieces of Funk whiteware line the storage shelves in museums, awaiting either restoration or (more likely) deaccession. This is to say nothing of glazes. When I was studying pottery in the 1990s, learning to formulate and make one's own glazes was seen as an essential part of the holistic, ethical realm of the studio. Although I hold my nose at the aesthetic qualities of whiteware, I grudgingly admit that as a sculptural clay body, it is resistant to cracking, forgiving during the drying process, and because of its stark whiteness, an inviting canvas for commercial glazes. In a 1992 monograph for the John Natsoulas Gallery, David Gilhooly had this to say:

> Stoneware was like blowing glass: very limited in what it was willing to let you do with it. White clay is the opposite. You can do anything with it. Potters hate white clay because it is ugly compared to stoneware, easy to work with, and garish when used with commercial hobbyist glazes.[21]

Using whiteware and commercial glazes was also freighted with the thrill of co-opting something illicit. Lucy Lippard's 1978 meditation on hobby craft, "Something from Nothing (Toward a Definition of Women's 'Hobby Art')" thoroughly unpacks the underlying sexism and classism that had made hobby craft a third rail prior to the emergence of Funk.[22] With their adoption of hobby aesthetics and materials, Funk ceramicists got to have it both ways, getting the amusement of something heretofore *verboten*, but also getting to wallow in their own perceived powerlessness. Famously, Robert Arneson appropriated the title of Duncan Ceramics' glossy hobby magazine for his first major piece with stamped lettering, *Yes, I'd say that Ceramics is the World's Most Fascinating Hobby* in 1966.[23]

Funk Wafts

As we have already established, Funk ceramics did not magically spring from Northern California. Instead, the rise of Funk was nurtured by a volatile mixture of material exploration, artistic rebellion, and low-brow sensibilities. It is interesting that Clayton Bailey, who I argue is patient zero of Funk ceramics, would ultimately move to California, but left a trail of Funk-empowered Midwestern students in his wake. In 1968, shortly before moving to California, Bailey put together a "Funk Festival" at the University of South Dakota in Vermillion, where he was teaching at the time. Bailey recalls:

> California artists Roy DeForest, David Gilhooly, David and Maija Zack are the invited guests. The students of the U.S.D. Art Department are well-prepared for the event. They make flights of ceramic police helicopters and rows of gaudy ceramic cowboy boots which await the Funk Artists from the West Coast. Upon their arrival, Maija Zack supervises the painting of the University armored car with psychedelic beasts, and together the artists produce a 2-hour T.V. interview and performance in which they discuss the stuffed animals borrowed from the University's natural history collection. The mangy menagerie includes an alligator, a wild pig, a giraffe head with its entire neck, and numerous tropical birds. The artists talk to the stuffed animals, and create a dust cloud, while moderator [Francis] Coelho's serious dialogue demonstrates the irrationality of logical thought.[24]

Clayton Bailey aside, Funk became a major export from the Bay Area and Davis. In 1969, Gilhooly left Davis to take a teaching position at the

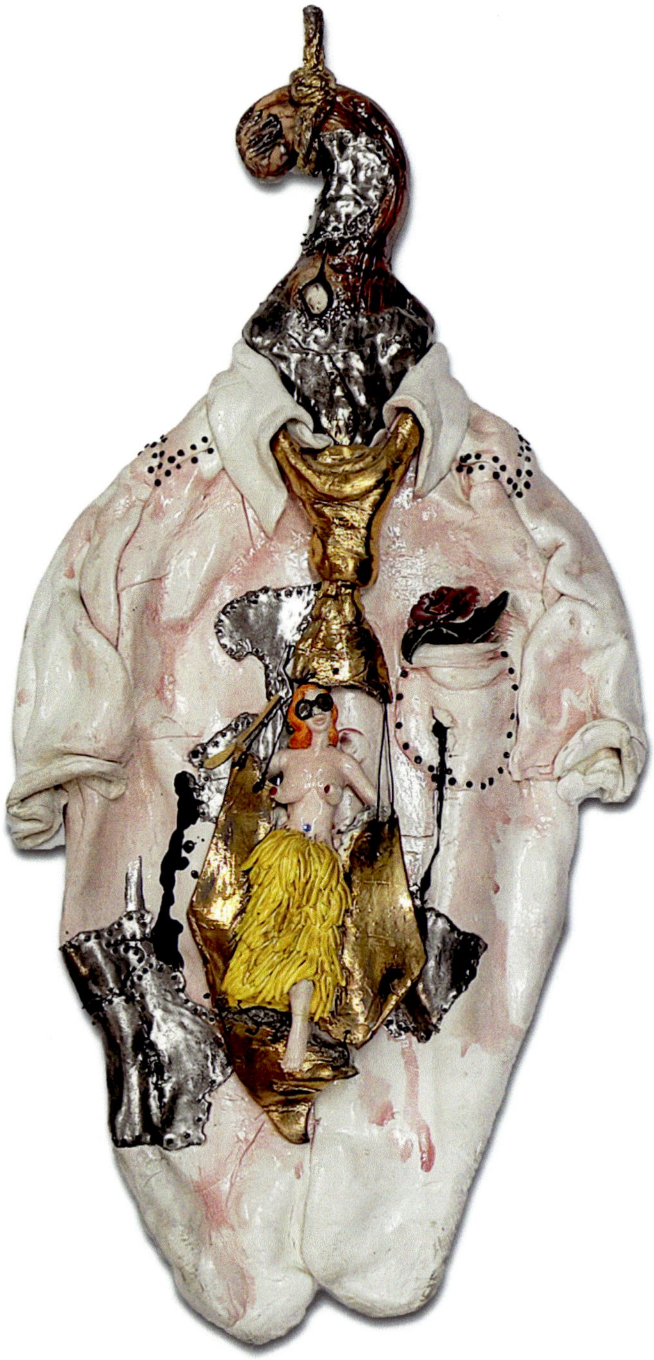

10 Victor Cicansky, Untitled, 1974. Ceramic, glaze, and overglaze luster

University of Saskatchewan in Regina. He was followed by David and Maija Zack (later Maija Peeples-Bright), whose Rainbow House in Haight-Ashbury served as the San Francisco headquarters for the Funk milieu. Regina native Victor Cicansky [fig. 10], who had met Arneson at a workshop at the Haystack School of Craft in Maine, received his MFA from Davis in 1970, then promptly returned to Regina to solidify its Funk scene. Artists like French-Canadian sculptor Joe Fafard put their own rural spin on Regina Funk.[25]

The phenomenon of Skangaroovian Funk in Australia began when artist Margaret Dodd arrived in Davis in 1965, and quickly gravitated to the ceramics studios at TB-9. Dodd immediately made an impact with her sculptures of automo-

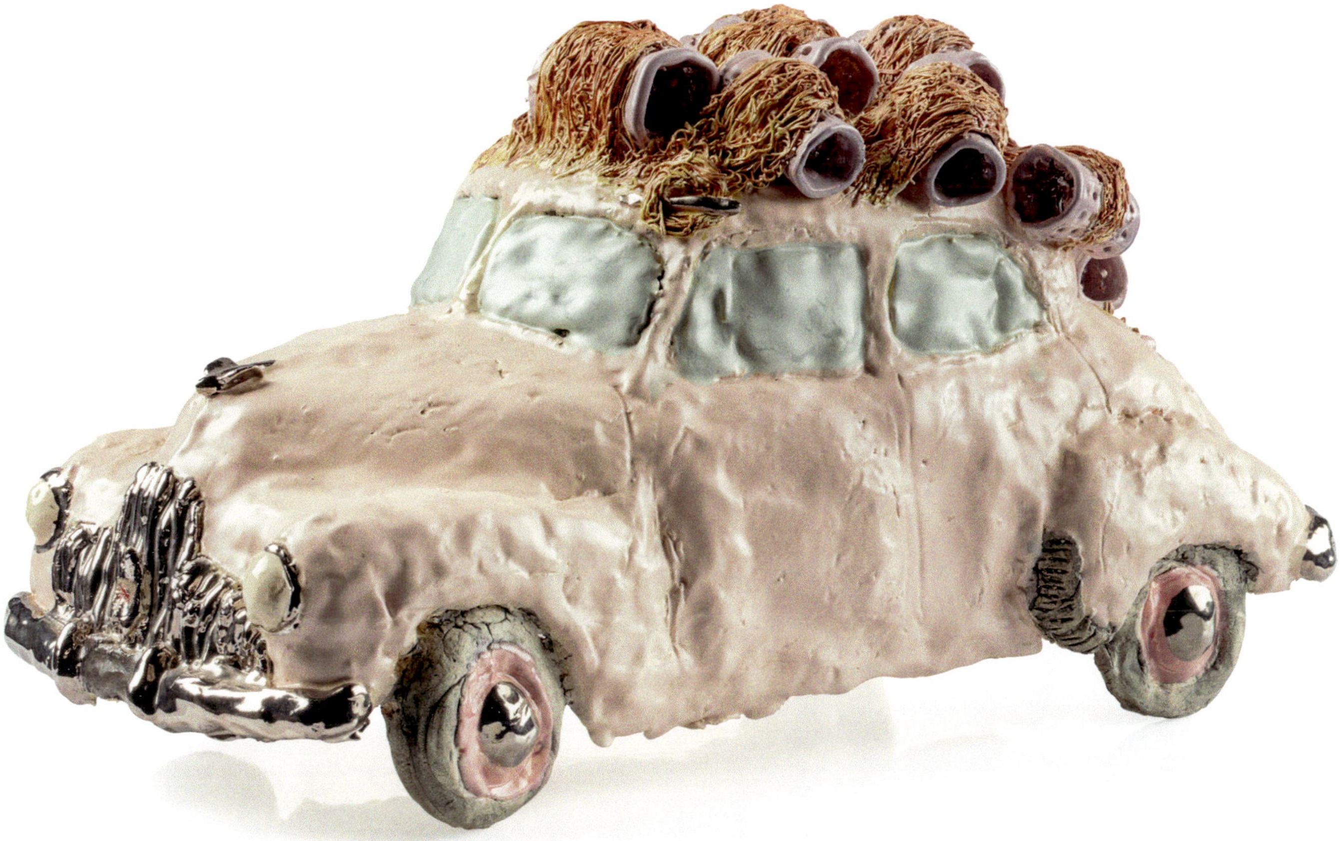

11 Margaret Dodd, *Holden with Hair Curlers*, from "This Woman Is Not a Car" series, c. 1977. Earthenware and glaze, 8 × 15 × 7 in. (20.5 × 40 × 18 cm). Art Gallery of South Australia; Catherine G. Brown Bequest, 2018

biles [fig. 11]. Reluctantly, she moved back to Australia with her husband after graduation, settling in her hometown of Adelaide. While Dodd was away, Bill Gregory, a British lecturer in ceramics, began laying the ground for an Australian ceramics revolution at Adelaide's South Australian School of Art. Gregory's sculptural assemblages of thrown pottery forms drew praise from Sydney critic Donald Brook, who wrote that, "his pots are absolutely useless ... it is ... as refreshing as drought breaking rain after an aeon of cider jugs with bucolic bodies like boiled oatmeal and orchid jars in sensitive toffee temmoku."[26]

When Dodd returned, she found a fertile artistic landscape, although she herself lived in the suburbs. Pregnant, and with some time to

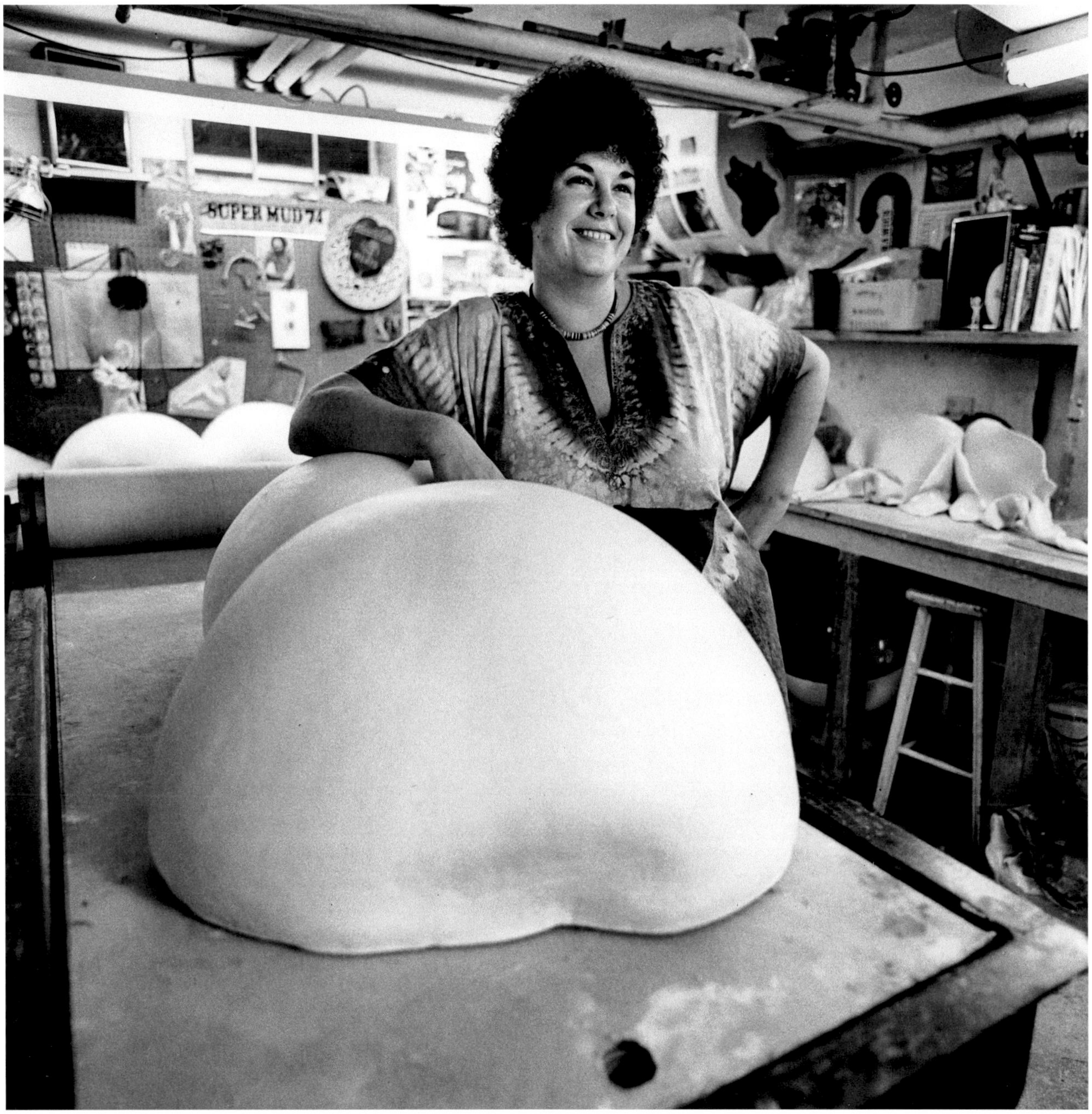

12 Judy Onofrio in *Studio Potter Journal*, V4 N2 Winter 1975–76

reflect, she began making sculptures of Holden cars, Australia's suburban automobile of choice. The Holden became a metaphor for the human body that Dodd would explore for the rest of her career. Other Skangaroovian compatriots included Olive Bishop, who created ceramic clothing as portraits, Aleks Danko, who made cerebral, process-driven sculptures based on common objects, and Paul Greenaway, whose Surrealist mini theater sets made full use of luster and porcelain paint.[27]

The Midwest also became a place where Funk flourished. Although she was a native of Spokane, Washington, Patti Warashina spent the mid-1960s teaching in Wisconsin and Indiana with her then husband Fred Bauer. Judy Onofrio moved to Rochester, Minnesota in 1967 and began making fleshy feminist sculptures—both large breast-like forms and labial landscapes coaxed out of clay slabs [fig. 12]. On the flip side, a clutch of male Midwestern professors like Dick Hay [fig. 13] and Curtis Hoard went through juvenile periods of

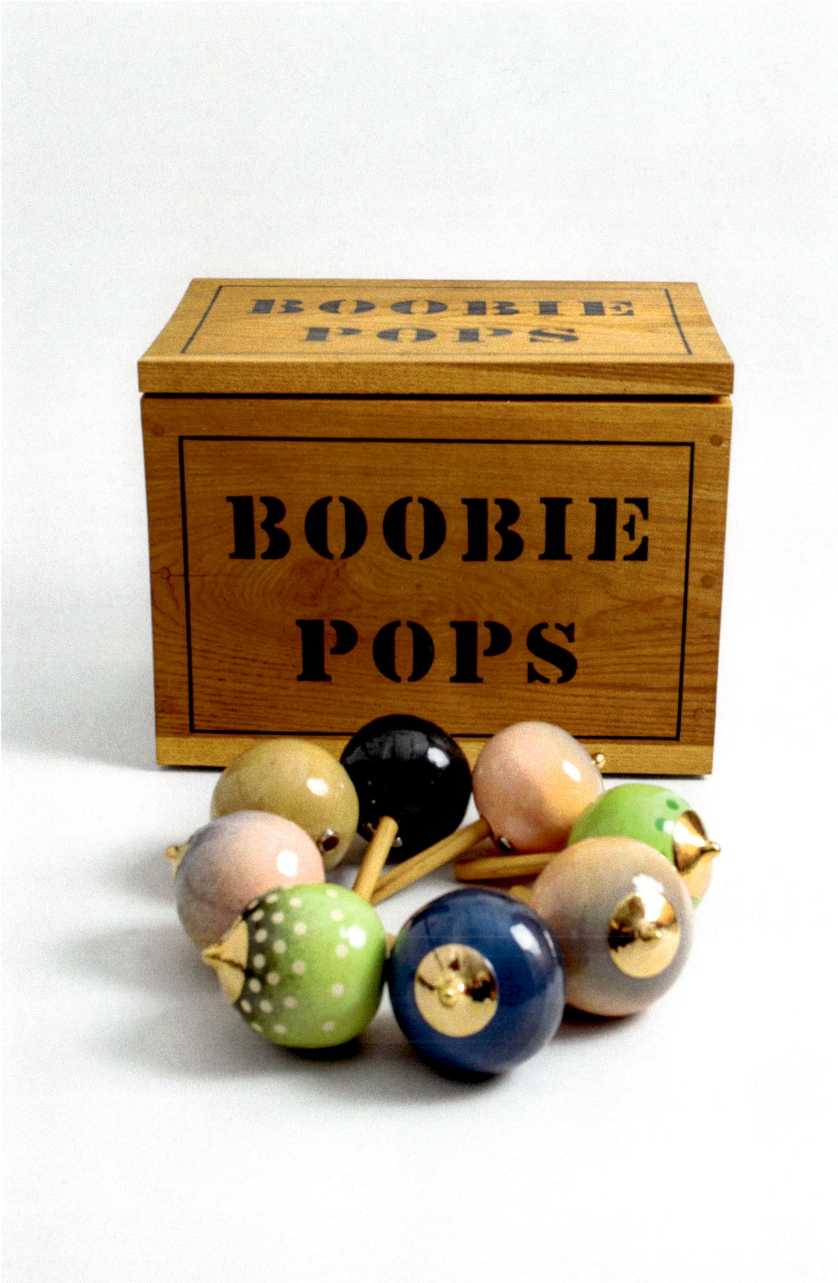

13 Dick Hay, *Boobie Pops,* c. 1974–75. Ceramic, wood, plastic, paper, and paint, box: 13 × 18 × 12 in. (33 × 45.7 × 30.5 cm), 8 "pops": 8 × 5 in. each (20.3 × 12.7 cm)

creating candy-colored breast ice cream cones, breast popsicles, and other male fantasy confections before settling into more sober work later in their careers.

On a national scale, the high-water mark for Funk ceramics as a discipline is arguably *Clayworks: 20 Americans*, which was held at the Museum of Contemporary Crafts in New York in the summer of 1971. Museum director Paul J. Smith, in his catalog introduction wrote that the exhibition "represents a group of ceramic artists with a *very* sensitive view of the world, who are engaged in making objects, usually in a series, to develop a particular theme with social, political, and sexual implications. Through their work, these ceramicists create a powerful commentary on present day society—its preoccupations and concerns, its faults and merits. Traditional concepts of 'good taste' are forfeited to emphasize the grotesque and the humorous."[28]

All of the artists represented in *Clayworks* were teachers, and aside from a handful of avowed West Coast artists like James Melchert, Robert Arneson, and Richard Shaw, the vast majority either hailed from or had taught in the Midwest. In what was exceedingly typical in higher education at the time, only two women were represented—Patti Warashina and Marilyn Levine. At its inception, Funk was apolitical, more interested in pushing social and material boundaries than political ones. By 1971, though, strong undercurrents of protest were coursing through Funk. In *Clayworks*, William Lombardo depicted a cow nibbling on the Washington Monument in *D.C. Lunch Break*. Philadelphia-based Ken Vavrek exhibited a series of ornate candelabra-like sculptures topped with bullets, and Raymond Allen showed a luster-covered slab emblazoned with silhouettes of the United States that emanated plastic tubes connected to a group of pigs [fig. 14].[29]

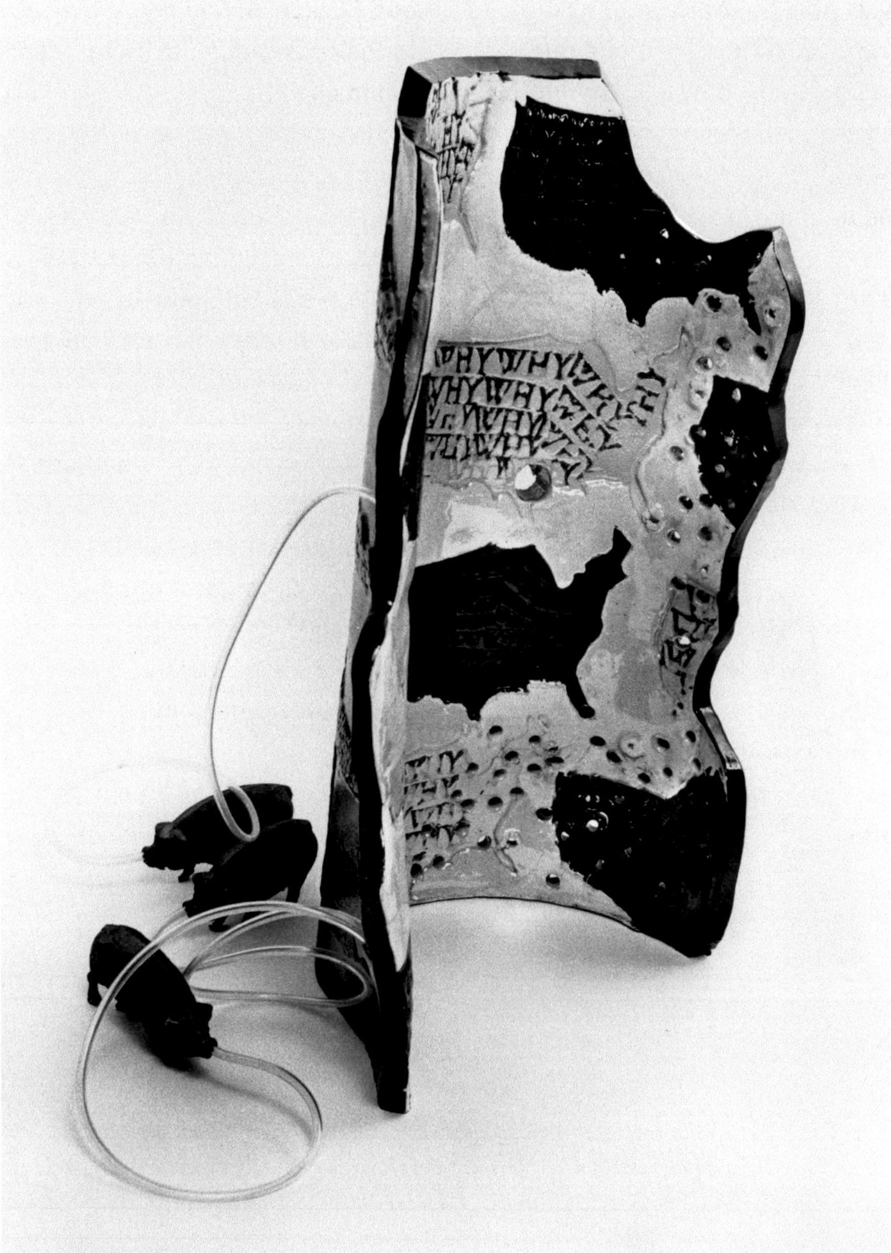

14 Raymond Allen, *Two More*. Earthenware, porcelain paint, and luster, 19.5 × 11 in. (49.5 × 27.9 cm)

FUNK FADES

Perhaps the absurdity of a bunch of tenure-track professors in the Midwest wielding porcelain paint, luster, and hobby glazes helped speed Funk's demise. With the exceptions of the California artists (and Patti Warashina), all of the Midwesterners moved away from the signifiers of Funk in their work. By the time of *Clayworks*, Arneson himself had abandoned his scatological premises and skin-crawling surfaces and had moved on to his formative experiments in self-portraiture. *Smorgi-Bob, the Cook* (1971), exhibited in *Clayworks*, was Arneson's first large-scale self-portrait. Although he had originally planned to use porcelain paint to color the self-portrait as chef and the forced perspective table full of food, he left the piece in stark white, which opened the door to working in new modes.[30]

The craft and art worlds were also shifting beneath Funk's feet. New opportunities for the most successful Funk artists like Arneson and Gilhooly continued, notably including *Ceramic Sculpture: Six Artists* at the Whitney Museum of Art in 1981. Fine art galleries like Braunstein/Quay in San Francisco and Alan Frumkin or OK Harris in New York all promoted ceramic artists to an international fine art audience. With the maturation of the craft market, galleries like The Hand and Spirit in Scottsdale, Garth Clark Gallery in New York, and Helen Drutt Gallery in Philadelphia brought higher price points and a cadre of devoted collectors.

The pendulum of style was also swinging away from Funk. The airbrush and decals emerged as more precise ways to achieve color on ceramic surfaces. Pottery moved away from 1970s granola stoneware, and toward more colorful and whimsical styles. Artists like Adriane Saxe, Ken Price, and Ron Nagle went on to create highly detailed works that were dubbed "Super Objects" by Garth Clark,[31] and artists like Marilyn Levine and Richard Shaw opened new frontiers in tromp l'oeil ceramics. David Gilhooly did a 180-degree turn from his ceramics to embrace Plexiglas constructions in the 1980s [fig. 15], and Clayton Bailey largely shifted his attention to the construction of metal robots created from found objects.

Pendulums always swing back, and Funk is once again in the air. Viola Frey has not been mentioned until this point. Although she utilized many of the same materials, techniques, and strategies of Funk artists, her work was always a bit too slippery and sophisticated to be slapped with the Funk label. Frey's sense of color was more indebted to European expressionist painters than to Pop and Funk, and her obsession with flea market finds was always too empathetic and academic for easy classification. It is Viola Frey's multivalent practice more than any that typifies the hybridity and ranginess of the new generation of ceramicists that have picked up the banner of squish, color, and humor.

Garth Johnson, Paul Phillips & Sharon Sullivan Curator of Ceramics, Everson Museum of Art

1 Rose Slivka, "The New Ceramic Presence," *Craft Horizons*, July & August 1961, 31–37.

2 Rose Slivka, *Peter Voulkos: A Dialogue with Clay*, New York Graphic Society, 1978.

3 From their inception, the *Ceramic Nationals* were designed to debut in Syracuse, then were sent to travel on a circuit of between eight to twelve different museums across the country. Over the years, most major museums, including the Metropolitan Museum of Art in New York, the Philadelphia Art Museum, and the Art Institute of Chicago played host to the exhibition.

4 Philip Rawson, *Ceramics*, University of Pennsylvania Press, 1984.

5 Janet Koplos and Willemijn Stovkis, *The Unexpected: Artists' Ceramics of the 20th Century*, Museum Het Kruithuis, 1998.

6 *Common Ground: Ceramics in Southern California, 1945–1975*, American Museum of Ceramic Art, Pomona, 2012, 135.

7 Mary Davis MacNaughton, *Revolution in Clay: The Marer Collection of Contemporary Ceramics*, Perpetua Press, 1994.

8 Garth Clark, et al., *Color and Fire: Defining Moments in Studio Ceramics, 1950–2000: Selections from the Smits Collection and Related Works at the Los Angeles County Museum of Art*, LACMA in Association with Rizzoli International Publications, Los Angeles, 2000, 123–156.

9 Mary Davis MacNaughton, *Clay's Tectonic Shift: 1956–1968: John Mason, Ken Price, Peter Voulkos*, J. Paul Getty Museum, 2012.

10 Kirk Delman, ed., *John Mason: Sculpture 1950–2010*, Ruth Chandler Williamson Gallery, Scripps College, 2010.

11 *XXI Ceramic National: Exhibition 13 November 1960/8 January 1961, Everson Museum of Art of Syracuse and Onondaga County*, Everson Museum of Art, 1960.

12 Warren MacKenzie, "Letters," *Craft Horizons*, November/December 1961, 6.

13 "Oral History Interview with Robert Arneson, 1981 August 14–15: Archives of American Art, Smithsonian Institution," *Archives of American Art, Smithsonian Institution.* https://www.aaa.si.edu/collections/interviews/oral-history-interview-robert-arneson-11807.

14 Alan Meisel, "Letter from San Francisco," *Craft Horizons*, July/August 1962, 42.

15 Clayton Bailey, "CLAYTON BAILEY'S CERAMIC CRITTERS 1960–1963." http://claytonbailey.com/critter.htm.

16 Peter Selz, *Funk*, University of California-Berkeley Art Museum, 1967.

17 Clayton Bailey, "A SHORT CHRONOLOGY OF THE ARTIST'S LIFE." http://claytonbailey.com/chronology.htm.

18 Ibid.

19 Bruce Breckenridge, *Clayton Bailey: Critters*, Museum of Contemporary Crafts, 1964.

20 Clayton Bailey, et al., *Clayton Bailey's World of Wonders*, Crocker Art Museum, 2011.

21 David Gilhooly and Kenneth Baker, *David Gilhooly*, John Natsoulas Press, 1992.

22 Not that Arneson and company were striking blows for feminism ... a 1966 article in the Davis Enterprise highlighted a ceramic sale by David Gilhooly and Peter VandenBerge, stating, "Modern works in the ancient media will be on display (incidentally and for sale) between 10 am and 6 pm and at the same time the artist's wives will be serving punch to cool the day." Ibid.

23 Jonathan Fineberg, *A Troublesome Subject: The Art of Robert Arneson*, University of California Press, 2013.

24 Clayton Bailey, "A SHORT CHRONOLOGY OF THE ARTIST'S LIFE." http://claytonbailey.com/chronology.htm.

25 Timothy Long and Sandra Alfoldy, *Regina Clay: Worlds in the Making*, MacKenzie Art Gallery, 2005.

26 Judith Thompson, *Skangaroovian Funk*, Art Gallery of South Australia, 1986.

27 Ibid.

28 Paul J. Smith, *Clayworks: 20 Americans*, Museum of Contemporary Crafts, 1971.

29 Ibid.

30 Jonathan Fineberg, *A Troublesome Subject: The Art of Robert Arneson*, University of California Press, 2013.

31 Garth Clark and Margie Hughto, *A Century of Ceramics in the United States, 1878–1978*, E.P. Dutton, 1979.

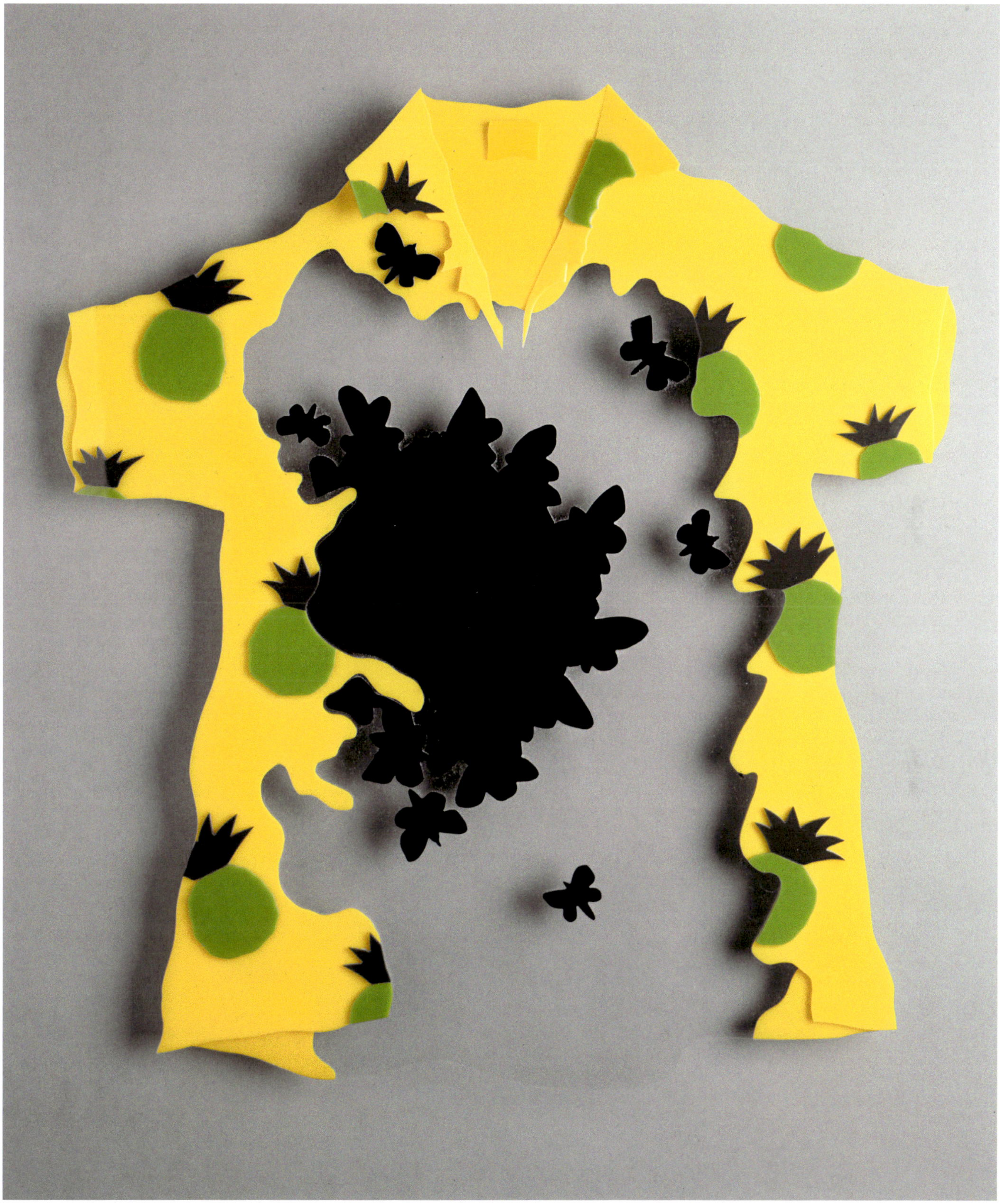

15 David Gilhooly, *Mothra*, 1991. Plexiglas, 26 × 24 × 1 in. (66 × 61 × 2.5 cm). Collection of the Hallie Ford Museum of Art, Willamette Salem, OR; Maribeth Collins Art Acquisition Fund, 2000

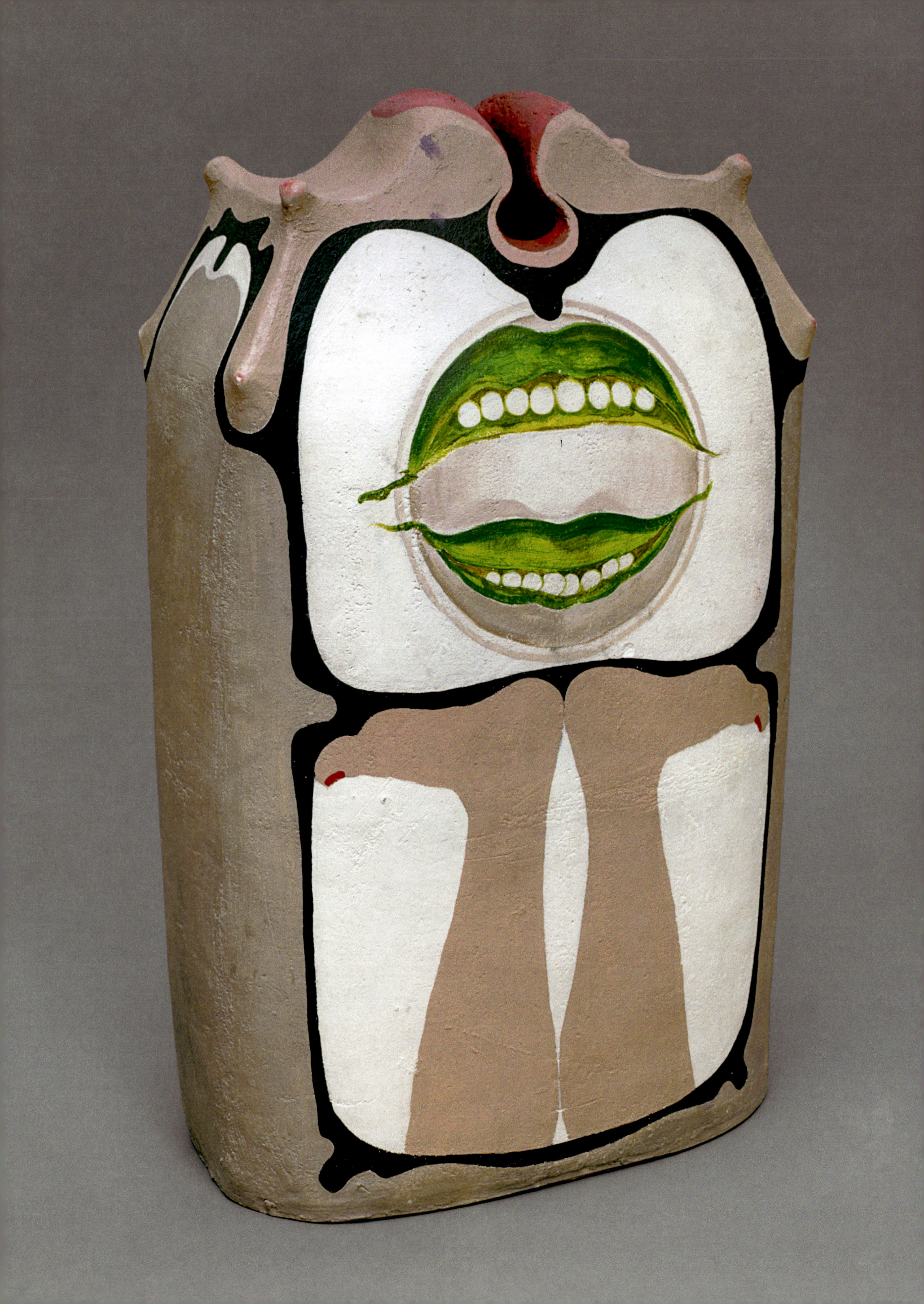

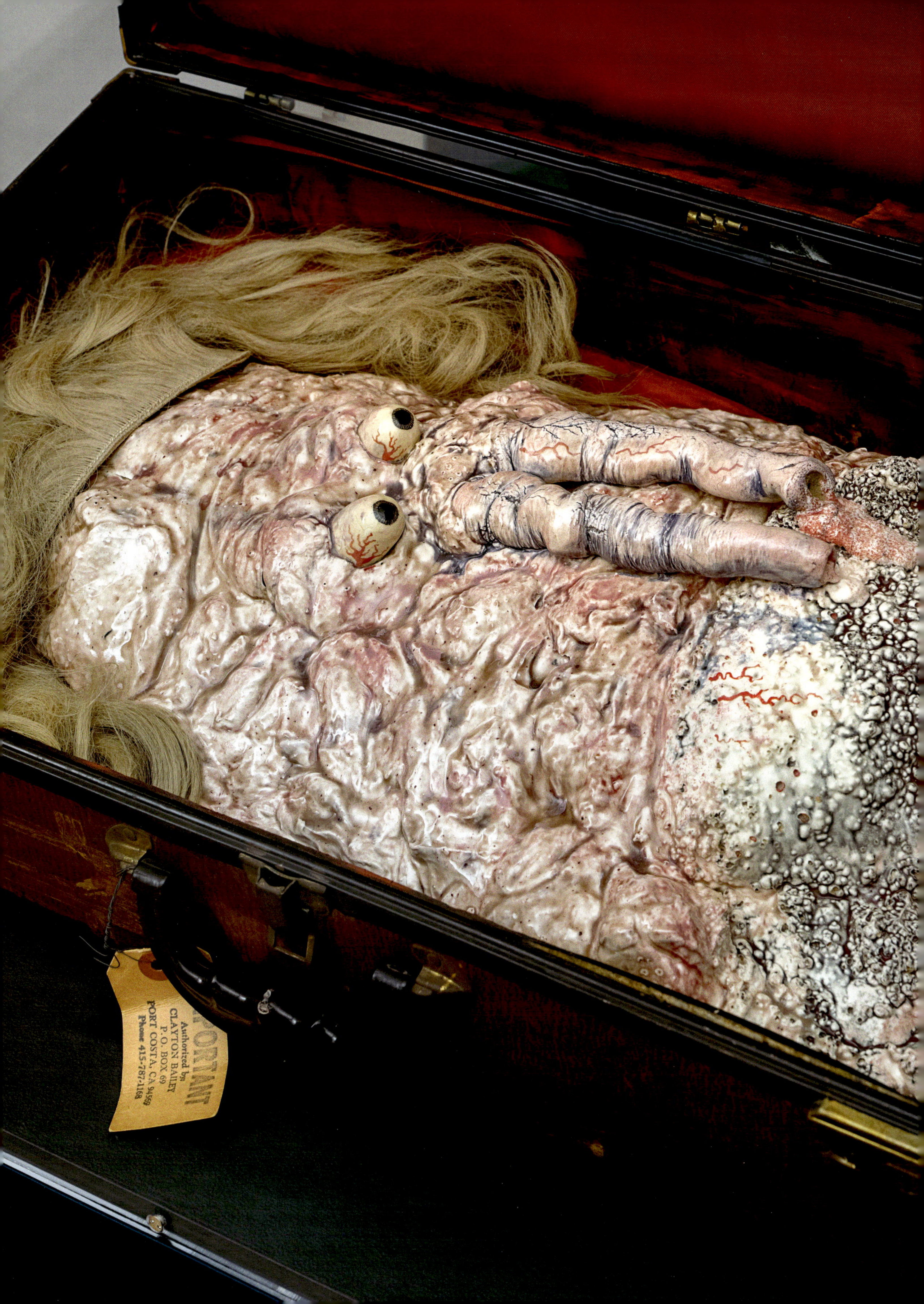
PORTANT
Authorized by:
CLAYTON BAILEY
P. O. BOX 69
PORT COSTA, CA 94569
Phone 415-787-1168

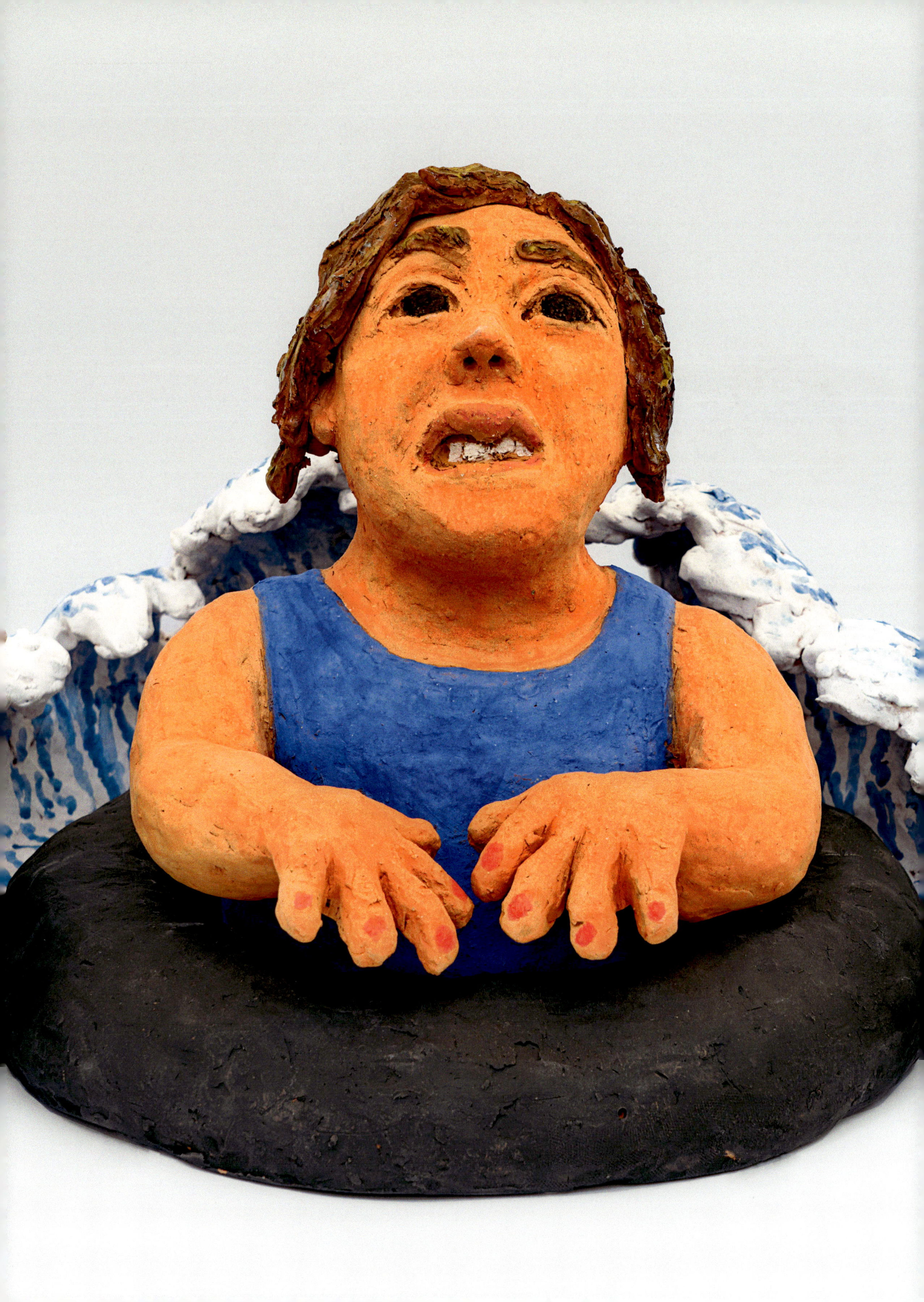

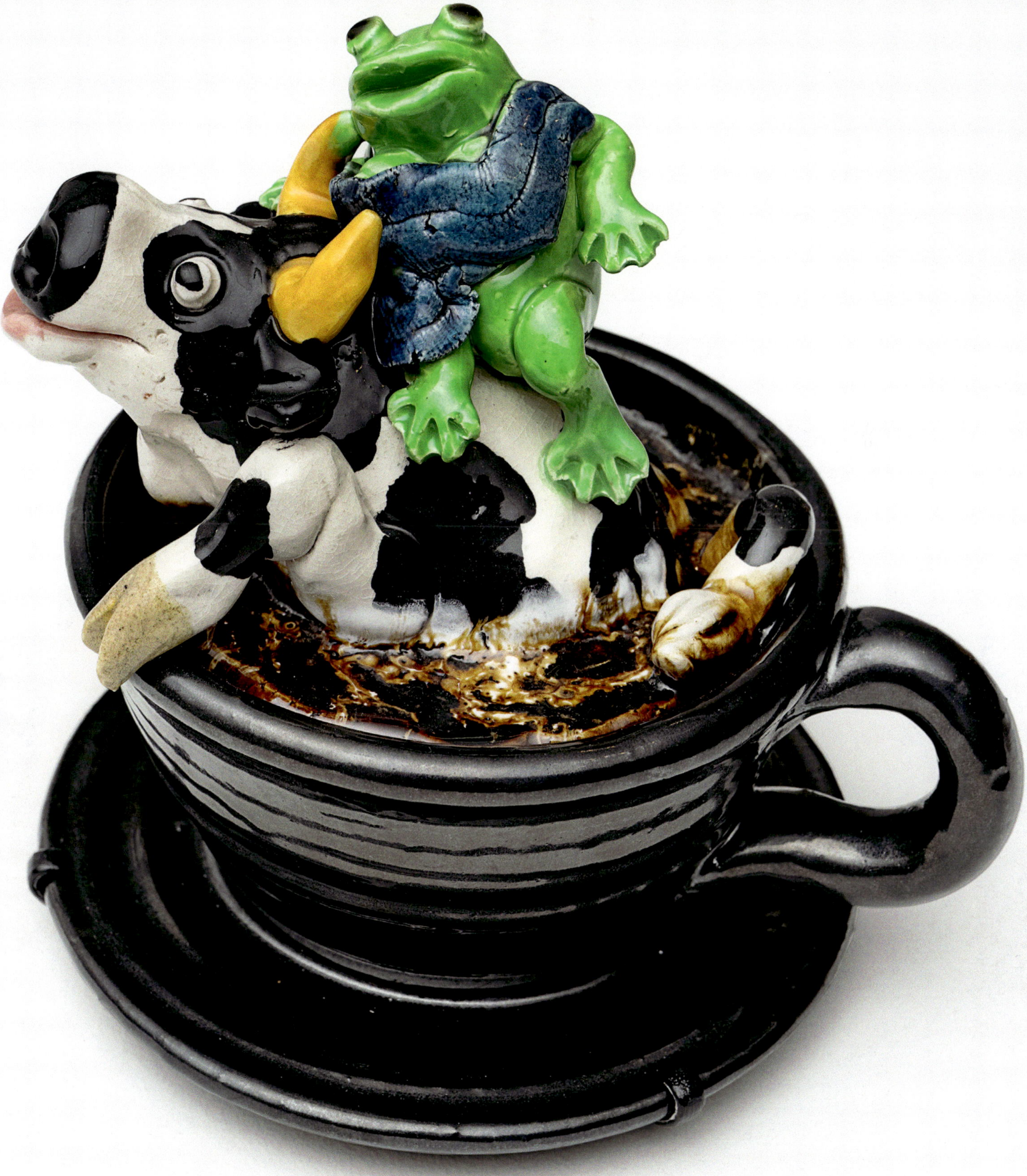

Biographies

Artists:

Alake Shilling (United States, b. 1993) has created a visual lexicon of soothing and comforting cute animals and plush creatures that embody the human condition. Shilling attended the School of the Art Institute of Chicago, followed by Los Angeles City College. She has had solo presentations at 356 Mission, CA, and Maitland Foley, CA. She has been included in group shows at the Hammer Museum, CA, The Rubell Museum, FL, Jeffrey Deitch, NY, Karma International, CA, and Steve Turner, CA. Her work is included in the collections of the Hammer Museum and The Rubell Museum.

Alex Anderson (United States, b. 1990) explores the intersection of the sublime in man-made and natural worlds, along with issues of race and cultural representation. Anderson received his BA in Studio Art and Chinese from Swarthmore College and his MFA in Ceramics from the University of California, Los Angeles. Anderson studied at the Jingdezhen Ceramic Institute in China, and is a Fulbright Grant recipient. His work has been exhibited internationally and nationally, including at the Orange County Museum of Art, CA, the American Museum of Ceramic Art, CA, Deli Gallery, NY, and Jeffrey Deitch, NY, among others.

Chris Unterseher (United States, b. 1943) is known for his intricate, deftly rendered narrative tableaux, often pulled directly from the pages of *National Geographic*. He recreated images of California scenes in clay along with their captions copy-etched on brass plaques. His work was the subject of a retrospective at the Sierra Nevada Museum of Art in 1981 and is included in many public collections.

Clayton Bailey (United States, 1939–2020) created eccentric and humorous sculptures depicting humans, robots, and other whimsical characters. Bailey received his MS in Art and Art Education from the University of Wisconsin-Madison. He taught at multiple universities, including California State University, East Bay, where he was until his retirement in 1996. Bailey was the recipient of the National Endowment for the Arts Grant and the "Golden Bear Artist of the Year" by the California Arts Council. Bailey's work is in many public collections, including the Racine Art Museum, WI, Smithsonian American Art Museum, Washington, D.C., Mackenzie Art Museum, Canada, and Asahi Shimbun, Japan.

David Gilhooly (United States, 1943–2001) worked from a handful of humorous themes in pressing together a vision of the universe unrivaled in its insight and creativity. His distinctive Frog World successfully bridged his passions for history, the physical sciences, and art. He received his MA from the University of California, Davis. He also worked as an educator at the University of Saskatchewan and York University in Canada. His work is included in many collections in the United States and Canada.

Didi Rojas (Colombia, b. 1993) has developed an extensive repertoire of sculptural shoes to address social-media-driven consumerism. She graduated with a BFA from Pratt Institute, NY. Her work has been exhibited in group exhibitions at the Museum of Modern Art, NY, Pablo's Birthday, NY, Yui Gallery, NY, Fisher Parrish Gallery, NY, Andrew Edlin Gallery, NY, Naughton Gallery at Queens University, UK and The Hole, NY. Rojas has had two solo exhibitions at Launch F18, NY.

Diana Yesenia Alvarado (United States, b. 1992) foregrounds the visual, cultural, and spiritual idiosyncrasies present in her hometown of South/East Los Angeles. Working primarily with clay, her hand-built sculptures can be characterized by their dreamlike glazing, accentuated sartorial details, and the animated faces of her distorted figures. She has been part of multiple group shows, including at Shulamit Nazarian, CA, Jeffrey Deitch, NY, The Hammer Museum, CA, Sow and Tailor, CA, and has had a solo presentation at The Pit, CA.

Genesis Belanger (United States, b. 1978) stages psychologically charged mise-en-scènes composed of idiosyncratic versions of everyday objects. Working across a multitude of handcrafts, Belanger conjures installations of unresolved tension with a vocabulary lifted from 1950s American advertising. In Belanger's practice, the body is absent, inviting the viewer to enter as a purposeful actor. In her immersive scenes, objects become surrogates for the female body. She has an MFA from Hunter College. She has had multiple solo presentations, including at The Aldrich Contemporary Art Museum, CT, and Le Consortium, France, and has been featured in many group shows.

Howard Kottler (United States, 1930–1989) used his art to satirize American popular culture. He applied glazes and decals to ready-made ceramic objects, rarely modeling and casting his clay later in his career. He earned his MFA at the Cranbrook Academy of Art, MI, and a PhD in Ceramics at Ohio State University. He was awarded a Fulbright Grant for study in Finland. He taught at the University of Washington in Seattle. His work is held in various collections around the United States.

Magdalena Suarez Frimkess (Venezuela, b. 1929) studied painting and sculpture in South America before a fellowship at the Clay Art Center in Port Chester, NY, brought her to the United States where she met her partner and long-time collaborator, Michael Frimkess. Since her first solo exhibition in 2014, she has been recognized for ceramics that capture pop culture iconography, ancient histories, and intimate memory. She has had solo exhibitions at White Columns, NY, kaufmann repetto, NY and Milan, and South Willard, CA. In 2024, her work will be the subject of a retrospective at the Los Angeles County Art Museum, CA. Her work has been part of many group exhibitions and is included in major collections around the United States.

Maija Peeples-Bright (Latvia, b. 1942) creates wildly inventive compositions bustling with animals. She earned an MFA from the University of California, Davis, and had her first solo exhibition at the Candy Store Gallery, CA, where she exhibited annually until 1991. Other solo exhibitions include those at Parker Gallery, CA, Nicelle Beauchene, NY, and Guerrero Gallery, CA. Her work has been included in group exhibitions at the Crocker Art Museum, CA, Venus Over Manhattan, NY, Berkeley Art Museum and Pacific Film Archive, CA, and Manetti Shrem Museum of Art, CA. Her work is included in several collections around the United States.

Maryam Yousif (Iraq, b. 1985) finds inspiration for her sculptures in Middle Eastern history, pop culture, and her women role models across time. She earned her MFA from the San Francisco Art Institute. Solo and two-person exhibitions include David B. Smith Gallery, CO, The Pit, CA, Andrew Rafacz, IL, and Guerrero Gallery, CA. Yousif's work has been featured in group exhibitions at The Pit, Center for Craft, NC, and Anglim Gilbert Gallery, CA. She was an AICAD fellowship at the School of the Art Institute of Chicago in the Ceramics Department.

Melvino Garretti (United States, b. 1946) creates ceramic sculptures and assemblage pieces with gestural marks that mine the improvisational pacing of free jazz. His expressionistic style imbues his totemic and polymorphic forms with lively chaos begetting surprising relationships. He earned his MFA from the San Francisco Art Institute. His work has been the subject of solo and two-person exhibitions at Parker Gallery, CA, South Willard, CA, and Vernon Garden, CA. His work has also been included in many group shows, including at Jeffrey Deitch, NY, and the California African American Museum, among others.

Natalia Arbelaez (b. 1983, United States) draws from personal narratives of her Colombian family's immigration, Indigenous South American cultures, and American identity to create work about hybridity and the ups and downs of life. She earned her MFA from Ohio State University. Her work has been exhibited internationally and is included in various collections, such as the Everson Museum, NY, Museum of Arts and Design (MAD), NY, Fuller Craft Museum, MA, American Museum of Ceramic Art (AMOCA), CA, and Institute of Contemporary Art, Miami, FL. She has been an Artist-in-Residence at the Harvard Ceramics Program, MAD, and AMOCA.

Patti Warashina (United States, b. 1940) is best known for her imaginative and figurative ceramic sculptures. She earned her MFA from the University of Washington, Seattle, where she later taught until her retirement in 1995. Her work has been featured in many exhibitions nationally and internationally and is included in multiple collections, including at the Museum of Arts and Design, NY, National Museum of Modern Art, Kyoto, and Smithsonian American Art Museum, Washington, D.C.

Peter VandenBerge (Netherlands, b. 1935) is known for his large stylized ceramic busts; earlier work featured anthropomorphic vegetables. He earned his MFA from the University of California, Davis. He taught ceramics at California State University, Sacramento, for over thirty years. His work has been exhibited at the Crocker Art Museum, CA, San Francisco Museum of Modern Art, CA, Smithsonian American Art Museum, Washington, D.C., Oakland Art Museum, CA, and Whitney Museum of American Art, NY, among other institutions.

Richard Shaw (United States, b. 1941) is a ceramicist and professor known for his trompe-l'oeil style. In Shaw's work, this term refers to his replication of everyday objects in porcelain. He then glazes these components and groups them in unexpected and even jarring combinations. Interested in how objects can reflect a person or identity, Shaw poses questions regarding the relationship between appearances and reality. He earned an MFA from the University of California, Davis. His work has been the subject of multiple solo exhibitions and can be found in many collections around the United States.

Robert Arneson (United States, 1930–1992) was a highly influential figure in contemporary ceramics known for his enduring sense of humor and critical gaze. From his earliest biomorphic and Surrealist Pop-inflected objects, to self-portraits and the later, more refined political work about war and race relations, he constantly pushed the limits of his subjects. He earned his MFA from Mills College, CA, and soon after was invited to start a ceramics program at the University of California, Davis, in 1962, where he taught until his retirement in 1991. His work can be found in major museums around the world, and has been featured in numerous exhibitions and museum retrospectives.

Ruby Neri (United States, b. 1970) envisions her figures of voluptuous women, beaming with frenetic energy, as various aspects of a single, fractured character, drawing on her own identities as a mother, lover, daughter, and artist. Her signature airbrushed or spray-glazed technique recalls her early years as a graffiti artist in San Francisco. Neri received a BFA from the San Francisco Art Institute, where she was a core member of the Mission School. Neri's work resides in the collections of the Brooklyn Museum, NY, Hammer Museum, Museum of Contemporary Art, CA, and Berkeley Art Museum, CA, among others.

Sally Saul (United States, b. 1946) has a penchant for bright colors and draws from day-to-day life to create sculptures exploring the complexity of the human condition. She earned an MA in American Literature from the San Francisco State University, CA. Her first survey exhibition *Blue Hills, Yellow Tree*, opened in 2019 at Pioneer Works, NY. Saul also presented a solo show at Almine Rech, Paris. She has participated in group exhibitions at Venus Over Manhattan, NY, Jeffrey Deitch, NY, Art Museum of West Virginia, The Aldrich Contemporary Art Museum, CT, White Columns, NY, and Lumber Room, OR, among many others.

Salvador Jiménez-Flores (Mexico, b. 1985) confronts colonialism and systemic racism through hybrid sculptures combining elements of humor and realism. He has exhibited at the National Museum of Mexican Art, IL, Grand Rapids Art Museum, MI, Urban Institute of Contemporary Art, MI, and Bemis Center for Contemporary Arts, NE, among others. He has been an Artist-in-Residence at Harvard University's Ceramics Program and Kohler Arts Industry, and received the Joan Mitchell Foundation Painters & Sculptors Grant. He is a 2021 United States Artist Fellow and Assistant Professor in Ceramics at the School of the Art Institute of Chicago.

Sandra Shannonhouse (United States, b. 1947) worked primarily in porcelain, making candies until 1980, after which most of her work is in cast metal to take advantage of the attenuated line that material makes possible. She has had many solo and group exhibitions throughout her career and several public commissions. Her work is included in the Manetti Shrem Museum of Art, CA, San Francisco of Modern Art, and Mint Museum, NC, among others.

Sharif Farrag (United States, b. 1993) merges classic ceramic methodologies with his own improvisational building techniques in order to represent his hybrid identity through clay. He received a BFA from the University of Southern California in 2018 and is currently an MFA candidate in Ceramics at the University of California, Los Angeles. In 2019 he was awarded a residency at the Skowhegan School of Painting and Sculpture, and he was a 2022 United States Artist Fellow. His sculptures are included in the collections of the Museum of Arts and Design, NY, and Rubell Museum, FL.

Viola Frey (United States, 1933–2004) created boldly colored figurative sculptures, paintings, and works on paper reflecting on culture, power, and gender dynamics. Frey's immense creative output delved into many aesthetic directions. Frey considered herself a bricoleur—a junk accumulator—and recontextualized her figurines and icons, philosophical ideas, and color theory freely to create new meaning and a dynamic back-and-forth conversation between media.

Frey's largest sculptures challenge traditional ideas of beauty and scale. She has been the subject of many solo exhibitions, and her work is included in multiple collections around the United States.

Woody De Othello (United States, b. 1991) is known for sculptures of quotidian objects that serve as monuments to the everyday. He completed his MFA at the California College of Arts in San Francisco in 2017. He received his BFA from Florida Atlantic University in Ceramics. Othello has exhibited widely, including at the Whitney Museum of American Art, NY, and the John Michael Kohler Arts Center, WI. His work is in many permanent collections, including the Institute of Contemporary Art, Miami, FL, the San Francisco Museum of Modern Art, CA, Seattle Art Museum, WA, and the Los Angeles County Art Museum, CA.

Yvette Mayorga (United States, b. 1991) creates work in response to the immigration stories of Latine immigrants using aesthetics of excess and confectionery goods. She holds a Fiber and Material Studies MFA from the School of the Art Institute of Chicago. She has exhibited at the Vincent Price Art Museum, CA, DePaul Art Museum, IL, Center for Craft, NC, Museo Universitario del Chopo, Mexico, and Los Angeles County Art Museum, CA. Her work was included in El Museum del Barrio's *ESTAMOS BIEN: LA TRIENAL 20/21* and acquired by the museum. Mayorga's first solo museum exhibition, *What a Time to Be,* will debut fall of 2022 at The Momentary, AR.

Contributors:

Angelik Vizcarrondo-Laboy (Puerto Rico, b. 1992) is a curator and writer of contemporary art and craft advocating for underrepresented communities, stories, materials, and approaches. She has curated and juried exhibitions across the United States, including at the Crocker Art Museum, CA, Mindy Solomon Gallery, FL, Center for Craft, NC, Jane Hartsook Gallery, NY, and Museum of Arts and Design, NY, among others. Vizcarrondo-Laboy has written for multiple exhibition catalogs and publications such as *Cultured*, *American Craft* magazine, and the *Journal of Modern Craft*. She is the creator and co-host of the *Clay in Color* podcast.

Garth Johnson (United States, b. 1973) is a writer, curator, and educator. He is the Paul Phillips and Sharon Sullivan Curator of Ceramics at the Everson Museum of Art, NY. Johnson is a self-described craft activist who explores craft's influence and relevance in the twenty-first century. Recent exhibitions at the Everson include *Renegades & Reformers: American Art Pottery* (2020), *Earth Piece: Conceptual and Performative Works in Clay* (2019) and *Key Figures: Representational Ceramics 1932–1972* (2019). His writing has been published nationally and internationally, with recent contributions to books *Repositioning Paolo Soleri: The City is Nature* (2019) and *Victor Cicansky: The Gardener's Universe* (2020).

Biographies edited by Angelik Vizcarrondo-Laboy, courtesy:

Jeffrey Deitch, New York and Los Angeles: Shilling & Alvarado

Sargent's Daughters, New York: Anderson

Parker Gallery, Los Angeles: Unterseher, Peeples-Bright, & Garretti

Arizona State University Art Museum, Temple: Bailey

John Natsoulas Gallery, Davis, CA: Gilhooly & Warashina

Didi Rojas

Perrotin, New York: Belanger

Smithsonian American Art Museum, Washington, D.C.: Kottler

kaufmann repetto, Milan and New York: Suarez Frimkess

The Pit, Los Angeles: Yousif

Natalia Arbelaez

Solomon Dubnick Gallery, Sacramento: VandenBerge

Frank Lloyd Gallery, Pasadena, CA: Shaw

Robert Arneson Estate, courtesy George Adams Gallery, New York: Arneson

David Kordansky Gallery, Los Angeles: Neri

Venus Over Manhattan, New York: Saul

Salvador Jiménez-Flores

Sandra Shannonhouse

Francois Ghebaly Gallery, Los Angeles: Farrag

Artists' Legacy Foundation, Oakland, CA: Frey

Jessica Silverman Gallery, San Francisco: Othello

Yvette Mayorga

Angelik Vizcarrondo-Laboy

Garth Johnson

Select Bibliography

Adamson, Glenn. "Chapter 5: The Amateur," in *Thinking Through Craft*. London: Bloomsbury and Victoria and Albert Museum, 2007.

Arneson, Robert. "Guardians: The Spirit of the Work," *Ceramics Monthly* 39 (April 1991), 50–54.

Baker, Tony Williams, John Natsoulas, and Terry Ann Tafoya. *David Gilhooly.* Davis, CA: John Natsoulas Gallery, 1992.

Camargo, William. "Diana Yesenia Alvarado's Sculptures Depict the Sounds, Smells, People, and Colors of Her Neighborhood," *Sculpture Magazine*, October 2020. http://amadeusmag.com/blog/diana-yesenia-alvarado-clay-sculptures/.

Candy Store Gallery records, 1968–2004, Archives of American Art, Smithsonian Institution.

Daniels, Diana L., ed., *Clayton Bailey's World of Wonders*. Exhibition catalog. Sacramento: Crocker Art Museum, 2011.

Falling, Patricia. *Howard Kottler: Face to Face*. Seattle: University of Washington Press, 1995.

Fineberg, Jonathan. *A Troublesome Subject: The Art of Robert Arneson*. Berkeley, CA: University of California Press, 2013.

Furman, Anna. "Woody De Othello's Extraordinary Monuments to the Mundane," *T Magazine*, March 17, 2022. https://www.nytimes.com/2022/03/17/t-magazine/woody-de-othello-art.html.

Helfand, Glen. "Artist Woody De Othello's Oversize Ceramic Sculptures Distort Household Furniture and Appliances." *W Magazine*, November 2019. https://www.wmagazine.com/story/woody-de-othello-artist-interview/.

Indrisek, Scott. "Genesis Belanger: Seduction and Repulsion," *Sculpture Magazine*, November 2019. https://sculpturemagazine.art/genesis-belanger-seduction-and-repulsion/.

Jones, Mady. *Oral History Interview with Robert Arneson (transcript)*, August 14–15, 1981, Archives of American Art, Smithsonian Institution. https://www.aaa.si.edu/collections/interviews/oral-history-interview-robert-arneson-11807.

Karlstrom, Paul J. *Peter Selz: Sketches of a Life in Art*. Oakland: University of California Press, 2012.

Karp-Evans, Elizabeth. "Woody de Othello Mixes Playful with Political," *Cultured*, December 2020. https://www.culturedmag.com/artist-woody-de-othello-sculptor-young-artists-2020/.

Kaufmann, Francesca. "Magdalena Suarez Frimkess: The Freedom in her Ceramics," *Harper's Bazaar*, October 1, 2020. (translation). https://kaufmannrepetto.com/site/web/app/uploads/2020/11/2020_Harpers-Bazaar.pdf.

Kelley, Ken. "Arneson in His Studio," *Style* (October 1987), 42–58.

Kingsbury, Martha. *Patti Warashina: Wit and Wisdom*. Exhibition catalog. Pomona, CA: American Museum of Ceramic Art, 2012.

Lesser, Casey. "Genesis Belanger's Uncanny Ceramics Help Us Cope with the Present," *Artsy,* October 1, 2020. https://www.artsy.net/article/artsy-editorial-genesis-belangers-uncanny-ceramics-help-cope.

Monte, James. "'Making It' Funk," *Art Forum*, Vol. 5, No. 10 (1967), 56–59.

Natsoulas, John, and Bruce Nixon. *Thirty Years of TB-9: A Tribute to Robert Arneson*. Davis: John Natsoulas Gallery, 1991.

Ngai, Sianne. *Our Aesthetic Categories: Zany, Cute, Interesting*. Cambridge, MA: Harvard University Press, 2012.

Ngai, Sianne, ed. *Documents of Contemporary Art: The Cute*. London: Whitechapel Gallery and Cambridge, MA: The MIT Press, 2022.

Nut Art. Exhibition catalog. Hayward: California State University, Hayward Gallery, 1972.

Paris, Harold. "Sweet Land of Funk," *Art in America* 55 (March 1967), 94–98.

Phillips, Lisa. ed. *Beat Culture and the New America: 1950–1965*. New York: Whitney Museum of Art, 1995.

Riedel, Mija. *Oral Interview with Sandra Shannonhouse* (transcript), July 22–23, 2015, Archives of American Art, Smithsonian Institution. https://www.aaa.si.edu/collections/interviews/oral-history-interview-sandra-shannonhouse-16277#transcript.

Ringiewicz, Abby. "Channeling the Funk: A Conversation with Artist Alake Shilling," *Amadeus*, June 2019. http://amadeusmag.com/blog/channeling-funk-alake-shilling/.

Rudick, Nicole. "Funk," in *What Nerve! Alternative Figures in American Art*. Rhode Island: RISD Museum, 2014.

Schwartz, Judy S. *Confrontational Ceramics: The Artist as Social Critic*. London: A&C Black; Philadelphia: University of Pennsylvania Press, 2008.

Schuster, Clayton. "Looking Back at the Strange and Surly History of Bay Area Funk Art," *Hyperallergic*, April 2017. https://hyperallergic.com/372519/looking-back-at-the-strange-and-surly-history-of-bay-area-funk-art/.

Schuster, Clayton. "Revisiting the Witty Work of 1970s Bay Area Nut Artists," *Hyperallergic*, July 2017. https://hyperallergic.com/390717/revisiting-the-witty-work-of-1970s-bay-area-nut-artists/.

Selz, Peter. *Funk*. Berkeley, CA: Berkeley Museum of Art, 1967.

Selz, Peter. *Art of Engagement: Visual Politics in California and Beyond*. Oakland: University of California Press, 2005.

Selz, Peter, Mowry Gaden, Joan Brown, Bruce Conner, Manuel Neri, James Melchert, and Peter Voulkos, *Funk Symposium*, April 28, 1967. Peter Selz papers, 1929–2014. Archives of American Art, Smithsonian Institution.

Shields, Scott A. and Mariah Carmen Briel. *The Candy Store: Funk, Nut, & Other Art with a Kick*. Exhibition catalog. Munich: Hirmer Publishers; Sacramento: Crocker Art Museum, 2022.

Smith, Paul J. *Clayworks: 20 Americans*. Exhibition catalog. New York, Museum of Contemporary Crafts, 1971.

Taragin, Davira S., and Patterson Sims. *Bigger, Better, More: The Art of Viola Frey*. Exhibition catalog. New York and Manchester: Hudson Hills Press; Racine Art Museum and Gardiner Museum, 2009.

Transmission Gallery. "Maija Peeples-Bright: Beyond the Candy Store," *Transmission Gallery*, April 2016. https://thetransmissiongallery.com/maija-peeples-bright-beyond-the-candy-store.html.

Ukwouma, Ezennwa. "The Search for Melvino Garretti," *Black Renaissance Noire*, Winter 2017, 104–113.

Valentine, Inez. "Childhood Cartoons Melt and Distort in Alake Shilling's Nostalgic Ceramics," *Elephant*, February 2020. https://elephant.art/childhood-cartoons-melt-distort-alake-shilling-nostalgic-ceramics-25022020/.

Various. Artists' surveys and letters. Archives of *Funk* exhibition, 1967. Berkeley Art Museum and Pacific Film Archive.

Vizcarrondo-Laboy, Angelik. "Sleight of Hand: The Fruitful Illusion of Humor in Ceramics," in *Sleight of Hand*. Asheville, NC: Center for Craft, 2020.

Vizcarrondo-Laboy, Angelik. "Seriously Cute: Six Artists Harnessing the Power Dichotomy of Cuteness," *Cultured*, November 2020. https://www.culturedmag.com/cute-contemporary-art/.

Vizcarrondo-Laboy, Angelik and Alex Anderson. *Clay in Color*, 2021. https://podcasts.apple.com/us/podcast/clay-in-color/id1581648957.

Wagley, Catherine. "Maija Peeples-Bright's Anti-hierarchical Utopias and the Art of World Building," *Carla* 22, November 1, 2020. https://www.culturedmag.com/article/2020/11/17/cute-contemporary-art.

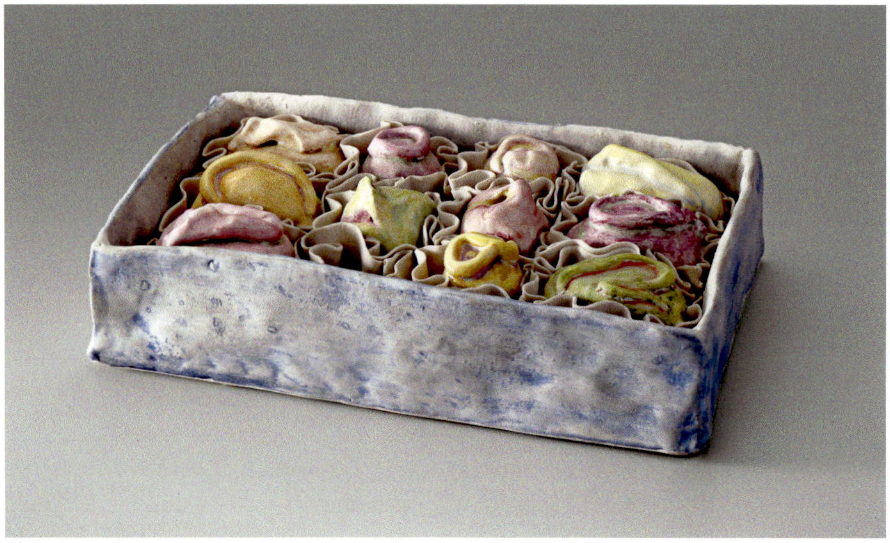

Photo Credits

IMAGE RIGHTS FOR THE WORKS OF:

Robert Arneson: © 2022 Estate of Robert Arneson / Licensed by VAGA at Artists Right Society (ARS), New York
Viola Frey: © Artists' Legacy Foundation / Licensed by VAGA at Artists Right Society (ARS), New York
Margaret Dodd: © Margaret Dodd / Licensed by Copyright Agency

IMAGES COURTESY:

Funk You Too!

The University of California, Berkeley Art Museum and Pacific Film Archive
Figs. 1–4a–c

Parker Gallery, Los Angeles
Figs. 5; 7 by Betty Warmack; 22 by Noam Rappaport; 31 by Paul Salveson

Robert Arneson Archives, Benicia, California
Figs. 6, 8–10, 14, & 39–42

Museum of Arts and Design, New York
Figs. 11–12, 19, 38, & 47 by Eva Heyd; 29 by Ed Watkins

© The Museum of Fine Arts Houston
Figs. 13 & 18 by Thomas R. DuBrock

Perrotin, New York
Fig. 15 by Pauline Shapiro

Didi Rojas
Fig. 16 by Didi Rojas

Jessica Silverman Gallery, San Francisco
Fig. 17

Peter Held
Fig. 20 by John Carlano

Everson Museum of Art, Syracuse, NY
Fig. 21

Crocker Art Museum, Sacramento
Fig. 23

Jeffrey Deitch, New York and Los Angeles
Figs. 24–25 by Genevieve Hanson; 26 by Josh White

Alex Anderson
Fig. 27 by Ed Mumford

kaufmann repetto, Milan and New York
Fig. 28 by Greg Carideo

Michael Rosenfeld Gallery LLC, New York
Fig. 30

Venus Over Manhattan, New York © Sally Saul
Fig. 32

Salvador Jiménez-Flores
Fig. 33 by Michael Tropea

San Francisco Museum of Modern Art © Sandra Shannonhouse
Fig. 34 by Katherine Du Tiel

Yvette Mayorga
Fig. 35 by Robert Chase Heishman; 36 by Yvette Mayorga

Adams and Ollman, Seattle
Fig. 37 by Leif Anderson, Area Array

Natalia Arbelaez
Fig. 43 by Chris Stone

Grounds for Sculpture, Hamilton, NJ
Fig. 44 by Bruce M. White

The Pit, Los Angeles
Fig. 45 by Jeff McLane; 46 by Chris Grunder

LGDR, New York © Ruby Neri
Fig. 48 by Charles White

Finding Funk

Smithsonian American Art Museum, Renwick Gallery, Washington, D.C.
Fig. 1 by Gene Young

Everson Museum of Art, Syracuse, NY
Figs. 2–3 by Jamie Young

Scripps College, Claremont, CA
Figs. 4–5 by John Trendler

American Craft Council Library & Archives, Minneapolis, Minnesota
Fig. 6 by Robert Buckman; 7 by Harold Myers; 8 & 14 by Bob Hanson

Curated Storefront
Fig. 9

Victor Cicansky
Fig. 10

Art Gallery of South Australia
Fig. 11 by Saul Steed

Judy Onofrio
Fig. 12

Indiana State University, University Art Gallery, Terre Haute
Fig. 13

Hallie Ford Museum of Art, Willamette University Salem, OR
Fig. 15

Additional

Jeffrey Deitch, New York and Los Angeles
p. 2 by Genevieve Hanson

Museum of Arts and Design, New York
pp. 4, 97, & 99 by Jenna Bascom; 96 by Ed Watkins

Perrotin, New York
pp. 6 & 10–11 by Pauline Shapiro

Robert Arneson Archives, Benicia, California
pp. 7 & 108

Sargent's Daughters, New York
p. 8 by Ed Mumford

Jessica Silverman Gallery, San Francisco
p. 14

kaufmann repetto, Milan and New York
pp. 15 by Andrea Rossetti

Parker Gallery, Los Angeles
pp. 16 & 75 by Paul Salveson

Francois Ghebaly Gallery, Los Angeles
p. 74 by Paul Salveson

Hallie Ford Museum of Art, Willamette University, Salem, OR
p. 76

Venus Over Manhattan, New York © Sally Saul
p. 98

Additional Image Captions

Page 2

Alake Shilling, *Baby Bear Loves Alake*, 2021. Ceramic, glaze, and enamel paint, 11.5 × 8 × 9 in (29.2 × 20.3 × 22.9 cm). Courtesy the artist

Page 4 & 96

Patti Warashina, *Pitter Podder*, 1968. Earthenware and acrylic paint, 25 ¾ × 15 ¾ × 9 ½ in. (65.4 × 40 × 24.1 cm). Museum of Arts and Design, New York; gift of the Johnson Wax Company, through the American Craft Council, 1977

Page 6

Genesis Belanger, *I Can See You From Way Over Here*, 2020. Stoneware, steel, powder-coating, lamp hardware, and electric cord, 39 × 17 × 6.5 in. (99.1 × 43.2 × 16.5 cm). Collection of Mr. Lorin Gu

Page 7

Robert Arneson, *Klown*, 1978. Earthenware and glaze, 37 ¼ × 19 × 19 in. (94.6 × 48.3 × 48.3 cm). Des Moines Art Center Permanent Collections; purchased by the Director's Discretionary Fund from the Gardner and Florence Call Cowles Foundation

Page 8

Alex Anderson, *Narcissistic Lemon with a Sour Audience*, 2022. Ceramic, underglaze, and luster, 22 × 22 × 3 in. (55.9 × 55.9 × 7.6 cm). Courtesy the artist and Sargent's Daughters, New York

Alex Anderson, *Narcissistic Orange with an Unbothered Audience*, 2022. Ceramic, underglaze, and luster, 22 × 22 × 3 in. (55.9 × 55.9 × 7.6 cm). Courtesy the artist and Sargent's Daughters, New York

Page 10–11

Genesis Belanger, *You Never Know What You're Gonna Get*, 2020. Stoneware and porcelain, 5 × 27 × 23 in (12.7 × 68.6 × 58.4 cm). Collection of Emmanuel Perrotin

Page 14

Woody De Othello, *Open Vase*, 2020. Ceramic, glaze, steel, and powder-coating, 14 × 16 × 13 in. (35.6 × 40.6 × 33 cm). Courtesy Mindy Solomon Collection, Miami

Page 15

Magdalena Suarez Frimkess, *Untitled*, 1999. Ceramic and glaze, 9 ½ × 5 ½ × 5 ½ in. (24.1 × 14 × 14 cm). Courtesy the artist and kaufmann repetto, Milan and New York

Page 16

Melvino Garretti, *I'm a Clown Just Horsin' Around*, 2020. Earthenware, glaze, and vintage textile, 16 × 10 × 5 ¾ in. (40.6 × 25.4 × 14.6 cm). Courtesy the artist and Parker Gallery, Los Angeles

Page 74

Sharif Farrag, *Trapped in a Pocket Watch Jug 2*, 2020. Porcelain and glaze, 9 × 7 × 6 in. (22.9 × 17.8 × 15.2 cm). Collection of Jeff Rosa and Elizabeth Satterwhite

Page 75

Melvino Garretti, *It's Only a Matter of Time...I Haven't Whipped Any Ass Around Here*, 2020. Earthenware and glaze, 17.5 × 10.5 × 10.5 in. (44.5 × 26.7 × 26.7 cm). Courtesy the artist and Parker Gallery, Los Angeles

Page 76

David Gilhooly, *Mothra*, 1991. Plexiglas, 26 × 24 × 1 in. (66 × 61 × 2.5 cm). Collection of the Hallie Ford Museum of Art, Willamette University, Salem, OR; Maribeth Collins Art Acquisition Fund, 2000

Page 97

Clayton Bailey, *Untitled*, c. 1972. Whiteware, underglaze, glaze, synthetic wig, and found suitcase, open: 8 ¼ × 30 ½ × 25 ¼ in. (21 × 77.5 × 64.1 cm). Museum of Arts and Design, New York; gift of Florence Rubenfeld, 2001

Page 98

Sally Saul, *Troubled Waters*, 2020. Ceramic and glaze 12.5 × 28 × 17 in. (31.8 × 71.1 × 43.2 cm). Courtesy the artist and Venus Over Manhattan, New York
© Sally Saul

Page 99

David Gilhooly, *Europa Version of Cowpachino*, 1993. White earthenware and glaze, 7 ¾ × 8 × 7 in. (19.7 × 20.3 × 17.8 cm). Museum of Arts and Design, New York; gift of the artist and Camille Chang, 1993

Page 108

Sandra Shannonhouse, *Candy Box*, 1975. Porcelain and porcelain paint, 2 × 9.5 × 5.5 in. (5.1 × 24.1 × 14 cm). Courtesy the artist